READYING THE REVOLUTION

THEATER: THEORY/TEXT/PERFORMANCE

Series Editors: David Krasner, Jen Parker-Starbuck, and Harvey Young
Founding Editor: Enoch Brater

Recent Titles:

Acting the Part: Audience Participation in Performance
E. B. Hunter

Theater, War, and Memory in Crisis: Vichy, Algeria, the Aftermath
by John Ireland

Readying the Revolution: African American Theater and Performance from Post-World War II to the Black Arts Movement
by Jonathan Shandell

Fantasies of Ito Michio
by Tara Rodman

Racing the Great White Way: Black Performance, Eugene O'Neill, and the Transformation of Broadway
by Katie N. Johnson

Chocolate Woman Dreams the Milky Way: Mapping Embodied Indigenous Performance
by Monique Mojica and Brenda Farnell

Democracy Moving: Bill T. Jones, Contemporary American Performance, and the Racial Past
by Ariel Nereson

Moving Islands: Contemporary Performance and the Global Pacific
by Diana Looser

Scenes from Bourgeois Life
by Nicholas Ridout

Performance Constellations: Networks of Protest and Activism in Latin America
by Marcela A. Fuentes

Interchangeable Parts: Acting, Industry, and Technology in US Theater
by Victor Holtcamp

Ruins: Classical Theater and Broken Memory
by Odai Johnson

Gaming the Stage: Playable Media and the Rise of English Commercial Theater
by Gina Bloom

Immersions in Cultural Difference: Tourism, War, Performance
by Natalie Alvarez

Readying the Revolution

AFRICAN AMERICAN THEATER AND PERFORMANCE CULTURE FROM POST–WORLD WAR II TO THE BLACK ARTS MOVEMENT

Jonathan Shandell

UNIVERSITY OF MICHIGAN PRESS

Ann Arbor

Published in the United States of America by the
University of Michigan Press
Manufactured in the United States of America
Printed on acid-free paper
First published January 2025

A CIP catalog record for this book is available from the British Library.

Library of Congress Cataloging-in-Publication data has been applied for.

ISBN 978-0-472-07718-2 (hardcover : alk. paper)
ISBN 978-0-472-05718-4 (paper : alk. paper)
ISBN 978-0-472-90480-8 (open access ebook)

DOI: https://doi.org/10.3998/mpub.12830358

The University of Michigan Press's open access publishing program is made possible thanks to additional funding from the University of Michigan Office of the Provost and the generous support of contributing libraries.

Dedicated to the memory and legacy of James Vernon Hatch:
whose scholarship, advocacy, and pedagogy
in African American theater history continue
to define the field.

Contents

Digital materials related to this title can be found on the Fulcrum platform via the following citable URL: https://doi.org/10.3998/mpub.12830358

Illustrations

Acknowledgments

The person most responsible for helping bring this book into being is Dr. LaDonna Forsgren of the University of Notre Dame. Many of the ideas that underpin the chapters that follow—and the original impetus to undertake the project in the first place—are thanks to both the knowledge and the generosity of this treasured friend and colleague. I also extend sincere thanks to other fellow scholars in the field of African American theater studies who assisted in ways both large and small in the book's development. Chief among these colleagues is Harvey Young—a friend, mentor, adviser, advocate, and supporter to whom I owe so much. Additional thanks to Soyica Diggs Colbert, Julius Fleming, David Krasner, and Khalid Yaya Long. I am grateful to those who toiled alongside me in many online "pomodoro" writing sessions, generously hosted by Robin Bernstein, Brian Herrera, and Patrick McKelvey. I also extend thanks to those colleagues too numerous to list who collaborated in sessions at the annual conferences for the American Society for Theatre Research and the Association for Theatre in Higher Education, where portions of the book were developed and presented over the course of several years.

Generous assistance with archival research (much of it conducted remotely during the Covid-19 pandemic) was provided by librarians and archivists at the Schomburg Center for Research in Black Culture, New York Public Library for the Performing Arts, Rose Library at Emory University, Institute of Jazz Studies at Rutgers University–Newark, and National Baseball Hall of Fame Museum and Archive. I received terrific assistance with illustrations from staff of the Schomburg Center Photographs and Prints Division, the Billy Rose Theatre Collection (NYPL Library for the Performing Arts), New York University Tamiment Library, University of Notre Dame Rare Books & Special Collections, and Michael Yoscary. Andrea Felder of the New York Public Library Permissions office was heroic in providing patient, prompt answers to my frequent cries for help.

This project was aided immensely by support that I am privileged to enjoy as a member of the faculty of Arcadia University. Two specific awards—the 2020 Dr. Norman Johnston Faculty Fellowship in the Humanities and Social Sciences, and a sabbatical for the 2022–23 academic year—were vital in supporting my research and writing, and in underwriting costs associated with securing illustrations. I am particularly grateful for the leadership and encouragement of Provost Jeff Rutenbeck in supporting my research. My faculty colleagues in the Theater Arts program are treasured collaborators and partners. Thanks to Kevin Glaccum, Mary Folino, Rob Napoli, and most especially to Kathryn Petersen for all that you took on to allow me the time and space to complete this book. My appreciation also goes out to the many wonderful students of Arcadia's Theater Arts program, past and present, who inspire me with their ambition, creativity, and investment in the work we undertake together. Thanks also to colleagues in Arcadia's Pan-African Studies Collective and the Center for Antiracist Scholarship, Advocacy, and Action (under the leadership of Doreen Lowry and Christopher Varlack) for their continuing interest in my scholarship.

To my parents, Fred and Susan Shandell, and my sister Stacey Ellison, thank you for a lifetime of unwavering familial love and support. I am grateful to my daughters, Ceil and Miranda, for the unique and inspiring young people they have become and their interest in their dad's work. And to my wife Robin—with whose unending love, companionship, patience, and support all things are possible. Though there's simply no way to express it adequately: thank you.

Introduction

In historical accounts of African American theater of the mid-twentieth century, one drama looms particularly large—Lorraine Hansberry's masterwork, *A Raisin in the Sun*. This play's initial 1959–60 run of 530 performances stands as the longest ever Broadway engagement for a drama by an African American playwright. Hansberry's meticulously rendered portrait of a working-class Black family's defiance of residential segregation in Chicago appealed to mass audiences both Black and white, and garnered effusive praise from the commercial establishment and mainstream critics. In her recent biography of Hansberry entitled *Looking for Lorraine*, Imani Perry notes:

> Lorraine Hansberry was the first Black woman to have her play produced on Broadway and the first Black winner of the prestigious Drama Critics' Circle Award. That first play, *A Raisin in the Sun*, is the most widely produced and read play by a Black American woman. It is canonical, not just in Black American literature but also in American arts and letters.[1]

A Raisin in the Sun now stands as a touchstone of African American culture of the civil rights era. The drama crystallizes the struggles, aspirations, and intensifying demands for justice and equitable opportunity that characterized Black American experience of its era. As the United States consolidated its position of postwar prosperity and global hegemony, and as Cold War political divisions intensified both domestically and internationally, *A Raisin the Sun* exposed troubling strains of white racist intransigence, capitalist inequity, and growing Black resentment and restlessness that pulled at the nation's social fabric. Most striking about the play for many was how Hansberry delivers her searing social critique in a manner that (at least upon first glance) "wasn't overtly political, didactic, or heavy-handed. She had chosen to write characters who were true, who were oppressed, who sought freedom, and who were also shaped by the society in which they lived. Her craft had grown too nuanced to read as propaganda."[2]

Scholars of African American theater and culture have justifiably celebrated this landmark play and the brief, phenomenal career of its playwright. (Hansberry was only twenty-nine years old when *A Raisin in the Sun* debuted on Broadway; her untimely death came in 1965, at age thirty-five, from pancreatic cancer.) Alongside Perry's biography are two recently published studies of Hansberry's life and work: Soyica Diggs Colbert's *Radical Vision: A Biography of Lorraine Hansberry* (a scholarly analysis of the playwright's intellectual life), and *Lorraine Hansberry: The Life behind "A Raisin in the Sun"* by Charles J. Shields. Other critical and historical analyses of *A Raisin in the Sun* abound within theater scholarship.[3] What is lacking within African American theater historiography is a broader investigation of the era within which that play sits—a transitional period between the conclusion of World War II in the mid-1940s and the rise of the Black Arts Movement and the emergence of Black Power politics in the mid-1960s. The works of other African American playwrights and performers of these years remain comparatively unfamiliar, obscured by the sizable shadow that *A Raisin in the Sun* casts on our historical vision. One primary goal of this study is to bring new attention to this underexamined and transformative period of African American theater and performance.

Some of the cultural and historical crosscurrents that shaped this moment reveal themselves within the public response elicited by *A Raisin in the Sun*. From one critical perspective, Hansberry's play won praise for fulfilling a need for direct, honest, and nuanced depictions of everyday Black experience of the mid-twentieth century. James Baldwin's tribute captures this dynamic vividly. "Never in my life have I seen so many black people in the theater," Baldwin notes. "And the reason was that never before, in the entire history of the American theater, had so much of the truth of black people's lives been seen on the stage. . . . [I]n *Raisin*, black people recognized that house and all the people in it."[4] Simultaneously, a different segment of the public (which included the white critical establishment) celebrated how *A Raisin in the Sun* evoked for them a rather different type of comfort and familiarity. Colbert notes how reviews published in major newspapers primarily "focused on the ways Hansberry's art and its politics fit into mainstream norms. Read against her contemporary Malcolm X . . . Hansberry's vision of Black freedom struggles proved much easier for mainstream American audiences to swallow, particularly as the winds of Cold War nationalism continued to pick up speed."[5] The popular appeal and continuing influence of *A Raisin in the Sun* owe much to the deft balance that Hansberry strikes with the play. The drama offers direct, unequivocal indictments of white supremacy and economic injustice in the United States at a fraught historical moment, in a manner that was impactful and meaningful for Black audiences, yet also comfortable for the predominantly white liberal public served by Broadway and the commercial theater.

Nonetheless, Hansberry's now iconic drama has had its detractors. According to Ben Keppel, though "*A Raisin in the Sun* was christened as the quintessential 'civil rights play'" within a few years (particularly following Hansberry's death), "*Raisin*'s historical reputation would fall." Within the increasingly militant Black political discourse of the late 1960s, the play became for some critics "a politically retrograde and aesthetically derivative sop that made the civil rights movement seem unthreatening to middle-class whites."[6] Harold Cruse is one such commentator, who disparages *A Raisin in the Sun* as a "most cleverly written piece of glorified soap opera" populated by artificial characters "who can be made to mouth middle class values, sentiments and strivings: platitudes that are acceptable to whites of the middle class."[7] Colbert, Keppel, Perry, and other Hansberry scholars challenge this critique as a selective misreading of the play (driven by Cruse's personal and ideological biases). Nonetheless the emergence of such a backlash against *A Raisin in the Sun* points to an important fault line of Black cultural discourse of the mid-twentieth century. As Lloyd Brown observes, *A Raisin in the Sun* became a key focal point for the era's "running ethnopolitical debates . . . between 'militants' and 'moderates,' Black 'extremists' and white 'liberals,' integrationists and Black nationalists, and so on."[8]

A prominent voice at one extreme of this discourse—whose writings came to epitomize the era's militant, nationalist cultural sensibility—was LeRoi Jones. When *A Raisin in the Sun* debuted in 1959, Jones (before he took on his nom de plume of Amiri Baraka) was a prolific poet and essayist in the downtown New York cultural scene. Jones had yet to turn to playwriting at this point in his career, and was not publishing any theater criticism. Thus his initial response to Hansberry's play was not publicly circulated at the time; he shares his initial impression of the drama in a later essay entitled "A Critical Reevaluation: *A Raisin in the Sun*'s Enduring Passion," composed to mark the play's twenty-fifth anniversary. There Baraka summarizes his original distaste (in alignment with Cruse's critique quoted above), as well as a subsequent evolution in his judgment about the drama:

> Young militants like myself [initially] thought Hansberry's play was part of the "passive resistance" phase of the movement, which was over the minute Malcolm's penetrating eyes and words began to

> charge through the media with deadly force. We thought her play "middle class" in that its focus seemed to be on "moving into white folks' neighborhoods," when most blacks were just trying to pay their rent in ghetto shacks. We missed the essence of the work—that Hansberry had created a family on the cutting edge of the same class and ideological struggles as existed in the movement itself and among the people.[9]

I quote this response at length not to dwell upon the critique of *A Raisin in the Sun,* but for what Baraka's reevaluation illustrates within African American theatrical culture in the postwar period—years before the debut of his own iconic breakthrough play, *Dutchman* (1964). Nationalist thought leaders like Baraka and Cruse disdained the politics of a pre–Black Arts "phase of the movement" as that phase unfolded, seeing the work of Hansberry and many of her contemporaries as tepid and "passive." The dramas of Hansberry and other Black playwrights seemed to them at the time too bourgeois, too beholden to an ideology of integration, and too dependent upon the sanction of white liberals to have a meaningful social impact. Only in hindsight does Baraka recognize an "essence" of "the same class and ideological struggles" shared by him and his Black Arts compatriots whose revolutionary movement was waiting in the wings.

Baraka's revised understanding of Hansberry's dramaturgy adds important context to our view of the underpinnings of the Black Arts Movement. Black nationalist artists and theorists of the mid-1960s and beyond—buoyed, as Baraka was, by a growing militant fervor that overtook African American cultural politics—sought to distinguish their own creative movement from the immediate past by wrapping their own efforts in the rhetoric of "revolution." Elsewhere, Baraka reflects on the period, "This was the era when, as Mao Tse Tung said, 'Countries want Independence, Nations want Liberation and The People want Revolution!' And as we used to quote him often, 'Revolution Is The Main Trend In the World Today!'"[10] Reflecting on the insurgent sensibility that propelled him out of the interracial bohemian cultural scene in Greenwich Village to found the Black Arts Repertory Theater School in Harlem, he writes:

> We wanted Black Art. We felt it could move our people, the Afro American people, to revolutionary positions. . . . We wanted an art that was revolutionary. We wanted a Malcolm art, a by-any-means-necessary poetry. A Ballot or Bullet verse. We wanted ultimately, to

> create a poetry, a literature, a dance, a theater, a painting, that would help bring revolution! That was what it was *all* about. That's what the whole movement and essence of The Black Arts was raised and forwarded by, the desire by Black youth to make revolution in the U.S.

These revolutionaries certainly saw white oppressors as their opponents; they *also* positioned themselves deliberately against those Black artists of the immediate past who had failed in their judgment to take up the banner of Black cultural revolution with sufficient fervor and defiance, whom they dismissed as "the 'whited out,' the bourgeois negroes, the backward."[11]

Critical studies of the Black Arts Movement abound that chart the ways that Baraka and his fellow travelers realized or fell short of their lofty goals of total cultural insurgency. The Black Arts Movement *did* in many respects mark a radical shift in both aesthetics and politics for the African American stage. More importantly, it served the movement's aims to position itself as completely untethered from the prerevolutionary status quo against which it rebelled. However, even the most deliberately self-styled revolutionary artists inevitably owe some debt—whether conscious or unknowing, acknowledged or unacknowledged—to those who preceded them and whose voices they may wish to render obsolete. Periods of evolution, experimentation, and measured progress (often easier to discern in retrospect) will pave the way for disruptive, revolutionary cultural changes. James Smethurst finds this dynamic operative throughout the literary genealogy of the Black Arts Movement:

> One can think of the beginning of the Black Arts and Black Power movements in the 1960s being enabled by a commitment to institution building by more strictly nationalist groups and individuals inspired by and complementing similar Left projects. In this way, we can see the rise of the Black Arts Movement as not simply a break with earlier ideologies, earlier poetics, and previous institutions. Of course, breaks did occur, and the dramatic staging of gestures of rupture and disaffiliation with earlier modes of racial politics was an important feature of the early Black Arts and Black Power movements. But the existence of such ruptures should not blind us to the continuities (and communities) of radical politics and poetics that would provide a matrix for the emergence of Black Arts institutions and ideology in a variety of locations across the United States.[12]

This study extends Smethurst's analysis by mapping within African American theater and performance the matrix of connections between the immediate postwar years and the Black Arts Movement that follows. The book's primary purpose is to demarcate—within an ostensibly "passive phase" of Black cultural production—some of the streams of continuity and influence that actively fueled the radical Black nationalist theater and performance culture of the late 1960s and beyond.

My historiographical approach follows a broader trend visible within scholarship on postwar racial politics. Narratives of the civil rights era have traditionally distinguished what is called a 'short,' 'classical,' or 'heroic' phase of the movement (1954–65) marked by mainstream legal and civic activism of an interracial coalition, from an ensuing 'militant' phase (1965–74) propelled by revolutionary rhetoric, a Black separatist ideology, and an embrace of more combative political tactics. This scheme of periodization has proven durable; but as Peniel E. Joseph argues, such a framing unfairly tarnishes the latter period "as an unabashed failure and a negative counterpart to more righteous struggles for racial integration, social justice, and economic equality." In the last few decades, historians have increasingly challenged the "simplistic binaries that frame the [classical] civil rights movement as a moral good in contrast to black power's violent predilections," and developed a more nuanced analysis of the postwar period as a time when "elements of civil rights activism and black power militancy coexisted in complex, combative, and novel ways. . . . Black power activism existed alongside civil rights struggles of the 1950s and early 1960s, and certain activists simultaneously participated in both movements. African American political culture between 1954 and 1965 is proving to be much more complicated, diverse, and heterogeneous than standard narratives of the era have depicted."[13] *Readying the Revolution* follows that scholarly trajectory, considering how the ideologies of integrationism and Black nationalism, and the strategies of liberal coalition-building and militant separatism, converged and cross-pollinated within the theater and performance culture of the mid-twentieth century.

Within that context, *Readying the Revolution* builds upon recent scholarly conversations that delineate a new historical framing for what has come to be known as the "long civil rights movement" (encompassing US racial politics from the 1930s to the 1970s). As Jacqueline Dowd Hall writes, the "dominant narrative" told traditionally by historians focuses primarily on "a short civil right movement that begins with the 1954 *Brown v. Board of Education* decision, proceeds through public protests, and culminates with the passage of the Civil Rights Act in 1964 and the Voting Rights Act of

1965." Such an approach narrows historical attention upon "a single halcyon decade . . . as a triumphal moment in a larger American progress narrative." Hall and other scholars have sought instead to circulate "a more robust, more progressive, and *truer* story—the story of a 'long civil rights movement'"[14] whose roots predate *Brown*, and whose continuity includes the upsurge of militancy and Black nationalism that continues beyond the mid-1960s. By including activities of the late 1940s within the scope of analysis, and by tracing points of connectivity and influence with the history of the Black Arts Movement, *Readying the Revolution* applies the "long civil rights era" paradigm to African American theater history. Black theater scholarship, too, is sometimes reliant on the mid-1960s as the focal point of a prevailing before-and-after scheme of periodization. This study seeks to complicate that interpretive approach, revealing the conjunctive and transformational essence of an underexamined phase in the history of Black theater and performance.

The chapters that follow take up Baraka's rethinking about *A Raisin in the Sun* and expand it into a wider analysis of Black theater and performance of the late 1940s to the early 1960s. My central thesis is that this purportedly "passive phase" of postwar African American theater and performance was in fact quite active with radical creativity that was even militant and nationalist at times. Not only was the theater of this period defiant in its own right; the works discussed in this book foreshadowed and helped energize the even more unrestrained radicalism that was soon to erupt within Black culture starting in the mid-1960s. Margo Natalie Crawford's theory of "Black anticipatory aesthetics" offers a useful critical lens: "Black anticipatory aesthetics is the art of not knowing what blackness will be; it is the art situated within the sustained dissonance of the earlier chords being heard, simultaneously, with the sounds that are just beginning to emerge."[15] The plays, performances, and artists discussed in *Readying the Revolution* are alive with a sustained dissonance created as Black artists anticipated a nationalist cultural uprising within the limitations of their comparatively more restrictive post–World War II and early Cold War cultural landscape.

The headwinds blowing across that landscape encouraged African American artists to proceed strategically in a way designed to *appear* more passive and restrained. As the United States emerged victorious from World War II, Black activists (in alliance with certain liberal-minded white partners) sought to leverage anti-fascist, pro-democracy rhetoric of the war effort toward the securing of long-denied fundamental rights. While Jim Crow segregation, racial bigotry, and inequality of opportunity remained entrenched in national life, some notable "cracks in the citadel of white supremacy" appeared starting in the late 1940s. These included incremental gains for African Americans in hiring practice and work opportunities, in access to education, in social and economic mobility, and in the consolidation of political influence. As Manning Marable observes, "The growing social and economic power of the black working and middle classes seemed to many to provide the basis for an entirely new political relationship between blacks and whites."[16] Certain gains were highly visible and potentially transformative. Jackie Robinson broke Major League Baseball's color line in 1947 (the focus of Chapter 1); in 1948, President Truman issued Executive Order 9981, designed to end segregation in the US military; a string of Supreme Court rulings—particularly *Morgan v. Virginia* (1946), *Sipuel v. Board of Regents of University of Oklahoma* (1948), *Perez v. Sharp* (1948), *McLaurin v. Oklahoma State Regents* (1950), and *Sweatt v. Painter* (1950)—advanced a long struggle to dismantle the legal infrastructure of racial apartheid in US education, setting the stage for *Brown v. Board of Education* in 1954. To be sure, massive inequities and harsh bigotry remained entrenched at the core of American society, and each measure of social progress stirred up a reactionary white backlash. Yet the era's developments provided some foundation for cautious optimism and hope for further progress among Black thought leaders. In that context, African American theater artists saw advantage in positioning their voices *within*—rather than in outright rebellion *against*—mainstream civil rights discourse. This was certainly Hansberry's aim with *A Raisin in the Sun*, even as she wove within her drama radical anti-supremacist, anti-capitalist, and anti-imperialist ideals. As Julius B. Fleming Jr. notes, "Black theatre and performance were vital to black citizens' efforts to grapple with the 'unfinished business' of emancipation" in the years of the 'short' civil rights movement. This study aligns closely with Fleming's project of bringing new attention to "the significance of black theatre to the postwar era of civil rights activism."[17]

Many of those in that era who yearned for a more defiant approach to racial politics gravitated toward the Communist Left. The Communist Party of the USA (CPUSA) had stood as the most consistent and well-organized radical voice agitating for racial equality and Black political empowerment since the 1920s: incorporating campaigns of racial justice activism within its wide-ranging anticapitalist agenda. As Mary Helen Washington notes, many of the era's most prominent artists and thinkers worked within what historians have labeled a vibrant "Black or Negro Popular Front": a network of political and cultural organizations aligned with the antiracist and anticapitalistic work of the Left. "Nearly every major black writer of the 1940s and 1950s was in some way influenced by the Communist Party or other leftist organizations,"[18] including (to list a just few prominent examples) writers W. E. B. Du Bois, Langston Hughes, Richard Wright, Gwendolyn Brooks, and Lorraine Hansberry, and actors Paul Robeson, Julian Mayfield, and Canada Lee. As Martha Biondi explains, in its politics and its creative efforts, the Black Popular Front encompassed some seemingly divergent strains of thought:

> In 1928 the U.S. Communist Party adopted the slogan "self-determination in the Black Belt" to signal its commitment to Black liberation alongside working-class organizing. Self-determination included support for a Black nation in the southern Black Belt, desegregation in the North and West, and full racial equality in the United States. This simultaneous embrace of Black nationalism and integrationism may appear contradictory, but it resonated with deeply rooted, and often interlocking, African American struggles for political sovereignty, cultural nationalism, and civil rights.[19]

The works of artists connected to the Black Popular Front reflected and wrestled with this mix of political aims, creating a capacious culture that housed intricate debates about the present realities and multiple future possibilities for African American citizenship. Many of the playwrights and performers discussed in the chapters of this book—including William Branch, Alice Childress, Theodore Ward, Beulah Richardson, and Ossie Davis—had some association (direct or indirect) with this radical leftist cultural network. As the chapters that follow will demonstrate, their creative works encompass the breadth of interlocking political ideologies—particularly its modes of Black radicalism—that characterized this fervent cultural environment.

Also influential for African American culture—particularly within the Black Popular Front, and to some degree for *all* Black writers no matter their political associations—were the domestic pressures that defined the early Cold War. Due to CPUSA's prominence in the struggle for racial justice, a suspicion pervaded US political circles "that anyone working against segregation or in the field of civil rights also had communist ties." Through a host of invasive and repressive methods, the FBI and other federal authorities relentlessly "targeted the black intellectual and cultural community of the 1950s,"[20] chilling (directly or implicitly) free expression for socially critical Black voices. Voluminous FBI files now document the detailed surveillance given to prominent African American artists and thinkers of the era. Blacklisting of suspected Communists and sympathizers derailed the careers of many notable cultural leaders. Those with even indirect or casual ties to the Black Popular Front found themselves persecuted, interrogated, and shunned—not only by McCarthyite red-baiters and the power brokers dominating Broadway or Hollywood, but also by certain "black middle-class leaders [who] attempted to divorce themselves from the communists as the reactionary trend was building across the country."[21] With Cold War paranoia heightening the risks of overt radicalism on questions of racial equality, Black theater artists of the late 1940s and the 1950s were compelled to raise their voices carefully and with some restraint. Through a range of creative approaches, they crafted performances whose critiques of white supremacy were bold and insightful, yet calibrated to ensure the artist's safety within a dangerous and repressive political climate. The measured tone in their expression does not automatically indicate a moderation of outlook or conservatism of ambition. For many plays and performances of the era, we must read beneath the surface of surviving texts and evidence to grasp the fullness of meaning that an artist sought and that an audience could experience in live performance.

Given these historical realities, for any analysis of this fraught period of African American theater history, the obvious bombast of the years that follow presents an inescapable point of contrast. The Black Arts Movement that erupts in the mid-1960s heralded a more overtly militant and nationalist trajectory for Black culture. Baraka's iconic 1964 play *Dutchman* stands as an important ignition point for the explosion of Black Arts theater that dominates the African American stage for more than a decade. Larry Neal, in his formative essay for the *Drama Review* in the summer of 1968, positioned the Black Arts Movement as "the aesthetic and spiritual sister of the Black Power concept. As such, it envisions an art that speaks directly to the needs and aspirations of Black America. . . . . The Black Arts and the Black Power concept both relate broadly to the Afro-American's desire for self-determination and nationhood."[22] The playwrights, performers, and theorists advancing this ideology conceived of their work as a distinct break from the more moderate, more integration-oriented approach of the immediate past. Such a view is evident in Baraka's reminiscence of the disdain with which he and his fellow "Young militants" initially viewed the "passive . . . middle class" sensibility of *A Raisin in the Sun*. Viewed through a lens of late-1960s and 1970s militant Black cultural nationalism, theater and performance of the immediate postwar years will undoubtedly seem more temperate, less brashly confrontational, and not nearly as totalizing in terms of an obliteration and reimagination of the white supremacist American status quo.

But the more that we view the past through that galvanizing lens, the greater the risk of obscuring a key dynamic of the post–World War II years. Whether to romanticize Baraka and other revolutionary playwrights for their disruptive boldness, or else to problematize the movement's indulgence in violent imagery and rhetorical excess, compartmentalizing the Black Arts theater from the years that preceded it within our historical vision serves to flatten the contours of a rich creative genealogy. Each chapter of *Readying the Revolution* accentuates the revolutionary implications of plays and performances crafted for a dynamic, proto-revolutionary moment in African American performance culture. The book presents for Black theater history a parallel to Nikhil Pal Singh's intervention in the political historiography of the civil rights era—a reconsideration of "the historical depth and heterogeneity of black struggles against racism" across a wide sweep of the mid-twentieth century.[23]

Readying the Revolution is interdisciplinary in its approach to African American theater history. Sections of the book look beyond traditional theater to consider performances by African Americans undertaken within other arenas—professional sports, leftist politics, and popular music—as part of a wider analysis of Black performance culture of the era. In this sense, the book expands into the field of performance studies, though it does not attempt to be comprehensive in that effort. Chapters that move beyond the stage into other genres where Black creative expression and racial politics intersect are offered selectively, to extend the book's central thesis about the less overt radicalism of the era across other cultural arenas. The chapters of the book are arranged chronologically by their focus, though the cultural activities discussed in each section often overlap with one another.

- Chapter 1 offers a critical reading of Jackie Robinson's performances both as a baseball player and as a public figure. Interpreting his athletic achievements and public life through a lens of performance, I argue that Robinson—despite the critiques of those who denounced him as accommodationist rather than radical—crafted a style of strategic resistance against marginalization and inequity, anticipating the cultural work undertaken by other African American theater and performance artists of the era.
- Chapter 2 analyzes three dramas written and produced during the postwar period that have been somewhat neglected in Black theater

scholarship: *Our Lan'* by Theodore Ward (1948), *Gold through the Trees* by Alice Childress (1950), and *In Splendid Error* by William Branch (1954). These plays presented striking theatrical visions of collective resistance against racial injustice. Each dramatizes groups of Black people uniting—righteously, forcefully, physically—in opposition to white supremacist political and social oppression, offering audiences of their era potent models of revolutionary Black political action.

- Chapter 3 examines the neglected theatrical legacy of playwright and performer Beulah Richardson (who later achieved prominence as an actress for theater, film, and television under the name Beah Richards). In her composing and staging of three mostly forgotten original performance texts of the early 1950s—*A Black Woman Speaks . . . of White Womanhood, of White Supremacy, of Peace, Genocide,* and *The Revolt of Rosa Ingram*—Richardson harnessed the visceral power of live performance to counteract the scourges of white supremacist, patriarchal, and capitalist oppression, and to move the public toward liberation and empowerment for African Americans, for women, and for all working-class Americans.
- Chapter 4 revisits Ossie Davis's 1961 play *Purlie Victorious* as a revolutionary comedy. Through analysis of the play text and its performance history, I argue that *Purlie Victorious* delivers—beneath its comic surface, and despite its popular commercial appeal for white audiences—a defiant vision of forceful Black uprising against white supremacy, one with profoundly disruptive implications.
- Chapter 5 examines two interrelated theatrical phenomena of the years 1961–64: the popular and highly controversial off-Broadway production of Jean Genet's play *The Blacks* at St. Mark's Playhouse, and Lorraine Hansberry's writing of her African-set drama, *Les Blancs*. Hansberry wrote *Les Blancs* in angry response to *The Blacks;* contrasts between these two works are abundant. Even so, this chapter argues that certain aspects of the off-Broadway staging of *The Blacks* were surprisingly aligned with the revolutionary spirit of Hansberry's drama. Both theatrical phenomena served as conduits for the era's burgeoning ideals of African American militancy in the face of white hegemonic oppression (within the United States and abroad).
- Chapter 6 reconsiders the artistry of singer/songwriter Nina Simone within the contours of cultural politics of the postwar years. The analysis centers on Simone's influential protest anthem "Mississippi

Goddam" as a performance text that links the ideologies of liberal integrationism and Black nationalism of the mid-twentieth century. The chapter situates "Mississippi Goddam" as a transitional moment within Simone's musical evolution from a mainstream performer with broad commercial appeal in 1950s and early 1960s to a muse of Black militancy, Black feminist advocacy, and fierce racial pride later in her musical career.

- A brief conclusion looks forward in history to consider connections between postwar African American theater and performance to the nascent Black Power political culture that emerged in the mid-1960s. Here I also briefly consider how the methodology of this study might inform scholarship on a new moment of productive upheaval in Black cultural politics ongoing during the writing of this book: Black Lives Matter. This conclusion speaks to my hope that this study can not only shed new light on theatrical activities of the past, but also point toward new perspectives on the artistic legacies of the present and future.

ONE | More Than "Guts Enough"

Jackie Robinson's Performances of Resistance and Integration

In February 1946, the New York chapter of the Baseball Writers' Association of America held its annual banquet—a private yearly gathering for members and invited VIPs. The event's proceedings traditionally included a comedy skit performed by association members lampooning the year's baseball news and notable personalities. That year, the talk of the sport was a certain notable player who, after one season with the minor league Montreal Royals, would likely be promoted to the Brooklyn Dodgers in the coming season: Jackie Robinson. As recounted by *New York Times* writer Arthur Daley, here is how the sketch performed at this banquet began:

> (*Curtain rises showing Southern mansion. Darky in satin knee breeches is dusting table with back to audience. He turns slowly, disclosing that upper part of uniform is a Montreal shirt. Waits for laugh, advances center, peers into wings.*)
>
> BUTLER: Looks lak de massa will be late dis ebning. (*Exits.*)

The "massa" of this fictional plantation, baseball commissioner and former senator Raymond "Happy" Chandler, enters and calls for his butler.

> CHANDLER: Robbie-eee. Robbie-eee. (*Butler enters.*)
> BUTLER: Yassuh, Massa. Here Ah is.
> CHANDLER: Ah, there you are, Jackie. Jackie, you ole woolly headed rascal. How long yo' been in the family?
> BUTLER: Long time, Kunl, marty long time. Ebber since Massa [Branch] Rickey [general manager of the Dodgers] done bote me from da Kansas City Monarchs [Robinson's former Negro League team].

CHANDLER: To be sure, Jackie, to be sure. How could Ah forget that Colonel Rickey brought you to our house. (*Aside*) Rickey—that no good carpetbagger! What could he be thinking of?

The scene continues in a similar vein. Daley describes the evening's entertainment as "healthy and wholesome" and assures readers that "no one's feelings really were hurt,"[1] presumably because only whites were in attendance. Not everyone found the premise of the performance amusing, however. In response to Daley's report, Wendell Smith—baseball writer for the Black newspaper the *Pittsburgh Courier,* who as an African American was barred from joining the Baseball Writers' Association—branded the skit a "Nazi Opera." Smith noted the irony of his white colleagues (many of whom had professed support for the integration of Major League Baseball in their newspaper columns) staging "this dastardly act behind closed doors. The parts were played by well-known writers . . . but their names were not made public for fear of being reprimanded."[2]

The private minstrel show mounted by the baseball writers magnifies the cultural backdrop to Jackie Robinson's entry into the major leagues. Whatever his on-field achievements or individual conduct with the Dodgers would come to be, this player's public image was always-already shaped by racial stereotypes and narrative tropes ingrained in the American cultural imagination for more than a century. Statistics provide an objective measure of a major leaguer's productivity in hitting, fielding, base running, and pitching. But our cherished "national pastime" is more than just a statistically measurable contest. It is also a public performance, a cultural genealogy, a civic spectacle, and a sacred ritual embedded deeply within the communal psyche. Accordingly, Robinson's acceptance by the public would inevitably be more than just a question of his on-field achievements, despite the many protestations to the contrary. For example, upon Robinson's transition from the Negro leagues to minor league play, Montreal Royals president Hector Racine proclaimed that "we are signing this boy because we think of him primarily as a ball player . . . we think it a point of fairness."[3] Racine was apparently unaware of how his diminutive language belied his claims to transcending racial prejudice. In a similar vein, Branch Rickey proclaimed about his prospect: "The American public is not as concerned with a ballplayer's pigmentation as it is with the power of his swing, the dexterity of his slide, the gracefulness of his fielding or the speed of his legs."[4] While on the Montreal Royals roster, Robinson played along with Rickey's rhetoric and urged the public to evaluate him "just like all these other players out here."[5] Yet, as the New York baseball writers knew and exploited for their own private amusement, the drama of Jackie Robinson's presence within white professional baseball was inextricably bound up in that most quintessentially American narrative of anti-Black racism.

Since the 1940s, the story of Jackie Robinson has been and continues to be refracted through lenses of white supremacy. Public commemorations of his career often depict Robinson as a disempowered laborer, whose opportunity to prove his worth to a skeptical public depended upon the bravery and generosity of paternal white protectors and rested on a capacity for enduring racist degradations without upsetting white sensibilities. Branch Rickey (known popularly as "The Deacon" and "The Mahatma") stands in such accounts as the mastermind and white savior figure, who single-handedly and courageously engineered the smashing of racist traditions, steered his charge through the perils of a hateful society, and protected Robinson from the potentially destructive consequences of his own aggressive tendencies. Such a narrative emerges from this familiar anecdote of the future Hall of Fame player's initial meeting with Rickey, which took place secretly in Brooklyn on August 28, 1945:

> "Mr. Rickey," [Robinson] said, "Do you want a ballplayer who's afraid to fight back?"
>
> Rickey's face wrinkled in mock rage. "I want a ballplayer with guts enough not to fight back!"[6]

Surveying numerous other accounts of Robinson's career written since the 1950s, David Naze finds within this historiography a troubling tendency to position "Robinson as a patient and silent participant in the endeavor to break baseball's color barrier" and to venerate Branch Rickey as the drama's real protagonist.[7]

Characterizations of Robinson as a cautious, conservative actor in the face of bigotry and degradation extend beyond the years of his baseball career into his later activities in business and politics. Away from the field and the clubhouse, Robinson pursued many business ventures and was a prominent voice within conversations about racial equality during the 1950s–1960s. His activities and associations regularly placed him at odds with more radical Black leaders and movements of the era. Robinson was a proud, lifelong Republican during an era when the GOP's shift toward conservative racial politics was well underway. He campaigned for Richard Nixon for president in 1960; in 1964, he championed New York governor Nelson Rockefeller's bid for the Republican Party presidential nomination (part of a long-standing political alliance and personal friendship between these two men). Robinson publicly criticized the tactics and the platforms of radical Black leaders and groups as harmful to the campaign for greater acceptance and opportunity for African Americans. Such a posture brought him harsh condemnation from certain Black critics and reinforced his image as someone far more moderate than militant in temperament.

Robinson's conservative politics, his distaste for radicalism, and his feuds with Black nationalist leaders have been thoroughly documented. However, to limit our understanding of Robinson to this political context is to miss something essential about his cultural influence and historical importance. "Frankly," Naze concludes, "this is where we have failed Jackie Robinson . . . . [W]e revere his reticence in the most tumultuous of times" so that we might take comfort in "a convenient legacy. Robinson's memory should be anything but convenient."[8] Seen from a different perspective, Jackie Robinson was an innovator and shrewd provocateur, who traversed a previously impermeable and oppressive social barrier erected around the nation's most treasured civic pastime; from that position, he strategically tested the limitations he faced, adapted his tactics of disruption, and explored new paths of resistance against white hegemony in ways often not immediately visible. While playing the game—I use that phrase both literally and figuratively—he skillfully performed defiance of the status quo and became an agitator for change. Viewing his athletic activities and public life through a lens of performance, this chapter argues that Jackie Robinson stands as a prototype for the work undertaken by Black theater and performance artists in the years following his major league debut. While he occupied the spotlight of the national culture's most cherished stage, and then later in retirement from baseball as he remained a focus of public attention, Jackie Robinson enacted strategies of resistance that would resound through Black performance culture of the decades that followed.

JACKIE ROBINSON AS A BASEBALL PLAYER

From his very first encounter with the Brooklyn Dodgers organization, Robinson's relationship with Major League Baseball was a performative endeavor. During his secret interview with Branch Rickey in Brooklyn, the Dodgers' general manager tested whether Robinson had "guts enough not to fight back" through mimesis—by provocatively "removing his jacket and rolling up his sleeves so he could act out all the hostile personalities that baseball's first Negro was likely to face." Rickey probed Robinson by impersonating beanballing pitchers, spike-flashing base runners, unaccommodating hotel clerks and waiters, biased umpires, and bigoted fans; each scenario was conjured to explore how this young player might respond. By the most popular account of the meeting, this was no dispassionate exercise for Rickey, "his shirt wet at the collarbone and under the armpits, his face gleaming with perspiration." His scene partner, too, got swept up in the emotion of the dramatized scenarios; by the same account, "Robinson was burning hot inside" in response to Rickey's performed provocations.[9]

Robinson well understood—without Rickey needing to explain it to him—that allowing himself to vent fully the rage that was "burning hot inside" would imperil his opportunity to upend history, and so he proceeded accordingly. In one dramatic enactment of an opposing player spoiling for a brawl, "Rickey waved his massive fist in Robinson's face, missing it only by a whisper. Robinson's nose twitched and his lips moved a bit. But his head was steady. 'I get it, Mr. Rickey, I get it . . . What you want me to say is that I've got another cheek.'"[10] This performance of acquiescence, despite a smoldering anger, aligns with a genealogy of Black performance that stretches back to slavery and the Middle Passage. Douglas A. Jones Jr. describes the songs and dances enacted by African captives on the decks of slave ships as "a system of coerced performance in which the slave, regardless of his degree of participation, contributed to his own abjection." Jones reads the delivery of these entertainments as a strategy of survival, racial solidarity, and subaltern resistance amid unspeakable oppression and degradation. From the plantation, to Jim Crow, and beyond, similar performed acts of acquiescence, stoicism, and nonaggression beneath the controlling gaze of oppressors help sustain the tenuous equilibrium between disempowered African Americans and those whites upon whose satisfaction their immediate physical survival depended. Such performances serve a dual function; while assuaging the slave masters, these gestures also united slaves with one another "in order to endure, and eventually resist, the wretchedness of their captivity." Thus, Jones argues, from its origins African American performance has functioned as "a *crucible of collective possibility*."[11] Robinson, though physically and spatially isolated from other African Americans while confined within the Dodgers' executive suite, was embarking upon a wider campaign of silent and steadfast resistance against social marginalization. It was a campaign he undertook in solidarity with his equally deserving Negro league compatriots not yet included in the narrative, and ultimately with all of Black America.

Robinson's immovability in the face of Rickey's provocations constitutes what Harvey Young terms "a performance of stillness" that makes physically manifest Black defiance against white control.[12] Rickey's imaginative role-playing exercise served (perhaps unintentionally) a concrete social function—to strengthen Robinson's capacity for safe navigation of the dangerous social situations that awaited him in the major leagues. In other words, the scenarios empowered Robinson as an emerging agent of social change to "practice a real act even though he [did] it in a fictional matter. . . . Within its fictional limits, the experience [was] a concrete one," and, in that sense, mirrored what Augusto Boal would later describe as "a *rehearsal of revolution*."[13] History has, regrettably and somewhat predictably, minimized Robinson's agency within this now apocryphal moment of Boalian performance and instead inflated the purported genius of his white scene partner.

Robinson's one-year stint in Montreal for the 1946 season was mostly free of ugly incidents of racism. The tactics rehearsed in Rickey's office received an early real-world test in just the second week of his first season with the Dodgers. On April 22, 1947, Brooklyn opened a three-game home series with the visiting Philadelphia Phillies. During the series, the Philadelphia club (under the leadership of Alabama-born manager Ben Chapman) employed vicious race-baiting. "Hate poured forth from the Phillies dugout," Robinson later recounted:

> "Hey, nigger, why don't you go back to the cotton field where you belong?"
> "They're waiting for you in the jungles, black boy!"
> "Hey, snowflake, which one of those white boys' wives are you dating tonight?"

Inwardly, Robinson seethed. "For one wild and rage-crazed minute I thought, 'To hell with Mr. Rickey's noble experiment.' . . . To hell with the image of the patient black freak I was supposed to create. I could throw down my bat, stride over to that Phillies dugout, grab one of those white sons of bitches and smash his teeth in with my despised black fist."[14] And yet—for himself, his team, and the larger social cause of African American liberation—Robinson made the strategic choice to mask that rage and redirect it toward his game play, with generative results. With the game scoreless in the bottom of the eighth inning, Robinson singled and then stole second base. His aggression on the base paths elicited a throwing error from Phillies catcher Andy Seminick, allowing him to advance to third base. Robinson then scored easily on teammate Gene Hermanski's single to center field. This was the game's only run, giving the Dodgers a 1–0 win, their first in a three-game sweep of the series.

Robinson's game-winning performance typified his mastery over what Koritha Mitchell terms "know-your-place aggression . . . a backlash of violence—both literal and symbolic, both physical and discursive—that essentially says, *know your place!*"[15] His play that day against the Phillies also illustrates a signature stylistic contribution Robinson made to Major League Baseball play. As Jules Tygiel notes:

> At the plate and in the field, Robinson radiated dynamic intensity, but his true genius materialized on the base paths. . . . "He brought a new dimension into baseball," says [former teammate and Dodgers executive] Al Campanis. "He brought stealing back [into the sport] whereas up until that time baseball had become a long-ball hitting game."

Robinson's weaponizing of his speed went beyond stealing bases. By dancing provocatively off a base and daring the defense to respond, by suddenly breaking for the next base when the opposition least suspected, by distracting pitchers and fielders and eliciting errant throws, he electrified his team's offense and flustered their opponents. In other words, this player "revolutionized major league baseball by injecting an element of 'tricky baseball,' so common in the Negro leagues"[16] into his play. Into a sport whose staid traditions and deliberate cadence might have been compared with classical music, Jackie Robinson infused the more improvisatory, syncopated energies of bebop.

There were two epilogues to Robinson's tense drama with the Phillies. In the next installment of "Jackie Robinson Says"—a regular column he wrote for the *Pittsburgh Courier*—Robinson took the high road in reflecting on the series: "Some of the Phillies bench-jockeys tried to get me upset last week, but it didn't really bother me. . . . In fact, the fellows who are sitting on the bench when I come to bat probably don't have much work to do. If they did, they'd be out there playing, wouldn't they?"[17] Then, when the Dodgers took their first road trip to Philadelphia the following month, Robinson joined Chapman for a staged tableau of reconciliation. The picture was orchestrated at the request of Phillies' management, who sought a counternarrative to the team's widely condemned racist behavior in the

Figure 1. Jackie Robinson (left) pictured in a photo with Philadelphia Phillies Ben Chapman (right) before a game between the Brooklyn Dodgers and Philadelphia Phillies on June 1, 1947. Photo: The Rucker Archive/Icon Sportswire.

earlier series in Brooklyn. Posing for the photo, Chapman refused to shake Robinson's hand, so the two men smiled holding opposite ends of a baseball bat. Robinson would later describe this photo-op as "one of the most difficult things I had to make myself do," but a few days later, took on a tone of magnanimity in his column: "Chapman impressed me as a nice fellow. . . . I don't think he really meant the things he was shouting at me the first time we played Philadelphia."[18] Such high-mindedness solidified the stance that Robinson promised Rickey he would assume toward his antagonists—assuring the continuation of his major league career and diminishing Chapman in the process.

Throughout his first two seasons with the Dodgers, Robinson stuck to his commitment to respond neither directly nor angrily to racist taunts. He endured beanballs from opposing pitchers, spikes from base runners while playing the infield, all manner of verbal abuse, and frequent threats from hostile fans. While he mostly maintained outward calm, he did find some opportunities to act upon his inner defiance—sometimes subtly, and at other times more overtly. One example came in an August 1947 contest against the St. Louis Cardinals. Robinson hit a soft grounder to the first-base side of the pitcher's mound, fielded by Cardinals' pitcher Harry Brecheen. Rather than toss the ball to first base for an easy putout, Brecheen placed himself menacingly along the baseline, with fists extended toward home plate. Robinson stopped running and allowed himself to be tagged out but did not retreat silently to the dugout. "You better watch out. You better play your position as you should," he warned Brecheen. "If you ever pull that stunt again, I'll send you right on the seat of your pants."[19] Robinson's first ejection from a game came during his second season, as part of a tense contest against the Pittsburgh Pirates. According to an account published in the *Courier* (a hometown paper for the Pirates, but also a consistent advocate for Robinson and other Black baseball players in the major leagues), during the game's second inning Robinson "went into a tantrum . . . as he vigorously protested" an umpire's call on the field. Two innings later, hearing Robinson continue to complain from the bench, umpire Butch Henline tossed him from the game: "Jackie came rushing out of the dugout as if he were possessed with the very devil itself and proceeded to give Henline a verbal lacing down that had all the characteristics of a three-ring circus."[20] Robinson was removed from the dugout and fined twenty-five dollars by the league. He would later write, proudly, that Henline "was treating me exactly as he would any ballplayer who got on his nerves. That made me feel great . . . One of the newspapers said it in the best headline I ever got. JACKIE JUST ANOTHER GUY."[21]

Looking back on the 1948 season, Dodgers manager Leo Durocher writes that "as the season progressed [Robinson] became testier and testier" with umpires, his teammates, and Dodgers management. "Having served out a year in silence, Jackie apparently felt he had the right to assert himself. Before I left [the Dodgers in July 1948], he was asserting himself with a vengeance."[22] His vengeance became even more noticeable with the addition of a second African American player to the Dodgers' roster that season. Roy Campanella, a Negro league star catcher since the late 1930s, had signed with the organization just a few months after Robinson had joined Montreal. Upon his promotion to the majors, "Campy" quickly became a friend and confidant for "Robby." The two shared segregated hotel and restaurant accommodations on road trips, exchanged advice and wisdom, made joint community appearances, and even purchased houses in the same Brookyln neighborhood. But differences between them quickly became clear. Campanella naturally personified an easygoing, turn-the-other-cheek approach that offered a clear contrast with Robinson's increasingly confrontational demeanor. In an unverified but frequently retold anecdote, Campanella reportedly once cautioned Robinson, "It may take ten years to go ahead but you can fall all the way back in one. . . . You got to walk a chalk line all the time. It's nice up here [in the major leagues]. Don't spoil it." Though the exchange was later disputed by Robinson, the story has persisted as "a favorite of white sportswriters, to highlight the difference between the Dodgers' black stars. Jackie . . . was the aggressive hothead, always 'popping off.' Campy, meanwhile, was passive, grateful to be in the major leagues."[23] William C. Kashatus interprets the contrasting reputations of Robinson and Campanella as reflective of "a fundamental dialectic in African American history itself, one that embodies a constant but inevitable tension between active defiance and passive resistance, aggression and docility, direct action and self-reliance . . . the differing philosophies of Booker T. Washington and W. E. B. Du Bois." This was more than just a question of who argued with umpires or walked silently back to the dugout. In the larger arena of racial politics, Robinson increasingly "considered [Campanella] an 'Uncle Tom' because he was an agreeable black man in a white world. Campanella's refusal to actively challenge Jim Crow irked Robinson." Conversely, Campanella found himself "unnerved by Robinson's outspokenness on civil rights issues and his combative behavior."[24]

The 1949 season marks a clear turning point in Robinson's major league narrative. In his autobiography, he writes, "Not being able to fight back is a form of severe punishment. I was relieved when Mr. Rickey finally called me into his office and said, 'Jackie, you're on your own now. You can be yourself now.'"[25] Though his own account gives Rickey primary agency over the change of performance tactics, Robinson's newly liberated style yielded his finest year as a major leaguer. With the persistent strain of quelling his anger removed, he posted career highs in total hits, batting average, runs batted in, slugging percentage, and stolen bases. And while there is no clear statistical measure of it, his productivity in protesting to umpires, delivering controversial quotations to sportswriters, jawing with opposing players, and sniping with league management also took a sharp upturn—a trend that would continue for the rest of his baseball career. Robinson was certainly cognizant of the risks associated with his change of approach: "As long as I appeared to ignore insult and injury, I was a martyred hero to a lot of people . . . But the minute I began to answer, to argue to protest—the minute I began to sound off—I became a swellhead, a wise guy, an 'uppity' nigger. When a white guy did it, he had spirit. When a black payer did it, he was 'ungrateful,' an upstart, a sorehead."[26] Robinson chose the course of outspokenness, nonetheless.

A June 1951 editorial in the *Sporting News* highlights the complexities of the new character that Robinson was playing on the public stage. In the paper's reckoning, Robinson had recently "appeared to have developed a persecution complex, in which he envisioned enemies among the umpires and opposing players," marking a distinct shift away from "the restraint and dignity that had characterized his previous progress in the game." For an era when jawing with umpires and jockeying with opponents during a game was a common and even expected part of competitiveness in professional baseball, the double standard behind the *Sporting News*'s sense of alarm is obvious enough. The anonymous (but most certainly white-authored) editorial goes on to praise Robinson for handling certain recent incidents (including a death threat from fans in Cincinnati, and an on-field collision with a Philadelphia pitcher) "lightly" rather than angrily. The editorial builds to this didactic conclusion:

> Robinson is a player to stir the spirit and admiration of all Americans, who, almost to a man, will respect quality and integrity of performance, allied with seemly deportment. However, they will resent and repel with all their force the agitator, the sharper with an angle, the fellow who is less than an American because he chooses to be a rabble rouser.[27]

Never were the national identities of other notorious baseball "rabble rousers"—from bygone legends like Ty Cobb and Rogers Hornsby, to many of Robinson's temperamental white contemporaries—subject to this type of criticism. The Phillies had justified their abuse of Robinson in his first season by arguing that "we're treating him just the same way we do any other player on a rival club"[28] and received no criticism for seeming "less than . . . American" for doing so. The risks associated with a Black player engaging in the exact same conduct were much higher; Robinson consciously assumed those risks, not only for himself but also on behalf of his teammates. "Many times when I made strong or controversial statements, I was not fighting for a personal thing. I was standing up for my team. I was saying things some of my teammates felt but were reluctant to say. The Dodgers appreciated this."[29]

Increasingly, Robinson's rabble-rousing took on (beyond the ordinary hard-nosed competitiveness celebrated from many players) an explicitly antiracist dimension. One telling example came in a 1952 series with the St. Louis Cardinals. Robinson on several occasions heard Cardinals players targeting him and his African American teammate Joe Black with torrents of abuse that included "the word 'n——r' linked with obscene nouns and adjectives." After years of habitually ignoring such remarks, at this moment, he publicly answered his tormentors by screaming back at them from the field. "Usually I don't give any sign I've heard them," he later told the *Pittsburgh Courier*. "But . . . it's been so long since I've heard anything this bad I just blew up about it." The incident inspired Dodgers president Walter O'Malley to lodge a formal complaint against the Cardinals with National League president Warren Giles.[30] A more vivid example came in late August 1956. Throughout the early innings of a game in Milwaukee, Braves pitcher Lew Burdette hurled racial insults at Robinson from the dugout. "He said something about a watermelon," Robinson told reporters. "I knew what he meant, and he knew what he was saying." Warming up at third base before the start of the third inning, a fuming Robinson aimed a throw not toward the first basemen where it belonged, but directly at Burdette's head in the dugout—narrowly missing him and striking the wall beside him. Asked about it later, Robinson was unapologetic.

> The thing that made me doubly angry is the fact that Burdette had the nerve to shout those racial slurs at me in spite of the fact that he has at least three or four Negro teammates on the Milwaukee team. How do you think they felt? They were there on the bench. . . . And I'm not through with Burdette yet. If he starts that stuff in Brooklyn when we play, I'll go after him again. He's nothing but a coward in my book.

The reporters who heard these statements acknowledged, "He means every word if it. . . . That Robinson's not a guy you can fool around with."[31]

This image of Robinson as fierce and defiant in the face of racial insults and unfair treatment has receded; the character of a patient, noncombative player whose forbearance deflated the public's bigotry takes its place in the national mythos. Such a vision soothes the fears of a country that prefers to avoid reckoning with the consequences of white supremacy and righteously angry Black responses to it. Arnold Rampersad's biography of Robinson reminds us of how the hero character we have constructed around Robinson obliterates a more disturbing truth from our historical memory:

> Robinson was always a symbol, both an individual human being and also a figment of America's guilty, shame-filled imagination. He was an exception even among the black players, whose conduct in facing the white world, during this first, tightly watched decade of

> racial integration, ranged mainly from congeniality, on the one hand, to rank obsequiousness, on the other. Only Jackie Robinson insisted, day in and day out, on challenging America on the matter of race and justice.[32]

The defiance against exclusion performed on the field of competition by Jackie Robinson was both consistent and strategic from the start of his association with Major League Baseball. Its valence evolved throughout his professional baseball career, but the challenge his various performances posed to the nation over fundamental questions of justice and fair play never wavered.

JACKIE ROBINSON AS ATHLETE-ACTIVIST

No matter his wish to be "just another guy" in the sport, this unique athlete could not avoid being written into the story of civil rights-era racial politics. Consequently—as a precursor to his later activity as a civic leader—Robinson found several opportunities during his playing career to shape (rather than to be shaped passively by) that political discourse. Whether from his own initiative, or in response to circumstances imposed upon him, through various performances on the public stage during his baseball career, Robinson promoted Black autonomy and actively resisted marginalization and silencing. Similar to what he displayed on the field and in the dugout, Robinson enacted his role as an athlete-activist with calculated savvy—showing a skill for testing (without defying outright) the oppressive systemic limits within which he operated.

A national political spotlight first shone on Robinson during his third season in the major leagues. On July 18, 1949, he received an invitation to testify before the House Unamerican Activities Committee (HUAC), to respond to controversial statements made by African American actor and singer Paul Robeson. With the "second Red Scare" in full swing, Robeson's infamy as a Communist sympathizer increasingly overshadowed his renown as a performer. Robeson had stirred up significant protest with an April 1949 address in Paris to the World Congress of the Partisans of Peace. The most controversial segment of that speech declares: "It is unthinkable that American Negroes would go to war on behalf of those who have oppressed us for generations against a country [the Soviet Union] which in one generation has raised our people to the full dignity of mankind."[33] To refute what was roundly interpreted as Robeson's anti-American prediction, HUAC sought an influential African American with an untarnished image to deliver a full public rebuke. In that role the committee placed a baseball player with no significant experience in public speaking, no expertise in Cold War geopolitics, nor any direct connection to Robeson nor his remarks. Because Robinson excelled on the field and had otherwise kept his public image free from controversy, he was the most recognizable and celebrated African American of the day, and thus fit HUAC's casting requirements perfectly.

Congress had set a stage, typecast their performer, and focused a national spotlight of attention. Robinson played along, fully aware that the proceedings had been orchestrated (as Congressman Morgan M. Moulder of Missouri reminded him during the hearing) "to combat the idea Paul Robeson has given by his statements" on behalf of "your country and your people."[34] The baseball star was somewhat reticent to take on this role before HUAC. "I was not sure what to do. . . . I didn't want to fall prey to the white man's game and allow myself to be pitted against another black man."[35] The stakes of the situation were heightened by Paul Robeson's earlier advocacy for desegregation of Major League Baseball, of which Robinson was a direct beneficiary. In a speech to the league's commissioner and team owners in December 1943, Robeson connected the public stage of professional sports with his own boundary-breaking theatrical appearance on Broadway in the previous year. He said, "To me the most indicative thing that has happened in the fight against racial discrimination is the reception that I've been given in 'Othello.' I was told before the play was produced that America was not ready to accept me or such a delicate theme, but I've never appeared before friendlier audiences."[36] He also spoke to the baseball owners of other experiences he had enjoyed as an All-American college football player—emphasizing the power of public performances (both artistic and athletic) as a catalyst for interracial unity. HUAC's public event aimed toward a much different outcome: with a lone Black actor summoned to recite before an entirely white panel of auditors a script engineered to emphasize division between two prominent African Americans.

Despite the risks and complications of testifying, Robinson saw an opportunity to affirm and renew before a national audience the birthright that African Americans shared with their white compatriots: an equal ownership stake in American democracy and the inalienable right to protest injustice, no matter the political environment. Mindful of opposition that some African American leaders had expressed to the news of the invitation from Congress, Robinson nonetheless agreed to testify. He collaborated with Branch Rickey and Lester B. Granger (the National Urban League's

Figure 2. Jackie Robinson testifies before the House Un-American Activities committee, July 18, 1949.

executive director, who had previously testified before the same committee) to craft a speech that blended pragmatism, patriotism, and defiant righteousness. His remarks nimbly spanned two divergent perspectives simultaneously. In one sense, Robinson sought to calm national fears by articulating some limited but sincere disagreements with the reports of Robeson's statements. (Robinson never saw a full transcript of the speech that he was asked to disavow.) As he hit those reassuring notes, he also looked to affirm the righteousness of *all* critiques of American white supremacy—even those articulated by Communist sympathizers.

The bluntest part of Robinson's words to HUAC reads: "Paul Robeson's statement in Paris to the effect that American Negroes would refuse to fight in any way against Russia . . . sounds very silly to me. But he has a right to his personal views, and if he wants to express them in public, that is his business and not mine." This prominent athlete and army veteran carefully assured the nation that, in the event of armed conflict against a foreign adversary, "most Negroes . . . [would] do their best to help their country win the war—against Russia or any other enemy that threatened us." His testimony concluded with a rhetorical flourish at Robeson's expense: "I've got too much invested for my wife and child and myself in the future of this country, and I and other Americans of many races and faiths have too much invested in our country's welfare, for any of us to throw it away because of a siren song sung in bass." Seizing on these strains within his remarks, the members of HUAC praised Robinson as "a fine young American" who has "rendered a great service to your country and to your people."[37] Media reports of the testimony focused largely on Robinson's direct retort to Robeson, hailing the Dodgers' young star as a loyal American hero.

Less noticed throughout the speech was an undeniable streak of protest. In giving the committee some of what it wanted to hear, Robinson also found the opportunity to validate the substance of Robeson's critique of American racism:

> The fact that it is a Communist who denounces injustice in the courts, police brutality, and lynching when it happens doesn't change the truth of his charges. Just because Communists kick up a big fuss over racial discrimination when its suits their purposes, a lot of people try to pretend that the whole issue is a creation of Communist imagination. But they are not fooling anyone with this kind of pretense, and talk about "Communists stirring up Negroes to protest," only makes present misunderstanding worse than ever. Negroes were stirred up long before there was a Communist Party, and they'll stay stirred up long after the party has disappeared—unless Jim Crow has disappeared by then as well.[38]

This passage precedes any direct mention of Paul Robeson in the testimony. Thus even as Robinson disputed the notion that African Americans might oppose a national war effort, he amplified Robeson and other Communists in their outcry against the nation's racial apartheid. The boldness of such a gesture—delivered in person to HUAC, by a political neophyte, amid a nationwide swelling of anti-communist paranoia—should not be overlooked. Contemporary and retrospective accounts mostly fall prey to what Naze calls an "oversimplification of the disagreement between Robinson and Robeson [that] blunts the edge . . . of Robinson's dissent."[39] In truth, the performance he delivered at the seat of American political power aligned directly (in its cagy rhetorical fashion) with the core of the critique Robeson had delivered from overseas. Thus, years before Robinson retired and put himself in the political arena, he showed sophistication with performing in the public eye. Like his "tricky baseball" play, he demonstrated how he could feint rhetorically to throw his opponents off balance, and then make a surprising advance in an unexpected direction.

At other times during his baseball career, Robinson's public statements were the source of (rather than a response to) political controversy. In one such instance, during an appearance on the nationally aired TV/radio interview show *Youth Wants to Know* in November 1952, a teenager asked Robinson whether he attributed the absence of African American players on the roster of the New York Yankees to racism within the organization. (The Yankees were among the last major league teams to integrate, doing so finally in 1955.) Yes was Robinson's frank answer, which he offered with a caveat that he considered the Yankees *players* to be "fine sportsmen and wonderful gentlemen" and that his judgment applied principally to the team's management. In a public uproar that ensued, Robinson rebuffed several invitations to recant or qualify his statement. "It seems to me the Yankee front office has used racial prejudice in its dealing with Negro ballplayers," he told the *New York Times*. "I may be wrong, but the Yankees will have to prove it to me. . . . The boy just asked me a question, and I answered it as simply and directly as I could."[40] When advised by baseball commissioner Ford Frick "to avoid the issue in the future," he answered Frick that "while I was not looking for any arguments with the Yankees or anybody else, I would give the same answer if I were every asked the same question again. . . . I have to live honestly with myself."[41] Robinson's statement elicited angry denials from the Yankees, and widespread condemnation in the press. "ROBINSON SHOULD BE PLAYER—NOT CRUSADER"[42] was the scolding headline in the next issue of the *Sporting News*. Even the *Pittsburgh Courier*'s Wendell Smith—a longtime ally and enthusiastic cheerleader—warned that "everyone should be very careful in these days and times about making such charges. . . . Robinson may be absolutely right about the Yankees, but we are inclined to think otherwise."[43] Whatever the validity of this judgment on baseball's most storied franchise, its clear utterance in national media demonstrated an evolution of Robinson's readiness for confronting publicly, rather than sidestepping, the pervasive racism of his sport.

A different short-lived but notable initiative during his playing career brought Robinson into the realm of publishing. In May 1953, he launched a new monthly magazine entitled *Our Sports* and served as the publication's founding editor. His first editorial column defined the mission of *Our Sports* as one of chronicling "the general participation of Negroes in all areas of the sports world . . . for the vast Negro audience." In addition to covering African American sports stars of national note, "Equal emphasis will be placed on the overwhelming bulk of activities on the *local level*; activities of Negro personalities that have never been covered by national magazines, local dailies or special sports publications."[44] The articles published in *Our Sports* cover a range of topics: athlete profiles, first-person accounts from Black sports figures (including Joe Louis, Josh Gibson, and Robinson himself), reports on Negro college squads and amateur athletics, and editorials exposing and decrying the persistence of Jim Crow inequality at all levels of competition. The venture was short-lived; only five issues appeared before *Our Sports* ceased publication in November 1953. Extant archives and documents (including Robinson's autobiography) provide no circulation or financial data for the magazine, and little insight into why it shuttered so quickly.

Though its lifespan was brief and its impact limited, *Our Sports* opens a tantalizing window into an otherwise obscured facet of Robinson's baseball playing years—his race consciousness. By 1953, Robinson had secured his status in the major leagues, won recognition as one of the sport's elite players, successfully expanded opportunities for the many Black players who followed him, and built a capacity for speaking, protesting, and rabble-rousing on the public stage. Even as these achievements transformed Major League Baseball and the nation, to what degree did this player remain (in the famous words of baseball writer Jimmy Cannon) "the loneliest man . . . in sports"?[45] Here, at the peak of his baseball success and with no background in journalism or publishing, Robinson created a new vehicle for fostering Black consciousness and pride in the sporting world; it was one way for him to rekindle his connections with a community of Black athletes that he had stepped away from in his historic move from the Negro leagues to the Dodgers. The limited lifespan of and lack of archival footprint left by *Our Sports* (beyond the five published issues themselves) now renders this project largely invisible within the historiography of Jackie Robinson during his years in Major League Baseball. But the project suggests that the sympathies and the activism of this influential Black performer were not *wholly* confined to an ideology of integrationism. *Our Sports* was a project animated by Black nationalist ideals.

ROBINSON AS ACTIVIST AFTER BASEBALL

In the second act of his public life, Jackie Robinson brought his antiracist ambitions into the arenas of business and national civic life. Following his retirement from baseball in 1957, until his health declined precipitously in the early 1970s, Robinson pursued various projects as an executive and entrepreneur and remained vocal in the realm of civil rights-era racial politics. He made frequent speeches and public appearances, joined marches and rallies, led fundraising campaigns, published editorials, lobbied elected leaders to promote economic opportunities for African Americans, protested Jim Crow segregation, and supported various politicians for office. His celebrity as a former athlete did not shield him from criticism in these endeavors; more likely, his prominence invited additional scrutiny and rebuke from those ideologically opposed to his approach, particularly other African American leaders. Within the cauldron of Black radicalism of the 1960s, Robinson personified for some a retrograde approach to pursuing social change. One anonymous and unforgiving letter sent to Robinson in 1962 proclaimed: "You have banished yourself from the Black Race. You are no longer one of us. You are a man without a race. The proud Black Race has ceased to recognize you as one of us."[46] A Brooklyn man wrote similarly in a 1963 letter to the *New York Amsterdam News*: "I do not consider Mr. Robinson a true black man. Rather he is a white mind covered by a black skin."[47] Surveying Robinson's various political activities and stances, Ron Briley describes him as "essentially a conservative" who "had little patience for black separatism and militancy."[48]

Sentiments like these are in large part a response to the public feuds that Robinson sustained with Malcolm X, Stokely Carmichael, Adam Clayton Powell, and other prominent and outspoken Black leaders. For example, in a second appearance in 1967 on the program *Youth Wants to Know* (the same venue through which he had labeled the New York Yankees' management as racist), Robinson remarked, "I don't advocate the Stokely Carmichael Black Power situation, because it can only get us in trouble. . . . If we're talking about getting in the streets, resorting to violence, creating disturbances, this cannot help anything. Black Power in this sense is just as bad as white power in that sense, so I'm opposed to it."[49] Robinson issued similar statements in print in various newspaper columns throughout the 1950s and 1960s. These sentiments, alongside his affiliation with Republican politicians, caused some to associate Robinson with that familiar and despised caricature of Uncle Tom. Such a view reinforces the prevailing narrative of his baseball career as one built upon white patronage, silent suffering, and conflict avoidance. Here, too, the story of Jackie Robinson merits a more capacious reconsideration. In his public life after retiring from baseball, Robinson displayed some willingness to experiment, to strategize, and to explore new paths of defiance that echoed his accomplishments both on and off the field during his time in the major leagues.

In February 1957, as he considered retiring from baseball rather than accept a trade from the Dodgers to the New York Giants, Robinson received a job offer to become director of personnel for the Chock Full o'Nuts corporation (which operated a popular chain of coffee shops). The leap from baseball to corporate management "seemed far removed from Robinson's interests and capabilities," but appealed to him as a new leadership challenge. According to Rampersad, the job offer from company president William H. Black came with a cynical hidden agenda, the "hope that Robinson would act as a buffer between his employees and the trade union movement which Black feared as a businessman."[50] The former baseball star's celebrity and public stature would surely be useful for the corporation as it sought to blunt growing demands from its mostly African American restaurant employees for fairer working conditions. Robinson, perhaps unaware of the political subtext, accepted the position. Once on the company payroll, he set about finding ways to support and advocate for company workers; no matter the agenda of management, he "saw himself as an advocate for the employees." Moreover, he took full advantage of the security and status that the job provided to sustain his political activism on other fronts throughout his time with the company. "Jack could not quite believe his luck in finding an employer so willing, whatever [Black's] reasons [for hiring him], to allow him the freedom he craved to speak out on civil rights."[51] His tenure with Chock Full o'Nuts was at times strained; Robinson was far from perfect in his performance as a corporate executive. Though the circumstances surrounding his departure from the company in early 1964 are somewhat murky, a key precipitating event was Robinson's angry protests to Black and other corporate executives over the hasty firing of six employees in retaliation for union-organizing activities.[52]

Following his departure, Robinson pursued a range of other business opportunities in finance, insurance, and housing. Some of these ventures found success—particularly his work with the Freedom National Bank, for which he served as founding partner and chairman of the board when it launched in Harlem in 1964. The bank quickly grew within its first five years into the largest Black-controlled financial institution in the country, serving Harlem's residents and Black-owned business, filling a void in the economic life of the community. Robinson remained active on the bank's board of directors and personally involved in its management until his health declined in the early 1970s. Other ventures, equally ambitious and community oriented, were less lasting. Throughout his business career, what animated Robinson's work was much more than a pursuit of personal financial gain. "As a would-be entrepreneur, Jack liked to quote the words of Malcom X, of all people, to the effect that he was interested in integrating lunch counters only because he wanted to own the cup he drank from, and counter on which his coffee rested, and the building in which the business was housed."[53] In that way, Robinson's ventures align the core philosophy animating *Our Sports*—namely, Black consciousness, autonomy, and pride, which values (despite claims to the contrary from his detractors) he held deeply and pursued earnestly.

As he developed his entrepreneurial ambitions, Robinson also deepened his engagement with national politics. Ideologically, Robinson supported the integrationist approach of the NAACP and conspicuously distanced himself from the era's radical Black nationalist voices. The NAACP awarded Robinson its prestigious annual Spingarn Medal in 1956—the first time an athlete had received the award—and appointed him later that year as national chairman of the Fight for Freedom campaign. He headlined a fundraising tour that drew huge crowds at events across the country: the start of many years of work on behalf of the organization. As tensions grew in the civil rights community between those who supported the NAACP's more cautious and legalistic approach and members of more confrontational groups such as Council on Racial Equality and the Student Nonviolent Coordinating Committee (SNCC), Robinson took notice, and at times called on the NAACP to take bolder action. In a 1958 press conference, after praising "the tremendous job the NAACP has done," he called on the group to "take a stronger stand. . . . I believe they have not done enough to gain confidence of the little man in the street. The average person is waiting to see the leaders take an aggressive stand."[54] The following month, he directly and personally criticized the group's executive secretary, Roy Wilkins, for a statement that seemingly endorsed a seven-year delay in enacting school desegregation measures. "For the head of the NAACP to agree with any delay in integration for seven years while the lawyers in Little Rock are fighting a two-and-a-half year delay is most unfortunate. Can you imagine how Daisy Bates and the kids in Little Rock would feel about such a statement?"[55]

Nor did Robinson allow his associations with the Republican Party to stifle him from criticizing certain party leaders and positions. A vocal "Rockefeller Republican" throughout the 1960s, Robinson's allegiance to the GOP was never blind nor absolute, particularly as the party lurched throughout the 1960s toward its "Southern strategy" of white supremacist race-baiting. Following the 1964 presidential nomination of Barry Goldwater (who defeated Nelson Rockefeller in the GOP primaries), Robinson proclaimed, "I never could nor never will buy Barry Goldwater. In my opinion, he is a bigot, an advocate of white supremacy and more dangerous than Governor Wallace."[56] As a delegate for Nelson Rockefeller to the 1964 GOP convention, Robinson led a small contingent of African American representatives in opposing Goldwater's candidacy, and in defending Rockefeller when his convention speech was booed and jeered by the party faithful. "Jackie Robinson is undoubtedly the leading light and spirit in a relentless fight for the party and the principles he believes in," reported the *Amsterdam News*.[57] When Rockefeller eventually toed the party line and endorsed Goldwater's candidacy, Robinson fired off to his longtime political ally and mentor a scathing letter: "It seems to me that to support [Goldwater] is to reject the ideals and principles for which the Rockefeller name has always stood. Your doing so is one of the most disappointing things that has ever happened to me."[58] He followed through on this principled stance by endorsing and campaigning for Goldwater's 1964 Democratic opponent, Lyndon Johnson.

These few examples of political disagreements with more moderate voices hardly qualify Jackie Robinson as a radical Black nationalist, but they echo (to varying degrees) the ways he responded to racial inequities within Major League Baseball. From corporate boardrooms, to Congress, to the floor of the Republican convention, Robinson understood his institutional constraints, seeking to leverage the goodwill he enjoyed within them to protest directly those very institutions when he deemed it necessary. His politics could never be identified as "revolutionary" in any immediate sense. And yet even one of his most prominent political opponents recognized the nuances of Robinson's position within a more sweeping narrative of racial struggle and progress. In a December 1967 column for *New York Amsterdam News*, Robinson relates this anecdote: "Malcolm X, the late and brilliant leader, once pointed out to me, during the course of a debate, 'Jackie, in days to come, your son and my son will not be willing to settle for things we are willing to settle for.' I am certain that this is correct and that this is the way that it should be."[59] Pursuing different ideologies and tactics, these two African American leaders found their own paths for performing antiracist defiance on the American stage so as to push history in the same direction. Jackie Robinson played quite a different character type than Malcolm X did in that drama, to be sure. But their legacies are closer in proximity than the two men themselves, their contemporaries, and many commentators since have discerned.

TWO | Staging Collective Black Resistance, 1948–1954

One distinguishing feature of drama of the Black Arts Movement was an overt and unapologetic embrace of violent imagery and stage action. "We want actual explosions and actual brutality," writes Amiri Baraka in his essay "The Revolutionary Theatre." "We must make an art that will function as to call down the actual wrath of world spirit. . . . This is a theatre of assault."[1] In one sense, Baraka's manifesto is a passionate cri de coeur against brutal white supremacy and its impacts on the everyday experiences and consciousness of African Americans; its language mirrors the graphic and bloody stage imagery that theater artists could employ to galvanize Black audiences toward revolutionary action. Baraka's shocking, heightened rhetoric seeks to differentiate a new, revolutionary movement in drama from the more cautious politics and the aesthetics (as he saw them) of the immediate past. Just as Black Power movement leaders sought to distance themselves tactically and temperamentally from the prevailing tenor of "classical" civil rights activism, so too did Baraka reject a theatrical sensibility he saw as beholden to antiquated notions of gradualism and liberal integrationism and to strategies of reasoned, nonviolent persuasion.

Baraka's legacy looms large over the historiography of Black theater of the mid-twentieth century. However, as Aimee Zygmonski notes, the Black Arts Movement was "an ever changing, ever evolving series of cultural productions" that defies easy summary or single attribution.[2] LaDonna L. Forsgren warns that "it is misleading to use the writings of male luminaries [principally, Baraka] to encapsulate the entire movement."[3] A wide range of Black Arts dramas (not just those by male writers) adopt the type of aggressive stance articulated in Baraka's manifesto—including *We Own the Night* by Jimmy Garrett, *The Bronx Is Next* by Sonia Sanchez, and Baraka's own *The Slave*. These and other Black Arts scripts concretize visions of violent, collective resistance by Black communities against the white supremacist status quo of the United States. Decried by some critics as dangerous incitements to real-world bloodshed, such dramas catalyze African American defiance of racial hegemony and aim to "teach [white Americans] their deaths" by projecting "horrible coming attractions of The Crumbling of the West."[4] Combining heightened theatricality with a politics of Black nationalist militancy, such plays capture the revolutionary anger that defined an explosive era in African American cultural politics. In contrast, works by African American dramatists from the late 1940s through the early 1960s can seem more tentative—both in style and in substance. Many dramas of the immediate postwar period appear to align with Barbara Ann Teer's critique of those Black artists "concerned with integration" who endeavor "to compete in an already established, highly competitive industry" centered on commercial success (primarily Broadway).[5] Critics often dismiss pre–Black Arts works as mere "'protest' literature" crafted within the "decaying structure" of a "Western aesthetic."[6]

Complicating that popular critique, however, are African American playwrights of the post–World War II years whose plays were, in their own ways, defiantly radical. Certain notable plays of the late 1940s and 1950s presented audiences with stirring visions of collective Black resistance. They give muscular voice to outrage and promote a radical sensibility that does not confine itself to gradualist tactics, nor singularly to ideals of pacifism and moral persuasion. In ways that have not yet been fully explored by extant historiography of African American theater, these dramas established an important precedent for the revolutionary upheaval in African American theater that would unfold later in the twentieth century. This chapter highlights three such revolutionary plays from the post–World War II / pre–Black Arts period: *Our Lan'* by Theodore Ward (1948), *Gold Through the Trees* by Alice Childress (1950), and *In Splendid Error* by William Branch (1954).

Each of these three plays calls upon African Americans to unite—collectively, righteously, forcefully, and physically—in opposition to violent white oppression. Accordingly, they exemplify a key transitional moment for Black theater in the United States. Ward, Childress, and Branch use the stage in ways that foreshadow and align with the militant energies of the Black Arts Movement. My analysis here focuses on each playwright's use of *strategic displacement* as a dramaturgical tactic. Working within the more constrained social climate of the post–World War II era, Ward, Childress, and Branch displace their narratives geographically and historically from their contemporary sociopolitical contexts. Such displacements afforded some protection for these writers from immediate political backlash against their radical messages and opened a liberating space to engage audiences with the necessity and the righteousness of standing boldly and physically against white racial terror. The plays' far-off and long-ago settings enable an indirect but undeniable engagement for contemporary audiences in the United States with the growing necessity of a Black revolution in the here and now.

The three plays discussed in this chapter all arise within the cultural and political context of the Black Popular Front: the hothouse of radical African American artistic expression fostered by leftist political movements of the 1930s–1950s. Artists working within the Black Popular Front drew inspiration from the antiracist politics of the Communist Party and the interracial American Left. As Brian Dolinar notes, radically minded writers like Ward, Childress, and Branch "found opportunities to promote their work among the network of artists and writers on the Left."[7] Racial politics *within* the American Left and the Communist Party were highly fraught. As the era progressed, many African Americans felt increasingly marginalized within leftist communities and thus grew skeptical of both the movement's sincerity with respect to racial equality and its real potential to achieve tangible progress on racial justice in the United States.[8] Nonetheless, crosscurrents of influence link the radical leftist culture of the postwar era and the revolutionary Black Arts tradition that followed in its wake. The dramas discussed here exemplify a moment of active transition and exchange within radical African American cultural expression: as class-based and interracially oriented leftist politics evolved toward a more distinctly race-conscious and separatist ideology of Black revolution. *Our Lan', Gold Through the Trees,* and *In Splendid Error* each brought that transition vividly to life for midcentury audiences in the United States and continue to capture its dynamics potently for us today.

THEODORE WARD'S *OUR LAN'* (1947)

Theodore Ward began his work on *Our Lan'* in 1940 as he enjoyed notoriety surrounding his 1939 drama *Big White Fog* (which was staged to acclaim by the Federal Theatre Project in Chicago and the Negro Playwrights Company in New York). *Our Lan'*—which bears the subtitle *An Historical Negro Drama*—grew out of Ward's desire "to find out how far back in American history there was the clearest expression of the Negro's comprehension of what was necessary for his own salvation."[9] He later shared this reflection:

> *Our Lan'* is a play about Reconstruction in the South, dealing *authentically* with the settlement of black freedmen on an island off the

> coast of Georgia by General Sherman with the promise that the Federal Government would confirm their title to Forty Acres and a Mule. However, they were eventually exterminated by Federal troops when the freedmen refused to vacate the island under the policy of the Johnson Administration, which restored the property to its former white owners despite their rebellion against the flag of the United States.[10]

The modifier "authentically" is the operative word here, as Ward sought to counteract white supremacist historical misrepresentations with a more accurate rendering of the nation's past. As Julie Burrell argues, *Our Lan'* was part of "an upsurge of black-authored, counter-hegemonic cultural texts combatting stage and screen distortions of the era" that spuriously romanticized the "Lost Cause" of the Confederacy and that demeaned Black men and women through condescension and stereotyping.[11] Ward's dramaturgy drew inspiration from W. E. B. Du Bois's landmark book *Black Reconstruction,* as well as from the work of historians Manuel Gottlieb, Elizabeth Lawson, and James Allen in emphasizing how emancipated African Americans in the South built self-sustaining agricultural communities after the fall of the Confederacy. Ward's rigorous historicism and his frequent use of traditional African American spirituals within the script create at first glance a distant and heightened dramatic essence. Yet the resonance of *Our Lan'* was by no means detached from everyday experience nor confined to the past. As Owen E. Brady notes, Ward's drama potently connects past and present, revisiting "historical experience to shed light on a contemporary social situation" facing the United States in the mid-twentieth century.[12]

Brady's detailed account of the textual history of *Our Lan'* outlines the work's evolution from pure melodrama (when first drafted in 1940–41) to high tragedy in its 1947 version. It was this latter iteration that garnered acclaim in its off-Broadway debut at the Henry Street Settlement theater in April 1947. That acclaim brought the play to Broadway a few months later (with new direction and some additional commercially minded revisions). *Our Lan'* depicts a group of former slaves—led by the heroic and selfless protagonist Joshuah Tain—whose ingenuity, hard work, and shared sacrifice transform a dilapidated cotton plantation on an island off the coast of Georgia into a thriving collective. Tension builds when news arrives of President Lincoln's assassination, and when the farm's former owner John Burkhardt returns to reclaim the acreage he once controlled. The African American farmers refuse to surrender their possession of the land or to

Figure 3. Photograph of a scene from the 1947 Broadway production of *Our Lan'* by Theodore Ward at the Royale Theatre, New York, NY.

submit to exploitative sharecropping contracts. Burkhardt returns with federal troops, seeking to dispossess the freedmen in enforcement of President Johnson's regressive Reconstruction policies. The defiance of Joshuah and his compatriots sparks a climactic confrontation in which the Black farmers stand off against heavily armed invading federal troops. The play concludes with Joshuah and his love interest Delphine locked in an embrace, awaiting their inevitable defeat as the sound of cannon fire brings down the curtain.

Around this plot, Ward layers a rich examination of history, economics, and racial politics. In alignment with Black Popular Front economic ideology, *Our Lan'* functions in part as a critique of American predatory capitalism. The play also highlights caste divisions within African American society and (with the introduction of a sympathetic white schoolteacher from the North, and a brief episode featuring disenchanted poor former Confederate soldiers) suggests the possibility of greater economic and social justice through working-class interracial alliances. The frequent singing of traditional African American spirituals (such as "Keep Your Hand on the

Plow" and "Deep River") provides a soundscape for the action and a celebration of the cultural and social genealogy that helped sustain Black communities in the South against historic oppression and constant threats of erasure. As Brady notes, folk elements serve multivalent purposes throughout *Our Lan'*: "Any revelation of the black spirit must of necessity carry with it the spirit of revolution."[13]

This revolutionary spirit—implicit throughout *Our Lan'*—reveals itself explicitly and boldly at several key moments. Soon after establishing themselves on the island, Joshuah and his compatriots get a visit from Hank Saunders, the plantation's former overseer. When Saunders challenges the new occupants' rights to claim the land and raise a cotton crop, Joshuah and Peltier (another one of the new settlers) respond defiantly:

> JOSHUAH: We goin' wuk. We goin' wuk all right. We goin' wuk right heah on de lan' what blongs t' us!
> PELTIER: Yeah! 'N Ah'd like t' see any man put me off this lan'!
> SAUNDERS: Mind your tongue, nigger!
> PELTIER (*quietly*) Spose yuh make me!
> SAUNDERS (*reaching for gun*) Why, confound yor black hide!
> JOSHUAH (*simultaneously with two others crowding him, pinning him in a vise between them*) Now jes er minute, Suh! Pay yuh best not t' start nothin' here!

Outnumbered, Saunders withdraws with a vague threat. "You jes stay heah. (*laughing*) Yuh'll learn!"[14] With that standoff, Ward stokes dramatic conflict and plants a seed of collective Black defiance that will germinate as his plot develops.

Saunders's threat comes to fruition months later, when Burkhardt returns, following a bountiful first cotton harvest by the new colony. The former owner, accompanied by Captain Stewart (an officer from the Freedman's Bureau) and a battalion of Union soldiers, intends to reclaim the farm and to compel its new stewards to sign exploitative labor contracts that would turn them into sharecroppers. Intervening historical events—the assassination of Abraham Lincoln, the inauguration of President Andrew Johnson, and the resulting shift in federal Reconstruction policies—have eroded the legal protections that helped the Black farmers establish their operation. "We already got this lan'! . . . we ain't goin' sign no contracts," Joshuah proclaims, telling Saunders: "'N if yuh know what's good fur yuh, yuh better git on off this ilun 'n don't come back disturbin' us in ouah homes no more" (128). As the new caretakers grow more defiant, Captain Stewart cautions them, "I warn you, violence won't get you anywhere in this case!" (129). But Joshuah is undeterred: "(*angrily*) We'll still be slaves till every man can raise his own bale of cotton 'n say, 'This is mine!'" The confrontation escalates:

> STEWART (*shouting*) Enough! . . . Either sign those contracts or get off the island!
> JOSHUAH (*ominously*) 'N spose we tell yuh, us ain't goin' do neither one?
> STEWART: You'll sign all right! (*warningly*) And if you commit any outrage, the Bureau will punish you with the utmost severity!
> JOSHUAH (*quietly*) Well, yuh might ez well git it straight. We ain't goin' sign!
> STEWART: . . . You defy my authority?
> JOSHUAH (*quietly*) We're free. You got no 'thority over us.
> STEWART (*after a moment*) Have you finished?
> JOSHUAH (*quietly*) Ez far ez *words* is consarned! (130)

The repetition of the stage direction "*quietly*" underscores Joshuah's calm determination; the Black farmers' resistance is fierce—but it is consistently principled and thoughtful, not rash or foolhardy. Stewart calls his soldiers to attention, and "*In a flash the Freedmen square off for battle. Grimly the two groups stand at bay. Stewart seems to be searching for a sign of weakness. Joshuah resolute and alert, with a sense of come what may*" (130–31). Stewart and his men withdraw temporarily, forestalling for a while the inevitable confrontation between the new caretakers of the land and federal troops.

As the play builds toward its climax, both Joshuah and Delphine pass up opportunities to flee, to compromise, or to surrender their claims to the land—despite the inevitability of defeat at the hands of well-armed Union soldiers who now do the bidding of the defeated wealthy white southern planter class. As the army gathers its forces and surrounds the colony, Joshuah rallies his compatriots: "Ah want you t' go t' yor posts, 'n jest remember: Aint nobody ever got nothin' worthwhile for nothin'. Some of ouah leaders don't understand tha. . . . We ain't many. 'N it's hard t' stand yor ground when yuh know deep down in your heart de best yuh can do is serve as er lesson" (139). In a final standoff with Burkhardt and Stewart, Joshuah repeats his claim: "This is ouah lan'. We done wukked 'n paid for it. Not only here, but all ovah this cruel South" (141). With that, the freedmen affirm their collective resolve to fight, fiercely and steadfastly, against a new form of enslavement. The play concludes with a melodramatic tableau of Joshuah and Delphine in tearful embrace, with an impending defeat looming.[15] Despite the tragic and unjust destruction of this enterprise in collective Black autonomy, the play's ultimate impact rests with the example it provides of militant, righteous opposition against white supremacist governmental force. Paul Robeson notes in his response to the play "the remarkable parallel between the valiant fight of the freed slaves during Reconstruction and the struggles which confront all darker peoples today. . . . Today, the oppressed and exploited millions of the earth are resolved to die rather than be forced back into imperialist and feudal bondage."[16] Alan M. Wald similarly emphasizes the play's implications for its own historical moment: "Ward's primary aim was to address the current, post–World War II dilemma of African Americans by disclosing the root causes of their oppression and dramatizing possible role models for sustaining the battle for liberation from racial and economic oppression."[17]

As the historical and political climate of the United States shifted in the postwar years, Ward found himself increasingly at odds with the ideology pursued by a younger generation of Black writers. As Michelle Y. Gordon notes, "Ward's politics conflicted with certain tenets and characteristics of the Black Arts Movement. . . . His Marxist politics clashed with many people's Cold War sensibilities and with some prominent visions of black nationalism and he disagreed publicly with some Black Power supporters' calls to crush 'the white man.'"[18] The shifting discourse of Black radicalism put Ward on the defensive, as evidenced in this published interview from the early 1970s: "There is a certain truth in all revolutionary movements . . . intrinsic to the play was the fact that Delphine and Joshuah and the other Blacks knew [their defeat] was coming, but still fought and died. They said, 'Fuck you.' In the historical, long run, nobody's going to stop that kind of courage and dedication. I call that revolutionary."[19] Indeed, if Ward felt a need to reassert his own "revolutionary" credentials amid a period of increasing militancy, *Our Lan'* offers strong support for his argument. The strategic displacement of his revolutionary vision toward nineteenth-century postbellum South should not distract anyone from the fierce urgency of Ward's clarion call to arms.

ALICE CHILDRESS'S *GOLD THROUGH THE TREES* (1952)

The "Dramatic Revue" *Gold Through the Trees* by Alice Childress shares with *Our Lan'* a strategy of projecting a contemporary revolutionary sensibility through a historical lens. This work contrasts markedly with Childress's more familiar plays of the period—such as her earlier one-act *Florence* (written in 1950, set in a train station in the segregated South) and her full-length drama *Trouble in Mind* (which debuted in 1955, depicting rehearsals for a lynching drama heading to Broadway). These more well-known Childress dramas illuminate present-day racism within everyday life in the United States through unified, narrowly focused, realistic storytelling. *Gold Through the Trees* is a more sprawling and expansive drama, depicting (as Lorraine Hansberry describes in her review of the debut production) "four different parts of the world, in five different times in history—Africa, 300 years ago; Haiti, during the overthrow of the French planters and Napoleon's army in 1849; the British West Indies today; and the United States during slavery. It ends once again in Africa."[20] While Childress's settings are distant both geographically and temporally, her vision of radical disruption of white hegemonic power was timely for postwar American audiences.

Gold Through the Trees debuted in April 1952 at Club Baron, a nightclub and performance venue founded in the late 1940s by the Committee for the Negro in the Arts (CNA) at Lenox Avenue and 132nd Street in Harlem. CNA, a community-based advocacy group for Black writers, had previously produced another work by Childress, *Just a Little Simple* (a stage adaptation of Langston Hughes's "Simple stories") in September 1950. The group was a prominent theatrical institution within the Black Popular Front, with strong ties to the Harlem Left and its interracialist cultural politics. Its avowed mission was "the integration of Negro artists into all forms of American culture on a dignified basis of merit and equality. It aims to help erase the persisting racial stereotype and to create employment for Negroes in the various art fields."[21] Elsewhere, CNA promoted their work "to stimulate the broadest possible action on the part of both white and Negro toward a solution of the problem which faces the Negro artist in all cultural media."[22] The group's pursuit of liberal integrationism, its support from white backers beyond Harlem, and the appeal of its theatrical productions to white critics and audiences drew criticism from cultural nationalists—most notably Harold Cruse. "From the very outset the Committee was interracial and included white Communists, white leftwing sympathizers and Left-liberals," Cruse notes, concluding that "since Negroes had no flourishing ethnic cultural arts institutions in their own community, pursuing this integration theme was like launching a campaign with no thought of building a starting base. . . . Negro radicals did not have an independent organization, *even inside their black community*."[23] Yet *Gold Through the Trees* does not conform to Cruse's critique of the group that first staged it. The play is an exam-

Figure 4. Photograph of a scene from *Gold Through the Trees* by Alice Childress at Club Baron, New York, NY. Photo: Courtesy of the Robeson Family Trust.

ple of what Mary Helen Washington identifies as Childress's "own distinctive brand of black-centered left radicalism"[24]—one that was in tension with certain tendencies of leftist culture in Harlem, even as Childress rose to prominence within that environment.

Childress elucidates her own distinctive Black radicalism in her essay "For a Negro People's Theatre," which appeared in the leftist newspapers *Masses and Mainstream* and the *Daily Worker* in 1950. Her treatise—which predates and foreshadows *Gold Through the Trees*—offers a vision of a theater that merges a populist, working-class perspective with a distinctively Black consciousness. The essay begins by recounting "a heated though friendly discussion concerning a Negro Theatre" Childress had with her leftist African American contemporary Theodore Ward. "He claimed that there was a definite need for such a theatre," Childress writes, "while I held to the idea that a Negro theatre sounded as though it might be a jimcrow [*sic*] institution." As Childress tells it, Ward's perspective won her over; her skepticism about the viability of a race-based theater soon gave way to a deeply held understanding of the need to empower African American artists to reject the white paternalism of the mainstream professional stage and to "turn our eyes toward our neighbors, the community, the domestic workers, porters, laborers, white-collar workers, churches, lodges and institutions."[25] In a renewal of W. E. B. Du Bois's empowering call for a "real Negro theatre" centered on new plays "about us . . . by us . . . for us . . . near us,"[26] Childress invokes the profound and quotidian beauty inherent in the lives of "my people" as the focal point for her Black theatrical aesthetic. A theatrical movement centered on everyday Black experience could become, Childress argues here, one of monumental political impact: "Its work is too heavy, its task is too large to be anything other than a great movement. It must be powerful enough to inspire, lift, and eventually create a complete desire for the liberation of all oppressed peoples."[27] With *Gold Through the Trees*, Childress puts her liberatory vision into practice. The play dramatizes stories of Black life from across time and around the world, in a call for emancipation from the global, historic inequities promulgated by white supremacist oppression.

The prologue that opens *Gold Through the Trees* introduces a narrator figure identified in the script only as "Woman." This character enters "*dressed as a woman of Ur . . . 2,500 years B.C.*"[28] to deliver a soliloquy that situates the ensuing drama within a rich, millennia-long narrative of Black diasporic history. This same figure reappears intermittently throughout the play, as a kind of spiritual tour guide who facilitates the journey across the play's numerous settings and storylines. In several episodes, she highlights the experiences of grief and mourning that link communities across the African diaspora. An early scene entitled "Africa" depicts a Queen and an elder woman bemoaning the abduction of men from their African village by white slave traders. In another episode called "On the Tree Top," the Woman becomes a mother in the South, "dressed in black from head to foot . . . [with] a long purple mourning scarf" (36), calling poetically, in vain, for her son. The reason for his absence is never specified, but easily enough surmised: lynching. Another episode includes performance of an original song entitled "Martinsville Blues," in memoriam to the "Martinsville Seven," who were executed by the state of North Carolina in 1951 on charges of raping a white woman. A monologue called "In the West Indes" describes hardships and starvation witnessed by a woman in Granada in the wake of a devastating hurricane, and the uncaring response of the island's white colonial authorities. These episodes center on the experiences and perspectives of working-class Black women, weaving a dramatic tapestry of pan-historical loss, struggle, and perseverance. *Gold Through the Trees* typifies "Childress's consistent foregrounding of Black women that, above all, differentiated her politics and art" from other African American playwrights of the era and "impacted her unwarranted neglect" from the historiography of radical Black theater of the mid-twentieth century.[29]

Interwoven with these vignettes of grief and heartache are other scenes that emphasize direct, active rebellion against white oppression. The first hint of the play's revolutionary politics comes toward the end of the "Africa" episode, where the sense of loss felt by the Queen and the Old Woman victimized by the slave trade transforms into defiance: "This word will bring forth spears. This word will bring forth the war dance," the women cry out, building the scene toward the performance of an "Ashanti War Dance" at its conclusion (29). The next scene, entitled "Stranger in a Strange Land," depicts a hotel laundry in Cape May, New Jersey, in the 1850s, where Harriet Tubman works to finance her campaign to liberate victims of chattel slavery in the South. When Harriet's partners, Lennie and Celia, voice frustrations and waver in their dedication to their enterprise, she seeks to harden their resolve with the story of her own escape from slavery. Her recounting introduces Tubman's famous phrasing that Childress employs as the play's title: "Don't you think I was scared when I run away? . . . When I found I had crossed that line! There was such a glory over everything. The sun come through like gold through the trees!" (33–34). The three women return to their work and recommit themselves to their just cause. Another scene, entitled "The Haitian Vendor," shows a brief exchange in "1791 . . . somewhere near Port au Prince, Haiti" between a Black slave named George and a mulatto peddler. The two surreptitiously exchange gruesome accounts of violent punishments inflicted upon those who have defied the autocracy of the island's white planters. The Vendor shares with George a key secret: "Touissant plans revolt." Proclaiming her allegiance with the impending uprising, the Vendor also bestows upon George a weapon: "In three days this poison is for the masters . . . the day we take to the hills . . . then we fire the city, even the arsenals . . . Then down from the hills, we will drive them to the sea."[30] The episode brings to life a chapter of history that was surely inspirational to a Harlem audience: the successful armed rebellion against French colonial control of Haiti that began in 1791 under the leadership of Toussaint-Louverture.

The play's concluding episode, entitled "South Africa," brings the play's action close to the present in portraying the resistance movement against apartheid as the three hundredth anniversary of white settlement of the country (April 6, 1952) approached. In the episode, John, an anti-apartheid activist, tells two associates, Burney and Ola, of the campaign that he will soon lead: "We shall break the laws by deliberately not observing them . . . we shall tear up our passes. We will walk where we please and when we please. We shall go on strike if we choose." John describes the movement as "a campaign of passive resistance. . . . We are not declaring war, we are declaring that we are men and women. We are going out into the streets to live and breathe as human beings. We would be free or dead . . . we cannot wait any longer" (44). In depicting Black resistance to apartheid, Childress stays true to the peaceful "Defiance Campaign" unfolding at the same moment that *Gold Through the Trees* debuted. An emphasis on the nonviolent nature of this revolution afforded some protection to Childress (who was under direct FBI surveillance at the time) and her collaborators from governmental retribution. Even so, John uses stark language to describe for Ola and Burney the inevitably brutal response that awaits: "It is very likely that many of us will be shot down . . . thousands of us may be jailed . . . many more carted off to the prison farms . . . many beaten cruelly" (44). The scene ends with a moment of optimism and shared resolve, with John proclaiming: "I am not sad or depressed. I feel very strong and certain . . . yes, even happy, Ola, for what comes." John concludes by dedicating his actions to his family, his community, and his people. As he recites their names, "*He is telling us why he is ready to die. . . .* For . . . my mother . . . my father . . . my sister . . . my people . . . for Burney . . . for me . . . for the little children . . . for freedom . . . for Ola." The curtain lowers on *Gold Through the Trees* with a rousing "*Finale: entire company onstage singing 'Didn't My Lord Deliver Daniel' or 'I'm On My Journey Now'*" (46).

Never does *Gold Through the Trees* depict violent acts of resistance directly. Rather, the play offers vignettes of inspiration, anticipation, and preparation associated with various episodes of mass Black defiance against domestic and global white hegemony. Its message for African American audiences of the early 1950s (if cryptic in its depiction) is nonetheless resonant: in the face of persistent persecution and suffering, righteous and militant opposition can and must arise. The CNA's staging of the revue, directed by Clarice Taylor and featuring an ensemble cast of ten African American performers (which included both Taylor and Childress), used movement, costuming, music, and visual iconography to emphasize Childress's diasporic vision. One reviewer's description of a theatrical effect created on the Club Baron stage makes this clear: "When the bars of a U.S. prison were shadowed across the face of the huge African mask background in the Martinsville scene, this it seemed to me was a successful artistic blending of the African and Negro peoples' struggles."[31] Offset from the present-day United States, and without directly depicting violence itself, Childress connects contemporary racial politics in the United States directly to the valiance of righteous Black warriors from across time and around the globe.

WILLIAM BRANCH'S *IN SPLENDID ERROR* (1954)

Another drama of the era to use history as a lens through which to consider contemporary revolutionary imperatives is William Branch's *In Splendid Error*. Set in 1859–60, *In Splendid Error* presents (by the playwright's own synopsis) "the little-known story of the relationship between Frederick Douglass and the fiery old abolitionist, John Brown, just prior to Brown's historic raid on Harpers Ferry." The play features an integrated cast and centers for much of its first two acts on establishing a contrast between Brown's bold abolitionist fanaticism and Douglass's more cautious and pragmatic approach to his antislavery work. However, the drama takes a distinct turn in Act 3, as Branch depicts Douglass embracing the necessity of militant action, even when such action might appear futile. Grounded in the legacies of two familiar icons of American history, the play transcends its dramatic milieu. As Alvin "Chick" Webb notes in his review of the debut production for the *Amsterdam News*, "The three-act play is topical, and could very easily be associated with the tense state of current day affairs."[32]

In Splendid Error received its first staging off-Broadway at the Greenwich Mews theater in October 1954. Branch's play was the first of several influential new dramas by African American playwrights presented by this groundbreaking company—whose white leadership committed the group to staging works of Black playwrights and to casting African American performers nontraditionally (in roles not defined by race). The debut of *In Splendid Error* bolstered the ascendant notoriety of William Branch (then just twenty-seven years old) following his earlier drama *A Medal for Willie*, which CNA had premiered at Club Baron in 1951. *A Medal for Willie* centers on the mother of slain Korean War hero Willie Jackson and her refusal to accept a posthumous medal for valor for her son, in protest of American racial inequities both inside and outside of the army. Branch later reminisced: "*A Medal for Willie* . . . pre-dated the Black Arts Movement by over a decade. The line: 'Willie shoulda had that machine gun over here!' [spoken by Mrs. Jackson in publicly rejecting her son's medal for fighting in Korea] was so 'radical' the reviewer for the *N.Y. Amsterdam News*, a black newspaper, said it was 'too strong' and suggested it be taken out of the play. It wasn't."[33] Similarly, *In Splendid Error* directly invokes the prospect

Figure 5. Alfred Sander as John Brown and William Marshall as Frederick Douglass in a scene from *In Splendid Error* by William Branch at the Greenwich Mews Theatre, New York, NY. Photo: New York Times.

of armed Black resistance at its climactic moment—a prospect as urgent in the 1950s as it was in the 1850s.

The opening beat of *In Splendid Error* provides a first glimpse at liberatory Black collective action: dramatizing the Underground Railroad operating out of the Rochester, New York, home of Frederick Douglass and his wife, Anna. Along with a local preacher named Reverend Loguen, Anna welcomes and provides for three rescued slaves, in advance of their passage across the Niagara River to freedom in Canada. Loguen shares a moment of pride with his partner on the success of their work: "Do you know how many we've taken care of already this year, Anna? Thirty-three!

Thirty-three free souls passing through our little station on the Underground Railroad."[34] This brief scene is part of a lengthy prelude to Branch's introduction of the core theme of the drama: the strategic contrast between Frederick Douglass and John Brown in pursuit of nationwide abolition of slavery. When the two characters first meet toward the end of Act 1, Brown shares his plan to lead a militia of fighters into the Blue Ridge Mountains to free slaves in Virginia and launch a wider war against slavery. Douglass is wary, but pledges to recruit support and funding for Brown's campaign. When other potential backers reject the plan, Brown discloses his intention to raid the federal arsenal at Harpers Ferry to obtain his needed munitions. "Can't you see it, Frederick? . . . the slaves rallying to the call . . . liberty travelling southward like a trail of fire!" Douglass is far from convinced: "It is impossible, insane! You must not even think of it. . . . You'd be attacking the United States Government. It would be treason!" Brown answers him defiantly: "Treason! Government! Laws! Blast them all to hell!" (117). A stark temperamental difference fuels the heated exchange that follows:

> DOUGLASS: And what of the slaves themselves—you want to help them, you say. Why then do you think of doing the very thing that will harm them most? Why bring the nation's anger on them? *You* may defy the federal government but they cannot.
>
> BROWN: But we will rouse the nation behind them! It needs rousing. It's cursed. It's dying. It needs to be startled into action. . . .
>
> DOUGLASS: Tell me, John: is there ever any justification for such unprovoked violence, even in pursuit of a righteous cause?
>
> BROWN: Yes! Yes, by God, I believe there is. If we cannot persuade the nation with words to purge itself of this curse, then we must do so with weapons. . . . Are you so far removed from slavery that you no longer care! . . . Have you carried the scars upon your back into high places so long that you have forgotten the sting of the whip and the lash? . . . Or are you afraid to face a gun? (118–19)

Brown fails to convince Douglass, but does inspire an ally of his named Shields Green to join the fight. Green (also an abolitionist hero from this period of history) has taken residence with the Douglasses in Rochester following his own escape from southern bondage. "Not agreeing to be whipped one day," Douglass explains about his guest, "he left his master with a wrenched arm, three loose teeth and a dislocated collar bone" (109). As Brown departs for Harpers Ferry, Green joins him, reinforcing Brown's comfort with the righteousness of violent resistance, and further isolating Douglass in his reticence to take up arms.[35]

In the next scene, Loguen brings word of the federal army's retaking of the arsenal, the capture of Brown and Green, and the issuing of an arrest warrant for Douglass as a coconspirator in the raid. Act 2 concludes with a tearful Douglass family vignette including Frederick, Anna, and their son Lewis, as the father prepares to flee to avoid arrest. Act 3 resumes six months later, with Douglass back home but profoundly distracted and having withdrawn from his leadership of the antislavery movement. George Chatham, a white abolitionist, implores him to rejoin the cause and address a large rally that evening. Brown's capture and subsequent execution triggered for Douglass a tragic recognition of his own failure. He shares with Chatham his painful confession:

> I have discovered that it is possible for a man to make a right decision, and then be tormented in spirit the rest of his life because he did not make the wrong one. There are times when the soul's need to unite with men in splendid error tangles agonizingly with cold wisdom and judgment. . . . John believed in his mission and however wrong he was he gave his life for it. But what have I done, except talk about it—I who have *been* a slave! . . . You are in the presence of a fraud! . . . do not believe that I can stand on a platform and look an audience in the eyes with this burning inside me: "*Are you afraid to face a gun?!!*" (131)

The Aristotelian model would have the tragedy end here, perhaps with the hero's suicide; yet Branch concludes *In Splendid Error* in a different vein—with a distinct and resonant turn away from pathos and toward the fallen hero's redemption. Chatham gives Douglass several gifts Brown bestowed on him as he awaited execution: Brown's musket, a "*torn, bespattered American flag*" from Harpers Ferry, and a personal note that reads, "Tell Douglass I know I have not failed because he lives. Follow your own star, and someday unfurl my flag in the land of the free" (132). His spirit renewed, Douglass agrees to speak at the abolitionist rally, striding off stage to the sound of a passing parade and a chorus of "The Battle Hymn of the Republic." Though Douglass does not explicitly advocate for violent attacks against the US government, the play's conclusion suggests the protagonist's embrace of the righteous armed action that underpinned the martyrdom of John Brown and Shields Green. Douglass's heart-wrenching remorse over his rejection of his friend's campaign, the iconography of the musket and war-torn flag, and the sound of the "Battle Hymn" to fife-and-drum accompaniment all converge at the play's finale to reconnect Douglass with the fight against slavery. Branch's clear implication is that Douglass has conquered his fear "to face a gun" for Black liberation, and that his is an example that all fighting for racial justice should strive to follow.

The Greenwich Mews's production of *In Splendid Error* was led by actor William Marshall, who had previously appeared in the 1951 Broadway revival of Marc Connelly's play *The Green Pastures* and several Hollywood films. The supporting cast included several other veteran African American performers: Clarice Taylor, Maxwell Glanville, and Kenneth Manigault. Critical response to the production is notable, in that both Black and white reviewers tended to praise the acting work of the cast and express some excitement about the play, while taking issue with Branch's rhetorical style. "Mr. Branch's new play showed further evidence of a serious talent," notes Miles Jefferson in *Phylon,* before lamenting that "the drama was handicapped by too much prosy dialogue."[36] Webb's review in the *Amsterdam News* celebrates *In Splendid Error* "as one of the best plays we have witnessed during the 1954 season" and lavishes praise on the cast, but tempers its praise with a note that the play's dialogue becomes "a trifle verbose."[37] The *New York Times* review praises Branch for a drama of "considerable eloquence and vigor," before noting that "the characters of history, for all their flesh and bones, lack the inner spirit of human beings. Neither John Brown nor Frederick Douglass comes completely alive, in spite of all their words and outer anguish."[38] Despite this mixed reception from both Black and white critics, *In Splendid Error* ran for almost four months at the Greenwich Mews, until January 1955.

If Branch struggled to balance historical dramatization with flesh-and-bones humanity or to restrain sufficiently his characters' verbosity, these are missteps that arise from the playwright's sizable dramaturgical ambitions in commenting on the nation's present crisis through strategic displacement into the past. Branch's own reflections on the play illuminate the scope of his project:

> I saw in the Douglass-Brown story certain parallels—remarkable and uncanny parallels—between the climate and events of the 1850s and those of the 1950s. Like Douglass, I found it hard to discard an ingrained belief that change could somehow take place without the necessity of outright overthrow of the government. . . . Like Doug-

> lass in the play, I found myself taunted by more revolutionary souls . . . [S]ociety needs both its fiery souls and its more reasoned thinkers, both its id and its super-ego.[39]

In the final moments of *In Splendid Error*, Branch brings his character Frederick Douglass toward this same realization: that fiery, revolutionary souls play an indispensable role in the national narrative he himself is helping to forge. History tells us that, following Brown's failed revolution, Frederick Douglass remained a leading orator and writer, but did not become a frontline combatant in the abolitionist cause. For the stage, Branch fashions Douglass as a converted revolutionary in spirit—a man reinvigorated by a newly discovered faith in the righteousness of militancy as a necessary tool for Black liberation.

In this manner, Frederick Douglass's evolution within the play encapsulates the wider moment of social and cultural transition within which it was crafted. As the center of gravity for radical Black politics shifted away from the Black Popular Front and toward Black Power, away from integrationism and toward cultural nationalism, away from nonviolence and toward militancy, William Branch and his contemporaries Alice Childress and Theodore Ward contemplated and documented this shift within their dramas. Their plays depict Black figures (both iconic and everyday heroes) from strategically distant settings and, in doing so, vividly capture contemporary urgencies and imagine future possibilities for revolution.

THREE | # Before We Knew Beah

The Revolutionary Performance Praxis of Beulah Richardson

For the 1968 Hollywood awards season, Beah Richards received Academy Award and Golden Globe nominations for Best Supporting Actress in a Motion Picture for her portrayal of Mrs. Prentice (the mother of Sidney Poitier's character, Dr. John Prentice) in the film *Guess Who's Coming to Dinner*. Richards had previously earned a Tony Award nomination for her work as Sister Margaret in the 1965 Broadway production of James Baldwin's play *The Amen Corner*. These new recognitions added to her renown as one of the nation's leading actresses of stage and screen. For all the accolades that *Guess Who's Coming to Dinner* brought to Richards (and to her costar, Poitier), the film provoked divided reactions from the public. James Baldwin notes that while white audiences and critics embraced this bourgeois family drama about the social implications of interracial marriage, "Black people particularly disliked *Guess Who's Coming To Dinner*. . . . It seemed a glib, good-natured comedy in which a lot of able people were being wasted. But, I told myself, this movie wasn't made for *you*."[1] Critic Maxine Hall Elliston echoes Baldwin's critique in blunter terms: "*Guess Who's Coming to Dinner* completely ignores the real issues. . . . The film coats, covers up, disguises and even hides the real problems of the racist Supernation. What this movie boils down to is—warmed over white shit."[2]

Richards herself may well have concurred with these assessments of the film that propelled her into national recognition. "Beah knew that [film] was a lie," Ossie Davis once commented. "At the same time, it was a chance at that level to make any statement at all. So she made it, and she made it with authority. She made even *me* listen to what she was saying."[3] Davis (who had costarred with Richards in the cast of his own play *Purlie Victorious*, discussed Chapter 4) knew well the dilemma with which Richards and all aspiring professional African American actors of her era had to wrestle. As Baldwin captures it, for these artists,

> It can become very difficult to remain in touch with all that nourishes you when you . . . are in the interesting, delicate, and terrifying position of being part of a system that you know that you have to change. . . . The industry is compelled, given the way it is built, to present the American people a self-perpetuating fantasy of American life. . . . *And the black face, truthfully reflected, is not only no part of this dream, it is antithetical to it.*

The strategy that Hollywood actors like Poitier and Richards pursued in the face of this dilemma was to "smuggle in a reality that . . . is not in the script."[4] Across her celebrated professional career spanning more than four decades in mainstream commercial film, television, and theater, Beah Richards conducted (as Baldwin conceived it) a skillful smuggling operation.

Far less familiar than Richards's professional acting work is a different artistic legacy forged by this same artist under her given name: Beulah Richardson. Between 1950 and 1953, before she was known as Beah Richards, Richardson wrote and performed a series of bold, experimental theatrical works of revolutionary political import that made no compromise to mainstream sensibilities or commercial imperatives. Working outside of the professional sphere, Richardson never enjoyed widespread visibility or acclaim for these theatrical works. Her plays of this period remain mostly unpublished and all but forgotten in the historiography of African American theater, though some recent scholarship has brought these activities of the early 1950s into greater visibility. Dayo F. Gore celebrates "Richardson's early years as a political artist and activist," highlighting her prominence within "a dynamic group of black women radicals" of the 1940s–1950s who "passionately asserted black women as powerful voices of resistance who could speak to multiple and interconnected forms of oppression."[5] Here I expand upon Gore's recovery of Richardson's activities by highlighting her groundbreaking theatrical praxis. This chapter examines in detail three original dramas that Richardson created and performed in the early 1950s. The creative activities discussed in this chapter constitute an important archive of revolutionary African American theater activity. They boldly embody "the resistant traditions of the Black Popular Front" while also offering a vital "link to the militant politics and aesthetics"[6] that transformed African American theater in subsequent decades.

The three dramatic texts analyzed in this chapter document the ambitions of an artist eager to depart from convention and experiment with theatrical form. Consequently, there is no easy way to label them. Two of the scripts—*A Black Woman Speaks . . . of White Womanhood, of White Supremacy, of Peace* and *The Revolt of Rosa Ingram*—resemble poems rather than plays in their formatting and presentation on the page. Several accounts from the era refer to these works as *poems*, and describe the author's live presentations of her texts as *readings*. In fact, Richardson often labeled herself a poet during the years she composed these works, as she was also writing and publishing poems not crafted for live enactment. A 1951 profile in the *Daily Worker* promotes Richardson as "A Negro woman poet, who is emerging as one of America's most powerful voices,"[7] even though her writings were not widely available in publication and were mostly known through performance. However, a third Richardson text discussed in this chapter entitled *Genocide* follows some of the familiar conventions of a traditional play script: with dramatic dialogue divided among distinct characters, and stage directions that envision theatrical presentation. Yet *Genocide* has no specified setting, follows no plot in any conventional sense, and might more accurately be described as a script for a political rally than as a *play*. Acknowledging the problems of taxonomy these texts present, this chapter interprets all three original works by Richardson as performance texts (in accordance with how the author first shared them with the public). These writings document a Black artist's innovative pursuit of new theatrical strategies to counteract white supremacist oppression and move the public toward liberation and empowerment for all African Americans—particularly for Black women.

By experimenting with form and utilizing nontraditional performance venues and formats, Richardson's artistic praxis sustained and invigorated revolutionary traditions within African American theater and feminist theater histories. As Margaret Wilkerson notes, Richardson's performances at leftist rallies, meetings, and other political and social functions connect to a longer history of "countless women who have performed their own poetry, prose, and drama in churches, clubs, and lodges—the original homes of black theatre in America."[8] Moreover, in taking the stage to speak her own liberatory truth through new aesthetic forms, Richardson joined a genealogy of women theater artists who (in line with Sue-Ellen Case's analysis) position themselves "outside of the dominant tradition of stages, characters, plots . . . [and who] explore new relationships to their own bodies and voices in performance and develop new kinds of plays," so as to more potently "perform within the parameters of their own unique experience."[9] Live, embodied presence within time and space was as vital to this artist's radical protest against American racist and sexist oppression as was the meaning of the words she crafted and spoke. This chapter investigates the substance of Richardson's writing and, more importantly, foregrounds how live embodied presentation of those texts was integral to their revolutionary meaning and impact.

Though Richardson (as Beah Richards) thrived as an actress on Broadway and in Hollywood, as a younger playwright and performer of her own writing, she labored outside of these commercial spheres, with limited resources. As a result, the records that typically document theatrical activity—printed programs, production photographs, design sketches, newspaper articles, published reviews, and the like—are virtually nonexistent, presenting a barrier in assessing the original performances of the works *as* performances. Where firsthand records are sparse, manuscripts of Richardson's dramatic writings offer some important clues about how those performances likely worked, and what their impact might have been. Kate Dossett's methodology for reading unpublished theatrical manuscripts from the "Federal Theatre era" is useful here. Dossett writes:

> Black theatre manuscripts . . . are also important vehicles in their own right, at the center of community debates about how race should be performed. . . . [T]o read black theatre manuscripts as dramatic texts and as historical sources requires we understand the communities who made them and for whom they were written.[10]

Situated within the sociopolitical context of the Black Popular Front and "Black left feminism"[11] of the postwar years, Richardson's writings and the few surviving accounts of their first public presentations open a window into a radical and transformative performance praxis. These are the archival remnant of an underappreciated chapter in a larger narrative of revolutionary African American theater of the long civil rights era.

A BLACK WOMAN SPEAKS . . . OF WHITE WOMANHOOD, OF WHITE SUPREMACY, OF PEACE

The most well known of Richardson's dramatic writings of the early 1950s is *A Black Woman Speaks . . . of White Womanhood, of White Supremacy, of Peace.* Richardson unveiled the work—a solo play, which she enacted herself—during the American People's Peace Conference in Chicago in the summer of 1951, with two performances hosted by the leftist organization American Women for Peace (AWP). As AWP reported, the first of those presentations "brought a spontaneous rising ovation from the 500 women in attendance," and the second recitation (held toward the end of the conference) was met with "the same response." The excitement elicited by *A Black Woman Speaks* brought immediate accolades to its creator: "In recognition of the deep significance of this poem Miss Richardson was presented a special award at the final session of the Peace Congress."[12] Gore reports that the enthusiasm that greeted those initial performances hastened "Richardson's ascent within a national leftist milieu in which she would come into her own as an artist, an activist, and a theorist," transforming her into something of a celebrity in activist circles.[13] A few months later, the journal *Freedom* reported how admirers were "moved to tears . . . [and to] cry out at the sight of Beulah Richardson," and described how "the deep affection and tears of other women" surrounded her in the wake of the Chicago gathering.[14] Following the conference, Richardson reprised *A Black Woman Speaks* at various leftist rallies, meetings, fundraisers, and other public events.

Amplifying the influence of this work was the circulation of the text in published form: first as a "poem" printed and distributed by AWP following the Chicago conference, and subsequently in a published volume of Richardson's writing entitled *A Black Woman Speaks and Other Poems*. The work was later reprinted alongside dramas by Alice Childress, Lorraine Hansberry, Ntozake Shange, and others within the anthology *Nine Plays by Black Women* (edited by Margaret Wilkerson), situating *A Black Woman Speaks* squarely within a genealogy of Black women's drama of the twentieth century. In her introduction to the anthology, Wilkerson speculates on the impact of Richardson's solo recitation of her play "for a white woman's organization in Chicago, Women for Peace. What a shock it must have been for this group to hear Ms. Richards's biting words, which emphasized white women's complicity in the oppression of black women and men."[15] Wilkerson's consideration of *A Black Woman Speaks* attests to the potency of its live delivery—how, beyond printed words, stage presence empowers the "Black Woman" performer to *speak* actively and demands that an audience confer attention and bear active witness. Discussing the play's utility as a pedagogical tool in an introductory drama course, Annette Wannamaker identifies how a live rendition of *A Black Woman Speaks* (even when recited spontaneously, within a classroom setting) "directly addresses and implicates the audience in ways that compel us to enter into a dialogue."[16] As one participant in the dialogue delivers her words aloud, the performance demands her listeners engage actively as interlocutors. Only through that active copresence can the revolutionary message of *A Black Woman Speaks* become fully manifest.

Richardson's text begins: "It is right that I a woman / black, / should speak of white womanhood."[17] These opening lines, spoken from the stage, serve as a multilayered metatheatrical reflection: reifying the raced and gendered identity of the speaker/protagonist, and affirming the "right" of those inhabiting the intersection of those identities to "speak" before an audience. This statement works partly as an *ante hoc* moral affirmation of arguments yet to come. It leads directly to a reminder of historical white supremacist brutality, as the speaker explains that the "blood" of African American men "chilled in electric chairs / stopped by a hangman's noose / cooked by lynch mobs' fire / spilled by white supremacist mad desire to kill for profit, / gives me that right." It also illuminates the implicit contract governing the event—which depends upon the sanction and participation of those also in the room. The audience, as a collective, takes on its own social identity and specified role in the drama:

> They said, the white supremacist said
> That you were better than me,
> That your fair brow should never know the sweat of slavery.
> They lied.
> White womanhood too is enslaved,
> The difference is degree.

This collective "you" identified as "White womanhood" functions throughout the drama as an antagonist to the speaker's "I." Given no words to say, "white womanhood" exists as a force opposing the emancipatory journey that the Black woman protagonist undertakes. "White womanhood stands in bloodied skirt / and in slavery, / reaching out adulterous hands / killing mine and crushing me."

To counteract that crushing force, the speaker challenges her listeners: "Let's look to history." The performance thus becomes an active struggle between two opponents over what must be learned from the past, and how to rescue the future. Lurking offstage, as an unseen character in the drama, is the male "white supremacist"—whose oppressive manipulation divides white womanhood against the Black woman protagonist: "He, the white supremacist, fixed your minds with poisonous thought: / 'White skin is supreme' . . . / And you did not fight, but set your minds fast on my slavery, / The better to endure your own." Though situated in dramatic conflict against one another, the protagonist and antagonists of *A Black Woman Speaks* share a common affliction—male supremacy—and thus their fates are inextricably linked.

This theatrical conceit empowers *A Black Woman Speaks* to become something more than a straightforward denunciation of racism in the

United States. In performance, the piece functions as an embodied, personified act of direct resistance against oppression jointly undertaken between actor and audience, playing out in real time and space. White women in the audience must reckon directly with their relationship to the disturbing historical truths of racial injustice and misogyny presented by the narrator; those in the audience who do not in their everyday lives fall under the category of "white womanhood" must set aside their familiar identities and assume that character as coparticipants in the theatrical event. Under the umbrella of the "you" to whom the protagonist speaks, all listeners must wrestle directly with white women's complicity in a litany of historical crimes perpetuated by a brutal white capitalist patriarchy: including chattel slavery, white rape of Black women, Jim Crow discrimination, the Ku Klux Klan's racial terrorism, and the wrongful convictions of innocent Black defendants. It is the speaker's embodied rejection of that pattern of complicity that animates the dramatic action: "The white supremacists used your skins / to perpetuate your slavery. / And woe to me. / Woe to the boy Emmett Till. / And woe to you!"

A Black Woman Speaks builds toward a climactic challenge that the protagonist issues to her listeners. Earlier in the play, she confesses, "I would that I could speak of white womanhood as it will and should be, / when it stands tall in full equality." The Black woman's journey through history brings her to a destination that was at the outset merely a wish—the rejection of the racial barrier that divides white women from their Black sisters. The play culminates in an appeal for unified struggle:

> What will you do?
> Will you fight with me?
> White supremacy is your enemy and mine. . . .
> Remember, you have never known me.
> You've been seeing me as white supremacy
> would have me be,
> and I will be myself—
> Free!
> My aim is full equality.
> I would usurp their plan!
> Justice
> Peace
> and plenty
> for every man, woman and child
> who walks the earth.

This is my fight!
If you will fight with me, then take my hand
and the hand of Rosa Ingram, and Rosalee McGee[18]
and as we set about our plan
let our wholehearted fight be:
PEACE IN A WORLD WHERE THERE IS EQUALITY.

The speaker extends her hand and invites a physical response, its grasping, to enact a new alliance against white patriarchal oppression and for peace and equality. The speaker's extended hand stands in for the hands—and, symbolically, the sociopolitical fortunes—of two notoriously oppressed Black women, and thus of *all* Black women marginalized in the United States. Did spectators at the 1951 Chicago Peace Conference reach toward the playing area to clasp Richardson's hand, which she surely extended toward them at this moment in the performance? No surviving account specifically says so, though one witness reported that "Negro and white women bowed their heads in understanding, in grief, in anger and outrage" at the culmination of *A Black Woman Speaks*.[19]

The play's orientation toward "white womanhood"—as both the subject it "speaks of" and the presumed audience it speaks *to*—adds complication to its position as a work of revolutionary theater. A new movement of Black nationalist artists and thinkers that would arise in subsequent years would come to reject art based on "traditional appeals for equal justice in a white-dominated nation."[20] Larry Neal repudiated any approach to drama oriented toward moral persuasion: "The Black Arts Movement eschews 'protest' literature. It speaks directly to Black people. Implicit in the concept of 'protest' literature . . . is an appeal to white morality." Neal's pointed critique of the failings of "Black intellectuals of previous decades" seems to fall squarely on a work like *A Black Woman Speaks,* which embraces the tactics of moral argumentation and the strategy of interracial coalition building preferred by the postwar cultural Left.

However, when fully considered as a dynamic performance text, Richardson's play transcends Neal's category of "protest literature" and emerges as a provocative example of radical, confrontational African American performance praxis. A staging of *A Black Woman Speaks* will take up questions of social justice distinctly "from the viewpoint of the oppressed" and align with Neal's call to pursue the "destruction of white ideas, and white ways of looking at the world."[21] The live event compels spectators to occupy a particularly delicate position within the nation's brutal white capitalist patriarchy—one that is simultaneously both oppressor (white) and oppressed (womanhood). How will they align themselves when challenged in that moment of live reckoning? Will they reaffirm their subservience to the white male supremacists who keep them entrapped in their own form of servitude, or will they unite with the oppressed Black sister standing alone before them and offering a path toward liberation? The active choice must be made and confirmed with a gesture: the linking of hands. The play's confrontation of white supremacy is not passive protest but rather is immediate, active, and physical: an antecedent of Augusto Boal's "poetics of the oppressed," which reconfigures the apparatus of performance so as "to change the people—'spectators,' passive beings in the theatrical phenomenon—into subjects, into actors."[22] It is expressly through live interaction in a theatrical milieu that "Richards' piece works to radicalize both black and white subjectivity."[23]

GENOCIDE

An October 1951 *Daily Worker* article relates how, in the wake of her celebrated performances of *A Black Woman Speaks* in Chicago, Richardson relocated from her home in Los Angeles "to New York and introduced several new poems to enthusiastic audiences." Proclaiming her a "genius of U.S. Negroes" and a "New Negro People's Poet," the article documents Richardson's concerns about counterrevolutionary forces within US culture that were "increasing pressure . . . on Negro artists" to soften their voices and to "do [the] dirty work" of those who would suppress radical dissent coming from the Left. Richardson viewed such pressures as "part of a program to kill off our militant culture and art, and we can't let it happen." Stepping into her new position of prominence within militant leftist culture, Richardson emphasized the theatricality of her creative work, explaining that "her poetry is 'written to be heard primarily.'"[24] The next opportunity for audiences to hear Richardson's words brought to theatrical life came in the following month, with the performance of her play *Genocide.*

Genocide was composed as a dramatic text to complement another revolutionary document of the era. According to a note in the manuscript, the play was "especially written for the meeting held at Riverside Plaza, in New York, in November 1951, to launch the book-petition of the Civil Rights Congress, *We Charge Genocide: The Historic Petition to the United Nations for Relief from a Crime of The United States against the Negro People.*"[25] This petition—written primarily by CRC executive director and prominent civil rights lawyer William L. Patterson—"detailed a long history of racial discrimination, economic exploitation, and violence against African Americans in the United States, taking the groundbreaking step of framing such concerns as a human rights issue deserving international intervention."[26] In this 240-page account, Patterson and the CRC exhaustively catalog 152 separate lynchings, and contend that ten thousand or more killings of African Americans had gone unreported since the abolition of slavery. In support of its charges, the petition also implicates the United States government in a litany of historical legal and extralegal injustices against African Americans. Soon after its public unveiling, Patterson delivered copies of the petition to a UN delegation in Paris in December. Around the same time, a group of signatories led by Paul Robeson delivered copies to UN headquarters in New York. *We Charge Genocide* never received any official response from the UN, and the document proved divisive within Black political discourse. Nonetheless, its publication inspired national and international discussion that, as historian Charles H. Martin argues, "expanded the intellectual boundaries of the contemporary racial debate, offering genocide as an alternate theory to explain American race relations."[27] Richardson once described *We Charge Genocide* as a treatise that was both "terrible—and magnificent. . . . I think I've always been aware of the effects of a policy of genocide, though it took William Patterson and the CRC to make me see it as a policy of government. . . . Life in America means death for Negroes in a hundred thousand forms, all practiced or supported by the government."[28] With her play *Genocide,* this artist channeled her theatrical voice in bold support of Patterson and the CRC's agenda.

Genocide resembles a traditional dramatic text more closely than do *A Black Woman Speaks* and *The Revolt of Rosa Ingram*. The play consists primarily of a dialogue between "The Negro Woman, 1st Voice," and a "Chorus of 10 voices" that answers her in unison. 1st Voice begins the drama by presenting herself, bodily, to the audience: "Look at me. This furrowed brow, these scarred hands, this gaunt body, these bursting veins. These are lines because of pain . . . ancient pain" (1). The character soon delineates the action that elicits her speech: "Look at me! . . . I've come, stepping from the printed page to lay my case before the conscience of mankind. . . . Now you must see that I am flesh and blood. . . . You must see that I am black and because of that, a strange democracy has been practiced upon me" (1–2). The chorus of voices becomes her ally, responding to her arguments and pleas with affirmations, and with encouragements to "say it plain." As with *A Black Woman Speaks*, for a staging of this play, the audience must serve as a silent antagonist—against whose implied opposition the 1st Voice asserts her frightening truth: "This American Democracy. . . . It kills me! . . . So it is the government's policy to make of me the enemy" (2). There are small roles within the drama for several white "children, ages 3, 5, 8, 15 and 21" (1), who enact a parable that demonstrates the maturation of white supremacist thinking. The parable starts with a "sweet child" of three, who progresses through stages of racial indoctrination to become a snarling, stone-throwing Klansman of twenty-one who "hates his poverty and he takes his rage out on me" (4). Stage directions provide descriptions of various lighting, sound, and music effects that help stitch together theatrically the play's episodes.

In addition to these conventional dramatic episodes, the script of *Genocide* includes within its dialogue several moments that introduce political speakers to the audience. According to the surviving manuscript, the first of these is a "white woman speaker" who was one of "fifty white women [who] went to Jackson, Mississippi" with the CRC to protest the death sentence of Willie McGee (an African American man wrongfully executed in May 1951 in Mississippi on flimsy rape charges). After delivery of this speech—its placement, but not its content, indicated in the script—the Chorus resumes the drama with a reminder: "But Willie McGee died, he was electrocuted and the women themselves harassed and persecuted. . . . White supremacists are not so easily defied, nor their doctrine easily denied" (5). The drama soon pauses again for another speaker, this one named explicitly: Ewart Guinier, a CRC lawyer and leading labor activist (6). Later, other guests become part of the theatrical presentation, silently, as notable victims of genocidal racial violence. The 1st Voice highlights their presence:

> Look here upon the stage. . . . See the widow Grayson, her fatherless five. Two of the Trenton six. . . . Olin Montgomery, a Scottsboro boy, Doris and John Mallard. . . . Here is Bessie Mitchell, too, all wounded by Genocide, still yet unafraid to petition for the punishment of this criminal government. (7)

A reverend then comes to the stage to deliver a "Prayer for Victims" (8). After announcements of several more speakers, the script culminates in the introduction of Patterson himself—announced by the 1st Voice and the Chorus as "a man among mankind! / A man who stands for right and for life. . . . You see he fights for democracy, for you, for me, for the world. . . . Listen to him and learn, fight with him and live. . . . We give . . . Mr. William L. Patterson!" (11). This is the final scripted moment of *Genocide*. In total, the play articulates a powerful theatrical indictment of the US government's culpability for decades of racial violence through an inventive fusion of dramatic dialogue, theatrical staging, poetic language, and political oratory.

Genocide presents to its audience an ambitious, multifaceted critique of white supremacy in the United States that aligns in many ways with *A Black Woman Speaks*. Supporting Patterson's analysis of contemporary racial violence, Richardson historicizes lynching and the executions of innocent Black defendants as a tragic continuation of the nation's original racial sins. The 1st Voice proclaims: "This government's policy toward me is ever changing but unchanged. . . . American enslavers came and chained my hands, my feet, my strength, my brain, my tongue. . . . Two hundred years of my unpaid labor made this country the nation it is now. And I don't need to go back to then . . . then is now for me" (1). Building its indictment of the federal government as an agent of genocide, the drama portrays the murder of Black Americans not as acts of personal bias from individual white criminals but as the foreseeable outcome of public policy: "It is the government's policy to make of me the enemy . . . and the white citizen, so deceived and armed with hate, has been shaped into a killer in these United States" (3). The back-and-forth between the 1st Voice and Chorus incorporates a leftist class-based critique: "And with all the killing, what's to be gained? Money for the rulers—injustice and death for the people black and white. American workers have a common enemy" (5). The play's dialogue builds toward a two-part call to action reminiscent of the final challenge voiced in *A Black Woman Speaks*:

> 1ST VOICE: White citizens, dare you take a neutral seat and see your sons and daughters shaped into beast, arsonist, rapist, murderers, thieves?
>
> CHORUS: No more, no more.
>
> 1ST VOICE: Black men and women, dare you keep silent tongue while they imprison black citizens who fight for your right to live?
>
> CHORUS: Speak up, speak out. . . .
>
> THIS IS A CLEAR AND PRESENT DANGER!
>
> 1ST VOICE: Citizens all, black and white, wake up, get in the fight!
> THIS IS A MATTER OF LIFE AND DEATH! (9–10)

This call leads directly to the introduction of Patterson, "the man who showed how Genocide applied to this government" (10), as the performance's culmination.

A *Daily Worker* report provides the only firsthand evidence I could find on *Genocide*'s debut performance. The description reads: "Among the participants, acting out their own lives, were the widows and fatherless children of recent lynch victims. Miss Richardson spoke the main narrative parts [of 1st Voice], and was aided by Negro speakers, including the actresses Hilda Haynes and Elyce Weir," who presumably were part of (or perhaps the entirety of) the chorus. The article also gives some details about one specific appearance within the event by "Mrs. Amy Mallard and her two children, whose husband and father, Robert Mallard, was slain by masked gunmen in Georgia in 1948," and describes a speech from "Mrs. Mallard, whose fiery words were woven into the drama" and delivered a direct challenge to "hypocritical words about 'freedom'"[29] from the US government. The article gives no other indications of who else spoke as part of this initial presentation, or how the play was staged.

Genocide may have had additional theatrical life beyond this debut production. According to Gore, Richardson "performed the piece at numerous events publicizing *We Charge Genocide*"[30] in the months that followed the launch of the petition. I found no published accounts of these performances, though the script provides a basis for some speculation about them. It seems unlikely that the same group of speakers detailed in the manuscript could be assembled for multiple presentations of *Genocide* in different cities. Presumably, Richardson could alter the script as circumstances demanded, to accommodate changes to the roster of guest participants at different events. It is possible that CRC used *Genocide* as a flexible dramatic template—to be modified for different presentations, as a tool in the group's ongoing campaign to promote *We Charge Genocide* and to compel a United Nations response to the charges against the US government. To expect members of the public to read and act upon the CRC's exhaustive and thoroughly researched petition would have been an improbable hope. Richardson's play distills and translates Patterson's historical analysis into a dynamic live experience—in which audiences must confront the realities of white American genocide and must directly face some of its survivors and the nation's fiercest critics. Having already experienced the emotive and persuasive power inherent in presenting her own voice as a "Black Woman" before a live audience, here Richardson endeavors to magnify the impact of her theatrical praxis by adding others' voices to her own, and by blending theatrical storytelling with tactics of direct political persuasion.

Despite the CRC's ambitions with the petition, *We Charge Genocide* elicited no meaningful action or response from those to whom it was addressed. The United Nations largely ignored the document, while the US government actively denounced the petition and its author—seizing Patterson's passport upon his return from Paris and launching a public campaign to smear him as a Communist sympathizer. Martin concludes that, due to substantial public backlash fueled by Cold War paranoia, "although it attracted interest from individual African Americans, the Genocide Petition failed to have a substantial impact on the black community."[31] Even so, one result of *We Charge Genocide* was the inventive play it inspired—which marked a refinement and an expansion of Richardson's use of the stage as a revolutionary tool in the fight for Black liberation.

THE REVOLT OF ROSA INGRAM

At several points in *A Black Woman Speaks,* Richardson invokes the names of notable individuals or groups—such as Crispus Attucks, Emmitt Till, the KKK, the Martinsville Seven—as examples supporting the play's critique of historic white patriarchal supremacy. One of these moments comes at the play's conclusion, when the speaker challenges "white womanhood" to "take my hand / and the hand of Rosa Ingram"[32] in the fight against racist and sexist oppression in the United States. At the play's debut in 1951, the name Rosa Ingram would likely have been familiar to those watching a performance at a leftist political event. Ingram (an African American mother of twelve children from Georgia) and two of her sons had been convicted and sentenced to the electric chair in connection with the 1947 death of a white man named John Stratford. Her trial and conviction, and an ensuing nationwide public outcry, were components of "one of the most significant civil rights cases of the decade . . . [and] proved a powerful touchstone for black communities and especially for black women activists" during the postwar years.[33] In 1953, with Ingram and her sons still imprisoned and facing a life sentence, Richardson took to the stage again to inspire radical action with a new play, *The Revolt of Rosa Ingram.*

The case of Rosa Lee Ingram, now largely faded from historical memory, galvanized advocates for racial justice for more than a decade. Ingram and Stratford were sharecroppers who worked adjacent parcels of land on a western Georgia farm.

> According to local newspaper accounts, Stratford had confronted Mrs. Ingram with a rifle after discovering several mules and hogs in his corn field. A fight between the two broke out, and several of Mrs. Ingram's sons came to her aid. When the melee ended, Stratford lay

> dead from several blows to the head. Arrested along with Mrs. Ingram, 40, were her sons Charles, 17, Wallace, 16, Sammie Lee, 14, and James, 12.[34]

An all-white jury convicted Ingram and two of her sons after a one-day trial, and all three were summarily sentenced to execution by the electric chair. Anger over injustices associated with the trial, the hasty convictions, and draconian sentences—heightened by public sympathy for Ingram as a mother and as a victim of white male aggression—mobilized a nationwide alliance of political groups, legal advocates, and journalists into a sustained campaign in support of Ingram and her family. As Gore writes, "The case pushed front and center black women's experiences with sexualized racial violence and provided an implicit and at times explicit validation of a black defendant's use of deadly force in defending her own life. That this defendant was a black woman protecting herself from assault by a white man lent even greater moral and political force to the cause."[35]

The author and performer who had so profoundly moved audiences with *A Black Woman Speaks* was perfectly positioned to contribute her own voice and physical presence to this cause. Working once again within the cultural program of the CRC, Richardson created and presented an original theatrical work that brought Ingram's political and personal plight to theatrical life. *The Revolt of Rosa Ingram* "was performed and circulated broadly" among CRC chapters and other allied leftist groups, helping solidify the influence of Richardson's dramatic writing "as the signature cultural articulation of these organizing politics" employed by Black women activists of the period.[36] Though evidence of performances is scarce, one firsthand report by the *Daily Worker* captures the emotional potency conveyed by Richardson in enacting her play. In December 1953, prominent Black activist Mary Church Terrell led a delegation of women to Georgia to lobby Governor Herman Talmadge for clemency and freedom for Ingram and her sons. Following a visit to the state capitol in Atlanta, the group gathered at the city's "Negro YWCA" and "heard the new poem by Miss Beulah Richardson, 'The Revolt of Mrs. Rosa Lee Ingram.' One of those listening was Mrs. Ingram's daughter, Mrs. Geneva Rushin. As she sat there, tears started down her cheeks. The rapt silence was followed by a thunder of applause as we all rose to pay tribute to this powerful Negro poet."[37]

The Revolt of Rosa Ingram employs a dramaturgical strategy different from that of Richardson's other plays discussed above. The text begins in an unspecified voice—akin to a narrator, or a chorus—who paints the scene: "The cell is bleak and cold. / Bleaker, colder to the innocent mother /

Imprisoned therein / Than to those prisoners grappling with thoughts / of remorse and regret."[38] But the drama soon shifts into the voice of Ingram herself: "How, why have I, me, / Rosa Lee Ingram, / come to this?" (2). The play shifts back and forth between these two voices, with Ingram's words distinguished on the page in underlined, indented lines, creating a dialogic dramatic experience:

> For she knows deep within her soul that
> that which was wrought in self defense,
> November fourth, nineteen-forty-seven,
> by her hand,
> was a human, humane thing.
>   How, then, does it come to this?
>   Here is justice turned upon itself! (1–2)

The *Daily Worker* account quoted above suggests that Richardson performed the entire work herself, employing the type of direct interaction with audiences she had exploited to such powerful effect with *A Black Woman Speaks.* Without more evidence, we must imagine how Richardson differentiated as a performer the layers of *The Revolt of Rosa Ingram* for her audiences—how she likely used shifts in tempo, vocal tenor, and physicality to distinguish the work's two voices.

As its title proclaims, the central action of this drama is a revolt. Though the play depicts Rosa Ingram as physically isolated and restrained, the character actively resists the logic of her imprisonment. Yearning to return home and reunite with her children, she contemplates the defense she provided for her sons against their white male attacker and achieves new insight:

> Is it not natural, necessary and right
> that we [mothers], who give life,
> should be first in the fight to defend it?
>   That is a part of this . . .
>   'Tis because I am a woman . . .
>   Surely that is a part of this . . .
> She sits transfixed,
> her eyes bright with this new knowledge.
>   But 'tis only a part. (4)

Driven to expand her understanding, Ingram achieves further clarity as she considers how the same values she taught to her children ironically contributed to their current imprisonment:

I taught my sons
you cannot love
where you deny defense and protection. . . .

That is part of it . . .
surely that is a part—
human decency does not fit the law.
What kind of law is it
that makes justice seem wrong
and wrong seem justified? (5)

The discovery that her sons now stand "punished for their decency"—as targets of "the law, the lawless law" (6) that criminalizes an honorable defense of their besieged mother—further propels the drama toward its climax. She then recounts her violent encounter with Stratford as if it were a biblical reckoning between good and evil:

But lo, this day there came upon me a
beast walking, talking like a man, but
who can understand the words he speaks
or the gun he carries in his hand . . .
Strike hard, my sons, hard as you can!
This is an evil thing. . . . It fell
down dead. Lo and behold, it was a man! (7–8)

Grappling with the death of her attacker, the protagonist absolves her sons of culpability and righteously concludes, "'Tis the lawless laws of this land / that killed this man" (8). The play's narrator confirms and extends the logic of this recognition:

It's the flaming cross
it's the hooded Klan
It's the landlords reaping the harvest
of other folks hands,.

It's the policeman's billy
the policeman's gun.
It's the lynchers running loose
and nothing's ever done.
It's jails packed full of innocent folks
with the real criminals judging in the courts. (9)

Here is the crux of the heroine's "revolt": her rejection and inversion of a white supremacist society's distinctions between "innocent folks" and "real criminals"—in the Ingram case and beyond. A denouement of sorts follows, with an expression of hope for the future: "But be calm my sons / men and women will come / must come / to defend a woman's right to her own body. / A sons right to protect his mother. / A human being's right to human decency" (10). As with *A Black Woman Speaks*, Richardson involves the play's audience in the drama, though here the confrontation and call to action are less immediate. *The Revolt of Rosa Ingram* does not directly address its spectators, but issues an implicit challenge for listeners to align themselves within the group of "men and women" whom the protagonist envisions coming to her aid. The dramatic character of Rosa Ingram—a stand-in for the real woman of that name languishing in a Georgia prison and facing death—charges the performance's spectators to move beyond spectatorship and take up the fight to restore justice.

In contrast with the political campaign in support of *We Charge Genocide*, the CRC's work on behalf of Rosa Lee Ingram met with more tangible results. After years of sustained public pressure, in August 1959, Rosa Lee, Wallace, and Sammie Ingram were granted parole and released from prison. *The Revolt of Rosa Ingram* served as one inspirational part of a multifaceted collaboration to redress an egregious injustice. As both playwright and performer, Richardson offered her era a vivid example of how Black theater artists might exploit the potency of live performance to radicalize the public toward revolutionary, liberatory social change.

BEULAH RICHARDSON'S OTHER DRAMATIC WRITINGS

In addition to the three plays discussed above, Beulah Richardson wrote several other works for the stage during this phase of her artistic life. A June 1951 byline for one of her published poems states, "She has written and produced two three-act plays." An October 1951 profile reports that "altogether, she has done eight poems, five plays, and a satire."[39] Several of these writings seem to be lost, with only scattered details for a few theatrical works surviving in various newspaper accounts. One play from this period, *And It Came to Pass*, was produced in May–June 1951 at the Negro Art Theatre of Los Angeles (a community ensemble founded in 1937 by Langston Hughes). The work was staged as part of an evening of short plays that also included Alice Childress's 1950 one-act *Florence* and another work entitled *Cotton Curtain* (a drama about the Korean War by a young local playwright named Frank Greenwood). The production ran for three weeks at the Masonic Temple in South Los Angeles. The Negro Art Theatre revived *And It Came to Pass* in August (along with *Florence* and another one-act entitled *The Button*) at the Lewis Metropolitan CME Church, in South Central Los Angeles.

Richardson cowrote *And It Came to Pass* with legendary actor Rex Ingram, who played the leading role in the production. By one reviewer's account, in contrast to the "down-to-earth drama" by Childress and Greenwood included on the same bill, this work was a "bit of fantasy" offering some relief from earthly situations.

> Ingram, in his masterful progression from the menial angel who was promoted because of his diligence and hard work, gives one of the finest portrayals of his career. From the subservient, humble custodian of the Lord's offices, he becomes a power-crazed dictator who brings a new set of commandments and tries to shape man in his own image.

This review describes the play as a "Rex Ingram monologue."[40] Its details are contradicted by another account that describes *And It Came to Pass* as a two-character play, in which "Rex Ingram and Bill Walker enact the roles of Satan and St. Peter."[41] Though it is not clear if this play discussed questions of race or gender explicitly, its engagement with themes of autocracy and abuse of power suggests a satiric reflection on a nation corrupted by social inequities and committing imperialist abuses on the world stage—in line with Richardson's leftist political leanings.

Another script from this period does survive, the three-act drama *One Is a Crowd*. Richardson began work on this play in 1950, though it would not be seen by audiences until decades later when staged in Los Angeles in the early 1970s. *One Is a Crowd* centers on a Black "retired night club singer"[42] named Elizabeth Dundee (referred to in the dialogue as "Lindy") and her attempt to avenge the deaths of her mother, father, and brother. The villain of the drama is a white senator (named only "the Southerner" in the script) whose rape of Lindy's mother decades ago set in motion a wholesale destruction of her entire family. After a surprise encounter with the senator at a party, Lindy seduces him into a meeting at her apartment, where she reveals her identity, confronts him with his crimes, and fatally poisons him. The play is essentially a sensational melodrama—with a simmering revenge plot, family secrets painfully revealed, formalistic language, multiple suggestions of sexual dalliance, a virtuous romance between young hero and ingenue characters, and a climactic onstage death scene to resolve the conflict. As such, it marks quite a departure from the politically radical and formally experimental theater that Richardson was also composing and performing in the early 1950s. It is striking that this potboiler belongs to the same playwright and originates from the same point in time as the other theatrical works discussed in this chapter.

One Is a Crowd may well have remained hidden from the public but for the playwright's collaboration (working as Beah Richards) in the late 1960s with Frank Silvera. Richards partnered with Silvera—a famed actor, director, acting teacher, and prominent champion of African American playwrights—to develop the play for a reading at Los Angeles's Our Corner Workshop in August 1968. That reading led eventually to a full staging at LA's Inner City Repertory Company in 1971, directed by C. Bernard Jackson, with Richards herself playing Elizabeth. (Silvera had died about a year earlier.) Describing her decades-long journey with *One Is a Crowd*, Richards told the *Los Angeles Times* that, since the play's original composition in 1950, "I've only changed a few words. Unfortunately, there's been no need to make changes, because things between blacks and whites haven't really changed all that much in the last 20 years. I wish everything in the play had to do with the past, but I'm afraid it has to do with today."[43]

Nonetheless, considered alongside her other stage writings, *One Is a Crowd* seems antiquated in its aesthetics and its driving sensibility. One reviewer found the drama "less a play in the conventional sense than an opera libretto, a slightly arbitrary succession of florid Big Scenes and bring-down-the-house arias [that] go from pretentiousness to pungency in a flash."[44] Within one of Elizabeth's operatic speeches, a glimmer of the author's radical politics emerges. As the play approaches its final poisoning scene, Lindy must first confront her piano player and love interest, Pagon (who faces his own trouble for having drunkenly attacked a prostitute the previous evening). Not yet aware of the truth of Lindy's past or her designs on vengeance, Pagon jealously accuses her of plotting to meet the senator for a romantic liaison. She responds to his intrusive accusations with this florid declaration:

> Look at me. Can't you see who I am? . . . I know who I am, what I am, and why I am as I am! I sat chained in that slaveship just like you. I stood on that auction block and was inspected and sold, just like you! I bore the lash and sustained the pain. I knew the mockery and the shame and picked my bale of cotton just like you! I escaped with the blood hounds at my heels just like you and did my share of the

> fighting too. How dare you set a boundary for me! How dare you! I am no male idea of shrinking femininity. I am no clinging vine. That's Charlie's shit and don't you bring it to me. Not me. I am a woman . . . a woman! I've had my fill of slavery and slavery's ideas. Don't you dare try to intimidate me. I have no more fear, I've used it up. Do you hear? I'll have no more of supremacy, neither white nor male.

Here is a glimpse of the radical racial and gender politics, fueled by a revolutionary historical consciousness, that are far more prominent in this playwright's other dramatic writings. Years later, Richardson remembered this monologue—delivered while shedding her wet clothes, after Lindy walks home through a rainstorm—as a high point of absorption for her audiences. "Not a single review mentioned that this child got completely down to the nitty-gritty," she declared proudly. "They didn't even see it! It was like I had all my clothes on!"[45]

The 1971 production of *One Is a Crowd* illuminated for the public new dimensions of a familiar actor's creative life. "What an actress she is!" the *Los Angeles Times* critic declared. "Those who know Miss Richards mostly from her crushed Mom roles in films like 'Guess Who's Coming to Dinner' have no idea of her extraordinary wholeness as a woman and as a performer."[46] Yet this sample of dramatic writing was notably unrepresentative of its author's radical theater praxis. What audiences did not see then, and what remains largely unfamiliar today, is how Richardson's bold creativity during the early 1950s blazed revolutionary new trails for the African American stage.

FOUR | Snatching the Bullwhip

Purlie Victorious as Proto-revolutionary Comedy

Around 1922 or 1923, police in Waycross, Georgia targeted an African American boy of five or six years old for humiliation. The officers apprehended the youngster on his way home from school and brought him (confused about why he was being detained) to the local station. At first, the policemen talked and joked with the boy in a seemingly nonthreatening manner. Suddenly, as the target of this attack remembered it many years later, "One of them took syrup and poured it on my head, and another gave me some peanut brittle and put me on the streets and told me, 'Go home now. Don't get into any devilment.'" Here is how, in adulthood, this individual assessed the white officers' intentions toward him:

> I always knew that that really was meant to tell me that I was a nigger and that I had a place and that I should keep in that place. As I think back on it, I think it was designed specifically to get my consent to the system of segregation. In other words, they had to ascertain whether I was going to be a good boy or a bad nigger. . . . I didn't feel threatened by the whole thing at all, but they had somehow "niggerized" me, and it lasted for many a year.[1]

This boy, Ossie Davis, would grow to become a celebrated playwright, actor, and activist: one of the African American theater's leading voices of the late twentieth century. Davis credited this lingering memory from his childhood as the primary inspiration for his most influential original drama:

> My play *Purlie Victorious* was, in a sense, my response to the time when they had poured the syrup on my head. I set out to write a very angry, vituperative play expressing all that had pent up in me, but I found that as I wrote it and read it back, it was so. . . . The language was so exaggerated, and the characters, the white folks, were so mean and the black folks were so holy that I read the stuff, and I

> started eventually to laugh at what I'd been writing, and eventually it ceased to be a play about a young angry boy and became a play about a preposterous preacher called *Purlie Victorious*, and we did it for comedy and for laughs.[2]

Finding a lighter side to his outrage, Davis lampoons white supremacy in the southern United States in the form of high comedy. *Purlie Victorious* utilizes satire, wordplay, exaggeration, and broad physicality to skewer the logic of Jim Crow. The comedy delivers an obligatory happily-ever-after ending that resolves its plot, affirms a moral order, rewards the deserving, and corrects wickedness and excess.

Beyond his childhood memories, another point of influence that Davis cited for *Purlie Victorious* was his experience working as stage manager for the 1953 off-Broadway production of *The World of Sholem Aleichem*, a theatrical adaptation of the iconic Yiddish writer's comic folktales. Davis's sustained encounter with "a play about Jews whose principal salvation in an absurd and oppressive world was laughter" inspired him to craft a laugh-inducing celebration of his own cultural heritage—one also responding to ludicrous patterns of oppression and injustice. "I felt right at home," Davis explains in a 1961 newspaper profile. "Sholem Aleichem's people were my people. They thought they had problems? Well I wanted them to look inside *my* closet."[3] This sense of cross-cultural affinity supports Mel Watkins's analysis that "black humor (like Jewish humor, perhaps the most prominent influence on the American humor tradition) is in many ways shaped by the minority status of its creators. The outsider or 'shadow' position of Jews and blacks in mainstream American society has given them a unique perspective on themselves as well as on the dominant or majority culture."[4]

Opening at the Cort Theatre on May 29 ,1961, *Purlie Victorious* enjoyed a nine-month Broadway run of 261 performances. This debut production featured Davis himself portraying the title role of Reverend Purlie Victorious Judson, alongside his wife and frequent collaborator Ruby Dee as the comedy's ingenue Lutiebelle Gussie Mae Jenkins. The original cast also included veteran Black actors Godfrey Cambridge, Beah Richards (the subject of Chapter 3), and Helen Martin, alongside white actors Sorrell Booke and Alan Alda. The Broadway success of *Purlie Victorious* sparked a subsequent production in Chicago, a 1963 film adaptation (featuring most of the original New York cast) entitled *Gone Are the Days*, and later, a 1970 musical adaptation called *Purlie!* Published in multiple editions, including several key anthologies of African American drama, *Purlie Victorious* now stands as the most widely produced and studied work within Davis's playwriting career that stretches over more than six decades.

At the time of its debut, *Purlie Victorious* elicited sharply divided responses from the public, as audiences and critics grappled with the implications of Davis's provocative comic technique. The playwright summarized his dramaturgical strategy in an interview with the *New York Times*: "Segregation is a ridiculous institution and it makes decent people do ridiculous things. Maybe if they can be made to laugh at it they can see how absurd it is."[5] Creative choices made for the original Broadway staging, under the direction of Howard DaSilva, supported this outlook. Photos and reviews capture the cartoon-style settings created by designer Ben Edwards, and the over-the-top physical, gestural, and vocal style employed by the entire cast, to highlight the slapstick nature of Davis's comic romp through the Jim Crow South. Many laughed along with this approach, affording *Purlie Victorious* mostly positive reviews and enthusiastic support from both Black and white audiences. Some, however, took issue with the playful treatment of a contemptible legacy of white oppression. As Davis reflects, detractors found his work "condescending if not demeaning. To them, we Negroes were locked in a life and death struggle against white, bigoted, Jim Crow oppressors. The cause was serious, and laughter was the last thing we needed at a time like this."[6]

The divided reaction elicited by *Purlie Victorious* points to the volatile cultural and political climate within which it appeared. The play's lighthearted approach, its commercial popularity, and (as will be discussed in detail below) the theme of racial reconciliation upon which Davis creates his comic resolution struck some artists and critics as out of joint with the urgency of Black freedom struggles of the early 1960s. As Davis reflects in his memoirs, the play posed to the public some vital and divisive questions: "Was *Purlie Victorious,* with all its laughter, its gags, its shtick and one-liners, an act of betrayal? . . . What place has laughter in a revolution?"[7] Such questions—which were thorny enough in 1961—take on a different valence considering developments in African American cultural discourse that followed soon after. Amiri Baraka's manifesto for a "Revolutionary Theatre" appeared just a few years later, calling for plays by Black writers that "will show victims so that their brothers in the audience will be better able to understand that they are the brothers of victims, and that they themselves are victims, if they are blood brothers. And what we show must cause the blood to rush, so that pre-revolutionary temperaments will be bathed in this blood."[8] Viewed by this searing light, *Purlie Victorious* appears quite conservative and conciliatory—perhaps even counterrevolutionary—in its outlook. The play's own rhetoric supports such an interpretation. As the comedy builds toward its madcap climax, just when its titular protagonist gains the opportunity to strike physically against his white tormentor (a Georgia plantation owner named Ol' Cap'n Stonewall Jackson Cotchipee), he refrains, and deliberately chooses a path of nonviolence and interracial unity. Purlie closes the play with a sermon that preaches fellowship between white and Black Americans: "Let us . . . stifle the rifle of conflict, shatter the scatter of discord . . . and grapple the apple of peace!"[9] With harmony restored through its protagonist's final choice to forgo vengeance and embrace reconciliation (an echo of Prospero in Shakespeare's *The Tempest*), *Purlie Victorious* seemingly arises from and speaks to those "prerevolutionary temperaments" that Baraka sought to purge from Black theatrical culture.

Here, however, I want to look beneath the play's surface and read against the grain of some of Davis's own statements about his work. As Henry D. Miller argues, "*Purlie Victorious* was, in many ways, a precursor of the ideas that were to form the militant and separatist movement in Negro life that [LeRoi] Jones [aka Amiri Baraka] was about to lead."[10] Following Miller's line of analysis, *Purlie Victorious* reveals itself despite outward appearances as a proto-revolutionary comedy with radical implications. A close reading of the script reveals how its comic qualities sit in palpable tension with its disturbing evocations of white hegemonic violence, theft, and sexual predation against African American communities. At a key moment in the action, Davis presents audiences with a gripping vision of armed Black uprising against white American oppression. While the play steps back from that brink at its conclusion, the moments that precede the comic rapprochement should not be overlooked. Its final tableau of interracial harmony fulfills generic expectations for comedy; yet that resolution also feels unsatisfying—purposefully so, I believe—and should not be fully credited at face value. What lingers more prophetically after the final curtain falls is the stirring image of a messianic hero's bold proclamation to his historically victimized and dispossessed people, "Arise and shine for thy light has come . . . [Our] enemy hath been destroyed!" (310).

Davis's account of his childhood experience calls to mind an oft-repeated aphorism (of uncertain origin, variously attributed to Mark Twain, Lenny Bruce, Carol Burnett, and other possible sources): "Comedy equals tragedy plus time." Though Davis had decades to reflect on his trauma, undoubtedly, his experiences of outrage and alienation evoked by racism in the United States were not confined to his youth. By depicting the persistent and pervasive menace of racial oppression in a comic register,

Purlie Victorious renews a rich tradition of subversive, socially critical Black humor that stretches back generations to the era of slavery. The Black comic tradition rooted in African American folk culture has been explored by several scholars—including Terrence Tucker, Bambi Haggins, Mel Watkins, William Schechter, and Lawrence Levine.[11] Tucker's study outlines a genealogy of "comic rage" through which Black comedians blend humor with anger. For Tucker, "comic rage" is

> an African American cultural expression that utilizes oral tradition to simultaneously convey humor and militancy. . . . Comic rage centralizes African American experience and, fueled by militant rage, uses a comic lens to examine the complexities and inconsistencies in the American national narrative. . . . [C]omic rage is a vital source of cultural expression that actively reveals the perpetuation of white supremacist hegemony through its mixture of tones and inversion of traditional discourse.[12]

Purlie Victorious deploys comic rage to expose, to mock, and to invalidate the absurd and maddening ideology of white supremacy in the United States and its pernicious effects. As the following analysis will demonstrate, the play's final reconciliation should not be understood as a straightforward endorsement of political moderation, nor as a negation of Black anger against centuries of white violence and theft, but as an illustration of the type of inversion of discourse to which Tucker refers. *Purlie Victorious* creates a productive, ironic dissonance between the infuriating nature of the social pathology that it explores and the buoyant comic spirit through which its story is told and resolved. Through that dissonance, Davis speaks evocatively to Black revolutionary aspirations of his era.

In contrast with Davis's approach, playwrights of the Black Arts Movement would follow quite a different approach in their explorations of comic rage. Comic dramas by Baraka, Ed Bullins, Ben Caldwell, Ron Milner, and others elicit laughter primarily through graphic, visceral shock—deploying grisly imagery and a separatist political sensibility in service of humor that proves far more savage in tone. These Black Arts comedies often secure their "happy endings" by envisioning brutal, unforgiving, and long-overdue comeuppances for white supremacists and their witting or unwitting Black accomplices in society. "Oddly enough," notes Daryl Dance in a 1974 analysis titled "Contemporary Militant Black Humor," "scenes replete with the sound of machine guns and the flow of human blood are wildly comic . . . [and] intended only for blacks—to awaken them to their heritage and a sense of pride, and to move them to revolution."[13] Much of *Purlie Victorious* seems to pull audiences in the opposite direction—not toward bloodshed, nor for the exclusive delight of Black audiences, but in affirmation of a spirit of "togetherness [and] each otherness" (318) across the racial divide. Davis himself emphasized these tendencies in promoting his work to the public. "What Martin Luther King is trying to do with love," he proclaimed in a 1961 interview, "I am trying to do in this play with laughter."[14] Elsewhere, Davis assured the public, "A lot of white people believe that the Negro is aching for revenge," he continued, "that as soon as he gets into a position of equality he's going to pay off some old scores. That's not true. If they can see us also laughing at segregation, they'll realize that we would like to forget about it, too, once it's behind us."[15] It is curious that Davis centers white spectatorship in envisioning the social impact of his own comedy.

Compounding the apparent counterrevolutionary implications of *Purlie Victorious* are Davis's deliberate uses of familiar and fraught racial stereotypes—including several common caricatures of African Americans derived from minstrelsy. Within the play's broadly rendered comic universe, one character proved particularly problematic: Gitlow Judson, the Cotchipee plantation's fastest cotton picker and (as Ol' Cap'n celebrates him) an epitome of "the old-fashioned, solid, hard-earned, Uncle Tom type Negra" (295). The play's foregrounding of this character—first enacted on stage by comedian Godfrey Cambridge—elicited pointed rebukes from certain Black critics. The *Chicago Defender*'s review notes with alarm: "There hasn't been so much 'Uncle Tomming' on a local stage in many years. Granted that it is all done purposely with a specific intent, the result is tasteless and dreary."[16] Many observers concurred; Davis acknowledges their discomfort by noting that "white folks already looked upon us as a race of clowns, incapable of acting like men. . . . What we needed from the theater [the play's opponents believed] was not buffoons, but heroes."[17]

The critical debates surrounding *Purlie Victorious* highlight a perennial flashpoint within African American cultural discourse: the tricky question of how Black writers might effectively address "a binary between humor that is 'genuine' and 'authentic' and that which is commercialized and mediated by white power."[18] For detractors, no matter Davis's larger purpose or intended message, the deployment of caricatures belonging to a white supremacist American culture placed *Purlie Victorious* on the less comfortable side of that binary. Whether in the final analysis one sees *Purlie Victorious* as validating and reinforcing existing stereotypes, or rather (as discussed below) inverting them productively, the inherent risks in reanimating the skeletons of a bigoted cultural legacy are impossible to ignore. Stage caricatures like Uncle Tom and Mammy are painful reminders of the persistent rot of white supremacy infecting the core of the American psyche, and of the pernicious role that the stage has played in spreading that contagion. Their very presence bolsters an interpretation of *Purlie Victorious* as backward-looking, as a drama that accommodates rather than disrupts the logic of American racial chauvinism.

But, as Simon Weaver argues, to think about comic images in terms of a strict binary can be reductive. Weaver's discussion of the "reverse discourse" of Black comedy posits that frequently "the images in [African American] humor both simultaneously 'play on' and 'play off' . . . long-established stereotypes," thus imbuing those images with "a simultaneous, and paradoxical, racist and anti-racist potential."[19] Davis countered his skeptics by pointing to this dual potential within his script. Conceding that his characters were crafted as "no-hold-barred buffoons," the playwright elucidates his antiracist aims in repurposing old racist tropes: "What I wanted was to gradually reveal inside the stereotypes, human beings who were diametrically opposed to the stereotypes."[20] Some observers credited his effort. "Is Mr. Davis poking mild fun at *us* for creating these types? I think he is,"[21] suggests one reviewer. Prominent African American critic Sylvester Leaks notes, "Never does the artist, Mr. Davis, laugh at his characters. He laughs with them. . . . Through [the play's] 'Uncle Tom' role one sees the duality of the black man's existence. Here one sees—aside from his distasteful role of pollyanna and sycophantic, the 'Uncle Tom' often times serving a useful purpose—that of a spy in the enemy camp."[22]

Such interpretations start to elucidate the potent double valences at work in *Purlie Victorious*—in alignment with centuries of Black comic tradition. As Mel Watkins explains, African American humor often exploits "the consequences of split vision—the ability . . . to see oneself and others from multiple perspectives."[23] This tendency arises out of the subjective experience that W. E. B. Du Bois's famously articulates as "double-consciousness": "One ever feels his twoness," Du Bois writes famously in *The Souls of Black Folk*, "an American, a Negro, two souls, two thoughts, two unreconciled strivings, two warring ideals in one dark body."[24] Watkins applies this paradigm to his analysis of African American comic traditions: "Du Bois's eloquent description of African America's psychological predicament provides a salient clue to the source and special tenor of black American humor."[25] Recognizing this distinctive quality of African American humor is key to any complete understanding of *Purlie Victorious*. To view the play

Figure 6. L to R: Ossie Davis, Helen Martin, Godfrey Cambridge, Ruby Dee, Beah Richards, Sorrell Booke (holding whip) in a scene from *Purlie Victorious* at the Cort Theater, New York, NY. Photo: Friedman-Abeles

straightforwardly, from a single vantage point only, is to miss the full "twoness" of its meaning.

"The Black tradition is double-voiced," Henry Louis Gates Jr. notes in his seminal work *The Signifying Monkey*. Gates identifies the cagy manipulation of simultaneous dual meanings as "Signifyin(g)," a rhetorical strategy at the heart of centuries of cultural expression in the African Diaspora. "Signfyin(g), in other words, is the figurative difference between the literal and the metaphorical, between surface and latent meaning. . . . Signifyin(g) presupposes an 'encoded' intention to say one thing but to mean quite another."[26] In the final act of *Purlie Victorious*, Davis gives his comedy a cagy double ending that presents audiences with two contrasting paths toward social justice for Black Americans. This double ending is Davis's gesture of Signifyin(g) on mid-twentieth-century racial politics. As with decoding the double-edged utterings of the Yoruba trickster Esu-Elegua, we can discern the full implications of *Purlie Victorious* by looking between and beyond the two simultaneous and competing voices through which it speaks.

The comedy begins with its title character's return to the Georgia plantation where his family has toiled for generations as slaves and sharecroppers. Having been driven away decades earlier by Ol' Cap'n Cotchipee, Purlie (now a reverend) reemerges with a plot to reclaim a $500 inheritance stolen by Ol' Cap'n from his Aunt Henrietta. He will use this money to reacquire Big Bethel Church, where his grandfather had preached, and to reestablish the congregation with himself in the pulpit. To execute the scheme, Purlie brings with him Lutiebelle (a domestic worker from Alabama), whom he has recruited to impersonate his deceased Cousin Beatrice (Aunt Henrietta's college-educated daughter). Purlie orchestrates this deception to fulfill weighty moral purposes: restoring the rightful wealth and ecumenical legacy of the Judson family and redressing the long history of oppression and exploitation that keeps the evils of chattel slavery alive in the Jim Crow South. On their arrival, Purlie explains to Lutiebelle:

> That ol' man runs this plantation on debt; the longer you work for Ol' Cap'n Cotchipee, the more you owe at the commissary . . . that's slavery! . . . just wait!—till I get my church;—wait till I buy Big Bethel back—(*Crosses to window and looks out.*) Wait till I stand once again in the pulpit of Grandpaw Kinkaid and all upon my people—and talk to my people—about Ol' Cap'n, that miserable son-of-a—. (281)

The score-settling is also personal, and seared into Purlie's flesh. His sister-in-law Missy explains to Lutiebelle how "that ol' man . . . took after Purlie so unmerciful with that bull whip twenty years ago" (286), motivating Purlie's long-standing quest for righteous retribution. "Big Bethel is my Bethel," Purlie declares: "It belongs to my people; I intend to have it back if I have to pay for it in blood!" (305).

Comic hijinks ensue as Lutiebelle stumbles in impersonating Cousin Bee, ultimately betraying the subterfuge to Ol' Cap'n. The plot thickens further through the intercession of two supporting characters: Charlie Cotchipee, Ol' Cap'n's liberal-minded but dull and naive son; and Gitlow, who seeks through most of the action to assuage Ol' Cap'n's abundant anger by singing the traditional spirituals "Ol' Black Joe" and "Gone Are the Days" and with constant reassurances that "you're the boss, boss!" (295). When Ol' Cap'n calls the local Sheriff and Deputy to apprehend Purlie and then attempts (following Purlie's escape) to force himself sexually on Lutiebelle, the play's tensions escalate toward an ultimate standoff. In a raucous climax, Purlie turns the tables on Ol' Cap'n and achieves his long-sought-after position of physical dominion over his abuser:

PURLIE: (*Snatches bull whip.*)
OL' CAP'N: Have a care, boy; I'm still a white man.
PURLIE: Congratulations! Twenty years ago, I told you this bull whip was gonna change hands one of these days!

This is the moment when Purlie, counterintuitively, pulls back and relinquishes his weapon. Davis resolves the plot with a deus ex machina flourish, as Charlie enters and announces his secret purchase of the deed for Big Bethel in Purlie's name. When Purlie offers to repay Charlie with $500 stolen from the plantation commissary, Charlie hesitates before accepting: "Well—all right," he finally agrees. "But only if . . . Would you let me be a member of your church?" Purlie agrees: "The doors of Big Bethel, Church of the New Freedom for all Mankind, are hereby declared 'Open for Business!'" The shocking turn of events smites Ol' Cap'n Cotchipee suddenly where he stands. "*GITLOW feels his pulse, listens to his heart, and lifts up his eyelids. Nothing.* The first man I ever seen in all this world to drop dead standing up!" (317).

A short epilogue depicts Ol' Cap'n's funeral service at Big Bethel, with Purlie offering posthumous words of grace for his tormentor: "For he who was my skin's enemy, was brave enough to die standing for what he believed. . . . He was a man—despite his own example." The play's final tableau sounds two contrasting notes to bring down the curtain. On one hand, Purlie's message to his new flock is an inspiring affirmation of Black pride and potential: "I find, in being black, a thing of beauty: a joy; a strength; a secret cup of gladness," Purlie extols. "Accept in full the sweetness of your blackness" (318). As Carol Bunch Davis points out, "By framing black cultural nationalism as a continuation of black Christianity, *Purlie Victorious* refuses cultural memory's prevailing narrative that situates them as mutually exclusive."[27] In the same sermon, the reverend also preaches faith in interracial fraternity and in the mechanisms of American democracy as the path toward a more just future for African Americans: "Now, may the Constitution of the United States go with you; the Declaration of Independence stand by you; the Bill of Rights protect you; and the State Commission Against Discrimination keep the eyes of the law upon you, henceforth, now and forever. Amen" (318).

Read on their own, these final words align with a counterrevolutionary reading of *Purlie Victorious*. With Purlie having seized the bullwhip—a potent symbol of the South's brutal white supremacist history—and with his enemy vulnerable before him, he refrains from striking back physically, and invests a curious faith in conventional legal remedies to racial injustice.

"We want our cut of the Constitution, and we want it now," he proclaims, "and not with no teaspoon, white folks—throw it at us with a shovel!" (316). To militant revolutionaries, such demands are bound to sound at best naive, and at worst destructive to the forceful pursuit of Black liberation. However, the hasty tying up of the plot is but one strain of Davis's double-voiced ending. The play's other voice, given full expression in the preceding scene, is a vivid, stirring theatrical engagement with the *possibility* and the *righteousness* of violent Black resistance to white racial terror. The implications of that gesture persist, even after the play doubles back on itself with its fantastical final twist.

Davis plants the seeds for the play's militant message much earlier in the action. When Purlie first arrives at the plantation and reunites with Missy, the play establishes the stakes for his return to Cotchipee County. "Twenty years ago it was, Purlie, Ol' Cap'n laid bull whip to your natural behind," Missy reminds him, to which he responds, "Twenty years ago I swore I'd see his soul in hell!" (282). Beyond his revenge on Ol' Cap'n, Purlie's reclamation of the pulpit at Big Bethel will fulfill his ambition to "lead the Negro people" and preach "the New Baptism of Freedom. . . . There is in every man a finger of iron that points him what he must and must not do" (285). Thus from the outset, Davis situates Purlie's return neither in terms of interracial communion nor as an assertion of US legal doctrine, but as a harbinger of overdue eye-for-an-eye vengeance and messianic liberation. "The South is split like a fat man's underwear," the reverend proclaims, "and somebody *beside the Supreme Court* has to got make a stand for the everlasting glory of our people!" (289, my emphasis)—signaling a clear understanding of the inadequacy of a purely legalistic approach to procuring justice for Black Americans. Purlie pursues a just redress for his people's victimization, using Lutiebelle's uncanny resemblance to the late Cousin Beatrice as the tool of his subterfuge. However, in Purlie's eyes she signifies something more exalted than merely the means to that righteous end. Rescued from servitude as a "common scullion in the white man's kitchen," Lutiebelle is to the reverend a vessel of historic race pride and power, whose glory he celebrates with soaring poetry:

> This Ibo prize—this Zulu Pearl—
> This long lost lily of the black Mandingo—
> Kikuyu maid, beneath whose brown embrace
> Hot suns of Africa are burning still: where—where?
> This brown-skinned grape! This wine of Negro vintage— . . .
> [A] dark and holy vessel,

In whom should burn that golden nut-brown joy
Which Negro womanhood was meant to be.
Then thousand queens, ten thousand Queens of Sheba:
(*Pointing at* LUTIEBELLE)
Ethiopia herself—in all her beauteous wonder,
Come to restore the ancient thrones of Cush! (284–85)

The alliance between Purlie and Lutiebelle—initially strategic and later romantic, in alignment with boy-gets-girl comic expectations—personifies the ascendant promise of Black political, cultural, spiritual, and diasporic power. With their union, the righteous quest for retribution against white supremacist violence and the flowering of racial pride for all Americans of African lineage converge.

The plan to recover Aunt Henrietta's stolen inheritance initially appears headed toward quick success. Though Lutiebelle's impersonation of Beatrice is rife with comic gaffes and malapropisms, the performance deceives Ol' Cap'n nonetheless. Purlie looks to seal the deal with flattery, by conferring on his former abuser the fake honorific of "Great White Father of the Year," in the presence of the local Sheriff and his Deputy. The hoodwinked Ol' Cap'n hands over a $500 bankroll (the amount owed to Beatrice), only to snatch it back when Lutiebelle errs by signing her own name (rather than Beatrice's) to the receipt. This misstep sparks the play's first eruption of violence between Black and white. Enraged at almost being duped, Ol' Cap'n vows to resume "something I started twenty years ago with this bull whip . . . (*Fastening his eyes on* PURLIE). Something I intend to finish . . . I'm gonna teach you to try to make a damn fool outta white folks." Purlie evades his lashes and a hapless pursuit by the armed Sheriff and Deputy, until his accomplice intercedes:

LUTIEBELLE: (*Stepping between the* SHERIFF *and* PURLIE) Don't you dare!
SHERIFF: What!
LUTIEBELLE: Insultin' Reb'n Purlie, and him a man of the cloth!
(*Grabs his gun arm and bites it.*)
SHERIFF: Owwww! (*She kicks him in the shin.*) Owwwwwww! (303)

In this madcap manner, Davis presents to his audience a stunning scene: physical Black resistance against the violent order of the Old South. As the melee continues, an errant punch from the Deputy (aimed at Purlie) catches Charlie square in the face—allowing Purlie and Lutiebelle to escape unharmed in the ensuing commotion.

That Charlie is the one to suffer the blow is apt. In one sense, the young man's liberal outlook on race relations stands in stark and sympathetic contrast to his father's extreme bigotry. Also in distinction to the boorish Ol' Cap'n, the younger Cotchipee is a meek, clownish, and inept figure. Stage directions describe him as *"a young white man of 25 or 30, but still gawky, awkward, and adolescent in outlook and behavior . . . very much oversized even for his age"* (291). Though adult in years, he is markedly immature in disposition: highly dependent upon the maternal doting of his longtime caretaker Idella and submissive in the face of his dad's bigoted bluster. "You are a disgrace to the southland!" his father upbraids him. "I could beat you with that bull whip—put my pistol to your good-for-nothing head—my own flesh and blood—and blow your blasted brains all over this valley!" Charlie can only answer with a timid, "Yessir," prompting Ol' Cap'n to seize him and demand, "You trying to get non-violent with me, boy?" (293).

Charlie does at times show flashes of sincerity about racial justice. At his first appearance, Idella nurses wounds he has suffered in a bar fight, for daring publicly to say things "friendly to the Supreme Court" (292). When reviewing commissary accounts with his father, Charlie speaks out against the exploitative business practices that keep the plantation profitable:

> According to this book, every family in this valley owes money they'll never be able to pay back. . . . How long do you expect them to stand for it? . . . How long before they start a-rearing up on their hind legs, and saying: "Enough, white folks—now that's enough! Either you start treating me like I'm somebody in this world, or I'll blow your brains out"? (294)

Such moral conviction and awareness of the righteousness of Black rage, while admirable for a white southerner, are overshadowed by Charlie's immaturity, timidity, and clumsiness. As Charlie suffers his lumps, the Judson family is mostly left to confront Ol' Cap'n and his badge-wearing accomplices on their own. After absorbing the Deputy's misdirected blow, Charlie disappears from the play until his improbable return at its conclusion. Even within a highly outlandish comic universe, the play's miraculous resolution delivered by this most unlikely "white savior" strains credulity. Is Davis suggesting that African Americans should invest hopes for restoring stolen inheritances and realizing human dignity in the hands of white liberals like Charlie? The playwright is surely not that naive; we must read his fantastical ending with a large dose of skepticism. The comedy's final flurry of events—Charlie's defiance of his father, Ol' Cap'n's spontaneous and peaceful passing, and the promotion of interracial Christian fellowship on the soil of the old Confederacy—are illogical to the extreme. But a more logical and compelling take on race relations in the United States can be found in the "false" ending that precedes this "true" resolution of the plot.

Purlie's righteous anger, inspired by Ol' Cap'n's decades of financial crimes against his family, is heightened by the events of the plot as they unfold. Earlier in Act 1, with his scheme exposed, Purlie escapes his second encounter with Ol' Cap'n's bullwhip and flees into hiding for two days. Upon his return, the reverend learns of new dangers. Ol' Cap'n's favorite "darkie" Gitlow has, in Purlie's absence, sent Lutiebelle to the "big house" to retrieve the money—alone. The frightening implications of this scenario are clear to Purlie:

> GITLOW: [Y]ou want to buy Big Bethel back or don't you?
> PURLIE: (*A glimmering of truth.*) I hope I misunderstand you!
> GITLOW: You said it yourself: It is meet that the daughters of Zion should sacrifice themselves for the cause.
> PURLIE: (*Grabbing up Missy's bat.*) Gitlow, I'll kill you—!

Lutiebelle enters at that moment, "*disheveled . . . with her hat completely askew,*" confirming Purlie's fears. She tells of Ol' Cap'n "sneak[ing] up behind me in the pantry . . . grabbing his dirty ol' hands on me . . . twisting me around and pinching me. . . . and then he, he . . . He kissed me!" (307). Though the details of this assault are not as brutal as were reasonably feared, its disclosure reignites Purlie's militant rage: "No man kisses the woman I love and lives! . . . I'm going up that hill, and I'm gonna call that buzzardly ol' bastard out, and I wouldn't be surprised if I didn't beat him until he died." This man of the cloth hurls a stream of profane violent threats out the window, toward Ol' Cap'n's mansion: "I'll break your neck off! . . . I'll stomp your eyeballs in! . . . I'll snatch your right arm outta the socket, and beat the rest of you to death!" Far from misplaced or irrational, Purlie's rage is appropriate and necessary—as Davis clearly underscores for the audience. "And what you suppose he'd a done to us if I'd a kissed his [love interest]," Purlie asks. "(*The one question too obvious to answer.*) And that's exactly what I'm gonna do to him!" (308). As Purlie storms off stage, Lutiebelle's and Missy's fears for his safety sit in tension with the prospect that appropriate retribution for years of racist crimes might at long last befall Ol' Cap'n. Awaiting Purlie's return or any news of the encounter, Lutiebelle confesses to Missy, "I wanted [Purlie] to get mad; I wanted him to tear out up that hill; I wanted him to punch that sweaty ol' buzzard in his gizzard—you think I was wrong?" The wise elder—knowing full well the historic victimization faced by Black women within the white southern patriarchy—answers frankly, "I should say not!" (309).

After tense hours of anticipation, Purlie storms triumphantly back on stage, declaring victory and brandishing two trophies from battle. First, he "*draws a roll of bills from his pocket for all to see*," before revealing another prize: "And that ain't all I got . . . *PURLIE slowly pulls out OL' CAP'N's bull whip*" (311). Purlie's gripping story of his confrontation and defeat of Ol' Cap'n dominates the next several minutes of stage time. The scene is a theatrical tour de force, one that Davis himself exploited to maximum effect in performance. For the plot, however, the story proves to be a red herring. Idella soon enters and reveals the truth, declaring, "That is the biggest lie since the devil learned to talk! . . . Purlie Judson! Are you gonna stand there sitting on your behind, and preach these people into believing you spent the night up at the big house whipping Ol' Cap'n when all the time you was breaking into the commissary!" (314). A cascade of revelations follows—that Purlie had *intended* to strike back at Ol' Cap'n and was on the cusp of doing so, and that Charlie intercepted and diverted him to save his father's life. "I had to get into that commissary, right then and there, open that safe, and pay him his inheritance," the son later tells his father, "even then I had to beg him to spare your life!" (316). This plot twist communicates a stern warning to white liberals and all white Americans: beyond conciliatory rhetoric, only through meaningful reparative action for the historic crimes of racism can justified and foreseeable acts of militant Black retribution be prevented. When Ol' Cap'n nonetheless persists in trying to arrest Purlie as the thief, the hero makes his final stand. This is when he recaptures the bullwhip to use for his vengeance, only to willingly relinquish it just a minute later. If his sudden turn toward forgiveness seems illogical, perhaps Davis's true message about racial justice lies elsewhere in the play's final scenes.

It is worth noting that Purlie achieves his moment of dominance with the assistance of a surprising accomplice. Even after Charlie confesses to stealing the $500 bankroll, Ol' Cap'n clings to his original accusation:

> OL' CAP'N: [I]t was Purlie who stole that money and I'm going to prove it. (*Starts to take out gun. GITLOW grabs gun.*) Gitlow, my old friend, arrest this boy, Gitlow! As Deputy-For-The-Colored—I order you to arrest this boy for stealing!
>
> GITLOW: (*With a brand new meaning.*) "Gone are the days—" (*Still twirls pistol safely out of OL CAP'N's reach.*)

Figure 7. L to R: Beah Richards, Helen Martin, Godfrey Cambridge, Ruby Dee, Ossie Davis (with arms raised), Cy Herzog, Roger Carmel, Sorrell Booke and Alan Alda in a scene from *Purlie Victorious* at the Cort Theater, New York, NY. Photo: Friedman-Abeles

Here, near the play's finale, Davis finally empowers Gitlow to emerge from behind the grinning mask of Uncle Tom and to complicate the caricature by resisting subjugation and allying with his people. This is the clearest illustration of how "Davis' play wrests segregation's symbols and iconography . . . away from their origins in minstrelsy and presses them into black cultural nationalism's service."[28] Does that gesture of inverting the stereotype, coming so late in the action amid a flurry of contrived events, deliver its intended payoff? Does it give us sufficient grounds for laughing *with* Gitlow, when (as some argue) the play's broad humor encourages audiences for most of the preceding two hours to laugh *at* him?

And how, ultimately, should we understand Purlie's inspiring tale of inflicting well-deserved comeuppance on Ol' Cap'n Cotchipee, after that story is revealed as a falsehood? "I felt the weight of his ol' bull whip nestling in my hands," Purlie narrates at the gripping climax of his story, "and the fury of a good Gawd-almighty was within me; and I beat him—I whipped him—and I flogged him—and I cut him—I destroyed him!" (314).

This, the comedy's first resolution, ultimately proves a "false" one. It is a fictional account spun within the fiction of the comedy, and its promise of long-sought and proportionate restitution for crimes inflicted on the Judson family soon vanishes. Nevertheless, while operative on stage, the tale is distinctly more logical, more creditable, and more inspiring than the outlandish "reality" that soon asserts itself to resolve the comedy. Purlie's story affirms African American strength, courage, and agency in confronting the evils of Jim Crow. The play's subsequent and more conciliatory "true" ending, by contrast, deprives African Americans of the power to act and invests hopes for racial justice in the hands of the hapless (if somewhat well-intentioned) offspring of the old Confederacy.

Purlie's story of revenge is not so much an outright falsehood as, he explains, "it was a parable! A prophesy! Believe me," he urges after Idella enters to warn of the approach of the still-living Ol' Cap'n, "I ain't never in all my life told a lie I didn't mean to make come true some day!" (314–15). This proclamation simmers with a double resonance. As a declaration to his family and his intended bride, Purlie reaffirms his continuing dedication to delivering his people from the wilderness of subjugation to the promised land of equality and empowerment. Simultaneously, for the playwright who penned these words (and first spoke them onstage as an actor), they capture Davis's lofty creative ambitions. With *Purlie Victorious,* he offered the public a theatrical parable of Black empowerment and triumph, and invested it with a hope to "make [it] come true some day!" With one voice, Davis conjures up a stirring vision of militant Black revolution. Then, in another register, he assures a potentially wary public of his continuing adherence to nonviolence, love, and faith in US jurisprudence. Though the latter voice seemingly replaces the former, the play's appealing "false" ending is "Signifyin(g)" on its flimsier "true" one. By offering a vision of Black revolution within a frame of comic diversion, Davis cleverly exploits—for his own radical purposes—"the dynamic and indeterminate relationship between truth on one hand and understanding on the other."[29]

As critical debates about *Purlie Victorious* unfolded, some African Americans provided key support for the comedy. The play's midtown run attracted ticket buyers well beyond traditional Broadway audiences. As Davis notes in a January 1962 essay, published in *Freedomways* as the production was running, the play "has never been a big 'hit' with the 'carriage trade,' the 'expense-account crowd.' . . . As a matter of fact, had Purlie been forced to rely on the normal avenue of Broadway patronage we would long ago have sunk and disappeared from sight. . . . It was, and is, the attendance of *my own people* at the box office that made the difference."[30] A *New*

York Amsterdam News report confirms Davis's assertion of racial pride: "Some nights the theater has been almost eighty percent Negro in audience." Such attendance was the result of vigorous community engagement and creative marketing efforts. Between performances, Davis and Dee made hundreds of "appearances at social clubs, churches, unions, schools and anti-segregation rallies."[31] They engaged some influential allies, "two Negro writers, [critic and journalist] Sylvester Leaks and [historian] John Henrik Clarke, . . . to promote theatre parties among groups, churches, and organizations in the Negro Community." Two months into its run, the *Amsterdam News* reported that "Mr. Leaks and Mr. Clarke have sold over 3,000 tickets to various groups from Harlem to New Jersey. Because of their efforts, more Negroes are seeing 'Purlie Victorious' than any other Negro play to ever hit Broadway." In describing his conversations with African American community groups, Leaks acknowledges the need to confront the comedy's potentially uncomfortable style of humor: "Mr. Clarke and I believe passionately in 'Purlie Victorious.' . . . Once we convince [people] that it is not a play that will embarrass them, the rest is relatively easy."[32] That *Purlie Victorious* could be sustained by a predominantly Black audience base (even on the "Great White Way") offered an inspirational model of artistic self-sufficiency. "For the first time since I started working in the theatre," Davis proclaims, "*my boss is the Negro people!* And I choose to believe that this fact has implications for the Negro artist, musician, performer—in his struggle to express himself and survive at the same time—that are revolutionary."[33] Launched within a white-dominated commercial theater economy, *Purlie Victorious* set a precedent of Black cultural autonomy that the Black Arts Movement would soon take up in Harlem, Newark, Chicago, and other African American communities.

One more anecdote supports a view of *Purlie Victorious* as a work with clearly revolutionary implications. Writing for a commemorative edition of the script marking the thirty-year anniversary of the play's debut, Davis reflects on the many leading African American leaders and thinkers who supported the 1961 production. He tells of Dr. Martin Luther King Jr., NAACP president Roy Wilkins, and even a ninety-three-year-old Dr. W. E. B. Du Bois attending performances and expressing their appreciation. Davis's account continues:

> Even more astonishing—Malcolm X, controversial minister of the Nation of Islam, also came to see. Malcolm was an uncompromising Black Nationalist who did not believe in integration, which is certainly what Reverend Purlie was preaching, so we waited with bated

> breath to hear what he would say. He was more than commendatory; he was enthusiastic. Anything that held the "white devil" and his racist practices up to scorn and ridicule had his approval.[34]

Elsewhere Davis reports Malcolm's assessment of the play as "revolutionary—the highest kind of Struggle he could imagine."[35] It seems that the era's most prominent Black nationalist leader, too, sustained hopes that a parable like *Purlie Victorious* represented a radical theatrical fiction that could someday come true.

FIVE | From *The Blacks* to *Les Blancs* and Beyond

Variations on Theatrical Outrage

On May 4, 1961, the US premiere of Jean Genet's play *The Blacks: A Clown Show* opened off-Broadway at the St. Mark's Playhouse in Greenwich Village. Genet describes his work as "a play for an all-black cast . . . written . . . by a white man, [and] intended for a white audience."[1] As such, this work occupies a complicated position within the history of Black theater in the United States. A highly abstract, multilayered, and at times bewildering drama, *The Blacks* inspired a range of public responses when it debuted in New York. Some thrilled at Genet's experimental bravura and provocative approach to theatricalizing racial animosity; others bristled at the play's problematic depictions of Black identity, its vulgarity, and its overarching cynicism; many dismissed the work as unnecessarily obtuse and impenetrable. Despite (or perhaps because of) this divided reaction, *The Blacks* became a popular sensation, sustaining a run of more than fourteen hundred performances that lasted until September 27, 1964. The variegated impact of this historic production is perhaps best captured by John McClain's review for the *New York Journal-American*, which describes the event as one "which fascinates and often overwhelms the audience. It will mean many things to many people, but it will bore none of them."[2]

Within the varying reactions that greeted the US premiere of *The Blacks*, one strain of criticism speaks to the production's striking effect on the nation's theatrical and political culture. Robert Brustein's review for the *New Republic* is most illustrative:

> Considering the fact that *The Blacks* is a ritual of murder, violence, and crime, enacted by Negro supremacists, and culminating in ceremonial slaughter of the entire white race, its thunderous success here is really rather astonishing. One would hardly be surprised if Genet's celebration of race hatred found favor with an audience of Black Muslims; but the play is now being praised by the same liberal

> community which so heartily applauded *Raisin in the Sun* for its benevolence, charity, and racial togetherness. . . . As such, the play may do a great deal of harm to the cause of inter-race relations.[3]

Putting aside Brustein's overly simplistic analysis of *A Raisin in the Sun* and his clumsy fear-mongering about "Black Muslims," the review's juxtaposition of astonishment over the harsh tenor of *The Blacks* against a rosy-eyed reverence for the soothing ambiance of *A Raisin in the Sun* puts into focus the frames through which the white critical establishment of the early 1960s encountered Black bodies and voices on stages in the United States. At one extreme, the yearning for a comforting call to benevolence and togetherness in alignment with white liberal idealism beckoned welcomingly. At the other extreme, the threat of unfiltered expressions of Black anger and resentment—not commonly given a platform, particularly in white-controlled commercial venues—loomed. Brustein was not alone in his alarm at identifying the latter sensibility expressed at the St. Mark's Playhouse. Other reviewers describe this production of *The Blacks* as one that enacts "a violent attack on the condescension of the white race," as a "ritual of hate for the Caucasian race . . . an angry, perverse, and cruel work," and as the embodiment of "racial antipathy on a scale which stretches across the globe and goes back to the ethnic roots of mankind."[4] That an entirely African American cast could, within a commercially popular production of a play by white French writer, shock mainstream critics in this manner affords *The Blacks* a distinctive position within American theatrical culture of the postwar era.

Perhaps the most familiar critique of *The Blacks* came on entirely different intellectual grounds. In a June 1961 essay published in the *Village Voice*, Lorraine Hansberry denounced Genet's drama for trafficking in "romantic racism" and a "new paternalism" in its vision of Black people primarily as exotic and violent primitives. "For all of its sophistication," Hansberry argues, *The Blacks* "is itself an expression of some of the more quaint notions of white men."[5] At the time her essay was published, Hansberry was working on a new play of her own that had "first began to form in the playwright's mind sometime in the late spring or summer of 1960." This drama centered on a reunion of three siblings from an African village after their father's death, amid an upsurge of anticolonial revolution on the continent. Hansberry's work on this script had begun prior to the off-Broadway opening of *The Blacks*. Her ex-husband and literary executor Robert Nemiroff explains:

> It was not, however, until May 1961 that the elements began to move into focus and the play was to find its final shape and title. This was in immediate visceral response to Jean Genet's celebrated drama *Les Negres (The Blacks)* which had its American premiere that month. The title was chosen half in jest, for the work-in-progress bore no direct relation to the Frenchman's tour de force, not in style or technique, nor certainly in the events and characters depicted.[6]

Hansberry wrote and rewrote this play, *Les Blancs*, as her health deteriorated from pancreatic cancer, leaving the drama unfinished upon her death in January 1965. The nearly five-year period of Hansberry's writing of *Les Blancs* overlaps significantly with the off-Broadway engagement of *The Blacks*. That historical coincidence, and Hansberry's defiant title, create strong linkages between these two works that otherwise might seem (as Nemiroff suggests) as divergent aesthetically, politically, and philosophically as one might imagine.

When *Les Blancs* finally made it to the stage in November 1970—in a version compiled and completed by Nemiroff, based on Hansberry's surviving manuscripts and notes—among the responses from white critics was a note of distress. Some reviewers recoiled, interpreting the posthumous work as "a bitter and disillusioned drama [that] ends in a welter of bloodletting," and as a play "that does its utmost to justify the slaughter of whites by blacks, and fails." One assessment offers the stunning conclusion that *Les Blancs* "advocate[s] genocide of non-blacks as a solution to the race problem."[7] I cite these reviews not for their critical insights (which are questionable, to put it mildly) but as indications of how, five years following Hansberry's death and a decade after she had begun crafting *Les Blancs*, nerves among the white critical establishment over theatrical expressions of Black militancy remained as raw as ever. Curiously, the clear activation of white fears of Black uprising links these two theatrical events to one another, and to their shared moment in African American theater history.

This chapter investigates the off-Broadway debut production of *The Blacks* and the script of *Les Blancs* as interrelated theatrical phenomena—highlighting how, despite contrasting outlooks from the two playwrights behind them, these theatrical undertakings of the early 1960s shared a key outcome. That these two phenomena would align as vessels for revolutionary Black expression seems counterintuitive, particularly given Hansberry's direct refutation of Genet's project. To support this argument, my analysis treats the *production* of *The Blacks* as a distinct object of analysis—

one whose meaning stands apart from Genet's authorial presence, even as it arises within the framework of a stage production of his script. As David Saltz argues, theatrical performance can be seen as a creative process wherein actors "tak[e] advantage of the text" to communicate in ways that function differently from the words they say. "Rather than the performance serving the text, the text serves the performance."[8] For the debut off-Broadway production of *The Blacks*, Genet's text was made to serve the expressive aims of its African American actors—apart from (or, more accurately, *despite*) the original script's deeply problematic racial ontology. Moreover, Hansberry's *Les Blancs* consciously refutes Genet's ontological perspective, and in doing so, aligns with the performance praxis that the African American cast of *The Blacks* employed on the St. Mark's Playhouse stage. Revisiting these two concurrent events and the surprising symbiosis between them reveals another path followed by African American theater artists toward the development of a militant theatrical sensibility, in a moment of prelude to the Black Arts Movement.

ENACTING BLACK ANGER IN *THE BLACKS*

Genet's preface to *The Blacks*, which was printed in the off-Broadway program, reads: "One evening an actor asked me to write a play for an all-black cast. But what exactly is a black? First of all, what's his color?"[9] Approaching Blackness as an epistemological quandary rather than a lived sociopolitical reality, Genet weaves a dense and often perplexing dramatic text steeped in condescension, racist stereotypes, and colonialist power dynamics. Its plot centers on a troupe of Black performers undertaking a nightly reenactment of the rape and murder of white woman, for the entertainment of a group of white courtiers from a colonial monarchy (Queen, Valet, Governor, Missionary, and Judge, all portrayed by Black actors in white masks). As the players complete that exercise (while interacting with both their onstage listeners and the theater audience beyond the proscenium), another story unfolds in parallel offstage: the trial and execution of a Black prisoner for his disloyalty to an ongoing uprising against the white colonial regime. After witnessing the retelling of the murder, the courtiers travel to the jungle to seek justice for the slain white woman. There the Black troupe members ceremoniously murder the white officials one by one. The play concludes with a suggestion that the entire sequence of events will restart again. Una Chaudhuri describes the multilayered, ever-shifting theatricality of *The Blacks* as an experience that "deliberately pursues confusion and actively fosters 'misunderstanding.' It is a process in which a series of apparently stable realities are progressively destabilized and denied . . . a subterfuge within a ritual within a performance within a play."[10] Heightened dialogue, music, dance, pantomime, and nested layers of metatheater add sensory and cognitive density to the theatrical experience that Genet embeds within the text of *The Blacks*.

While the script refers to no specific setting for the action, *The Blacks* depicts a society clearly organized around white imperial rule and Black anticolonial resistance. Genet's engagement with the racial politics of colonialism was a topic of much debate when the play opened in Paris in 1959—a discussion that was reignited for American audiences when the work crossed the Atlantic. That the same drama could strike some viewers as an angry antiracist screed and incitement to Black violence, and appear to others as "an insensitive, racist betrayal of the Black revolution" highlights its enigmatic nature. Genet's drama is highly visceral and incendiary, yet also consistently protean and disorienting. Chaudhuri's analysis offers a useful path through the drama's thicket of possibilities: "*The Blacks*, as I see it, is not a political play but rather the script or score for a political experience," most distinctive not for any clear authorial point of view expressed therein but rather for its "lack of final clarity."[11] With no coherent social thesis predominating, any staging of the drama can supply—thanks to the text's many ambiguities and lacunae—avenues for comment on racial politics that are *not* predetermined by the playwright. Here I want to focus on one distinct pathway of meaning charted by the first African American actors to interpret *The Blacks* for audiences in the United States. Viewed apart from the swirl of condemnation and praise that the play inspired, the off-Broadway cast's performance praxis signaled the swelling of a revolutionary sensibility within African American theatrical culture of the early 1960s.

The opening night cast of *The Blacks* overflows with names now recognizable, including James Earl Jones, Cicely Tyson, Maya Angelou, Roscoe Lee Brown, Louis Gossett, Helen Martin, Godfrey Cambridge, Charles Gordone, and Ethel Ayler. Other illustrious performers—such as Robert Hooks, Vinie Burrows, Abbey Lincoln, and Douglas Turner Ward, to name just a few—cycled into the cast throughout the production's lengthy engagement. The longevity of this production provided many African American performers of the era with professional opportunities. As Jones relates, *The Blacks* provided him and his fellow cast members a platform that helped support each artist's creative development. "I was in and out of the production seven times from 1961 until late in 1963. The production gave us all a home base. . . . One by one, we would leave to work on other projects, and come back again."[12] Those opportunities came with distinct demands and challenges, however. As seen within the public, the content of the play provoked strong and contrasting reactions from its actors. Maya Angelou recounts her distaste for Genet's script upon a first reading, a discomfort she never fully shed even as she invested herself in playing the white Queen: "*The Blacks* was a white foreigner's idea of a people he did not understand. Genet had superimposed the meanness and cruelty of his own people on to a race he had never known . . . I threw the manuscript in the closet, finished with Genet and his narrow little conclusions." Her husband and friends prevailed on Angelou to join the cast, however, and she ultimately came to view her involvement in the production differently. But tensions stirred by the script contributed to an increasingly difficult behind-the-scenes working dynamic. "Rehearsals began with a playground joviality and in days accelerated into the seriousness of a full-scale war. . . . Each day, tension met us as we walked into the theater and lay low like morning fog in the aisles."[13]

Also fostering an atmosphere of unease was the approach taken by Gene Frankel, the production's white director. Frankel approached *The Blacks* "as a form of hate therapy: where the ventilation of conscious and subconscious projections that are at the heart of all human difficulties are projected [and] we have an opportunity to literally air out our hatreds."[14] His combative approach to working with the cast (while in alignment with his directorial vision for the play) added combustibility to a tense environment. Stuart Little reports that "rehearsals were periods of sometimes bruising confrontation between the black cast and the white director. To Frankel . . . this was precisely the point of the American production," to leverage the play text as a device through which Black cast and white spectators could each make "nakedly plain the resentment and hatred they felt."[15] Roscoe Lee Browne reflects on "terrible moments" of uneasiness within the rehearsal process; the cast hashed out their difficulties together in a series of conversations that often lasted deep into the night, which Browne termed "the Mau Mau meetings."[16] A principle focus of these meetings was the cast's "resistance to Frankel's direction on the grounds that, being white, he was unable to understand black motivation."[17] As Jones reminisced, the overriding impact of *The Blacks* on its cast was fatigue—"more than just physical weariness—it was spiritual fatigue. There was a constant harangue. It was wearing." He nonetheless grew to appreciate his work in this production as a productive period marked by "intense stimulation to stretch and grow," and as "a landmark experience for me, one of those pivotal moments in a career, and I was grateful."[18]

Figure 8. A scene from *The Blacks* by Jean Genet at the St. Mark's Playhouse, New York, NY. Photo: Martha Swope.

Beyond professional challenge and exhaustion, *The Blacks* served for its African American actors as a vehicle for political expression that many found empowering, even liberating. That is a striking historical truth, particularly considering the justified critiques of the play among African American cultural leaders. Hansberry bluntly elucidates her disdain for a drama that she saw as "a conversation between white men about *themselves*" in which "the blacks remain the exotic."[19] In rejecting *The Blacks*, Hansberry was in agreement with fellow playwright and cultural critic Amiri Baraka. At a public forum held more than forty years later, Baraka reaffirmed his original impression that "the play is like a minstrel show." He pronounced *The Blacks* as antithetical to the Black Arts theater that coalesced a few years after the play's debut, which was by his own description "an actual eruption of an Afro-American cultural revolution in which we said we wanted an art that was identifiably Black, second we wanted an art that was mass-oriented, third we wanted an art that was revolutionary."[20] These and other critiques of Genet's work are certainly defensible. However, alongside the play's undeniable problems and blind spots were for its originating cast some empowering possibilities for exploring on stage ideals of Black militancy. The actors' mining of that potential helped to energize their performance praxis. This was a potent dimension of the St. Mark's Playhouse production, no matter the criticisms raised over the text with which their performances were forged.

Racial antagonism is the engine of dramatic conflict within *The Blacks*. The Black troupe's racial solidarity and shared antipathy toward white onlookers (and white society more generally) stoke that conflict. As a character named Village, who is the presumed killer of the white woman, contemplates reenactment of his deed, the other players spur him on: "What we need is hatred. Our ideas will spring from hatred. . . . Politeness must be raised to such a pitch that it becomes monstrous. It must arouse fear. . . . Since they [i.e., the whites] merge us with an image and drown us in it, let the image set their teeth on edge!"[21] Archibald—the troupe's leader and an emcee for the proceedings—inveighs to his collaborators as they perform: "I order you to be black to your very veins. Pump black blood through them. Let Africa circulate in them. Let Negroes negrify themselves. . . . Negroes, if they [whites] change toward us, let it not be out of indulgence, but terror" (52). Their performed act of racial killing is a prelude to more theatricalized bloodshed, as the white courtiers descend from their high perch above the stage to face their own staged executions. One of the Black players, Felicity, squares off against the white Queen and pronounces the extinction of this autocrat and the coming replacement of all that her colonialist oppression exemplifies:

> To you, black was the color of priests and undertakers and orphans. But everything is changing. Whatever is gentle and kind and good and tender will be black. Milk will be black, sugar, rice, the sky, doves, hope will be black. So will the opera to which we shall go, blacks that we are, in black Rolls Royces to hail black kings, to hear brass bands beneath chandeliers of black crystal. (106)

Just a few minutes later, the white courtiers "die" in a heap at the hands of the Black players, with Archibald delivering a harsh eulogy, "What we enjoyed was to kill you, to slaughter you down to your white powder, to your very soapsuds" (116).

In this stylized and disorienting manner, *The Blacks* offered its cast pathways to explore antiwhite, anti-supremacist, anti-imperialist longings in performance. Jones reflected on this dynamic in a 2016 interview: "It was quite a wonderful experience for us on stage because it gives a lot of chance to vent a lot of stuff, a lot of feelings, but it was theatrically controlled."[22] Vinie Burrows—not a member of the original cast, but a company member through much of the play's four-year run—reflected on her experience with *The Blacks*: "When we poured out our litany, it gave many Blacks in the audience a sense of power, and a sense that now someone was saying how we feel and how we've been treated."[23] Similarly, Angelou—whose role as the white Queen cast her as a target of (rather than a mouthpiece for) the expressions of hatred within the drama—relished the chance to play a part in conjuring such emotions. "I started enjoying my role," she explains. "I used the White Queen to ridicule mean white women and brutal white men who had too often injured me and mine. . . . The theater became a sardonic sanctuary where we sneered at white saints and we spit on white gods."[24] The thrilling nightly chance to inhabit scornful defiance of white supremacist power sustained the cast through their exhausting work of bringing the play (itself an expression of a French writer's problematic racial condescension) into theatrical form.

As these expressions of antagonism pour forth, the play's metatheatrical layering envelops other strains of social commentary. At several moments throughout their ceremonial enactments, the Black company of players pause their activities to highlight the larger implications of their own performative work. Near the outset of the festivities, Archibald informs his courtly auditors, "We embellish ourselves so as to please you" (10), underscoring how feigned displays of Black servility pervade white supremacist social contexts and disguise genuine feelings. This social dynamic returns later and extends into the auditorium, when the character Newport News (an ally of the troupe not involved in the reenactment) reminds his peers, "Though we can put on an act in front of them (*pointing to the audience*), we've got to stop acting when we're among ourselves" (82). The interplay of performed Black subservience and the hegemonic white gaze pervades the theatrical event, as outlined in Genet's preface:

> This play . . . is intended for a white audience, but if, which is unlikely it is ever performed before a black audience, then a white person, male or female should be invited every evening. The orga-

> nizer of the show should welcome him formally, dress him in ceremonial costume and lead him to his seat, preferably in the front row of the orchestra. The actors will play for him. . . . But what if no white person accepted? Then let white masks be distributed to the black spectators.

Such instructions align with Baraka's nationalist critique of the play quoted above, as well as various critics' dismissals of *The Blacks*. Yet by mirroring beyond the proscenium the drama's onstage social arrangement—that is, the Black actors performing for white spectators and/or for Black people disguised as white people—a performance of *The Blacks* will make tangible on stage Frantz Fanon's conception of racial ontology within a colonialist context: "Not only must the black man be black. He must be black in relation to the white man."[25] Angelou remarks upon her own discovery of the truth behind Genet's theatrical conceit: "Blacks did sneer from behind their masks the rulers they both loathed and envied." Angelou and her castmates used the opportunity to perform *The Blacks* to explore the prospect of "throw[ing] off the yoke which dragged us down into an eternal genuflection."[26]

One additional layer of narrative surrounds the onstage events of *The Blacks* that are visible to the audience. Intermittently throughout the action, Newport News arrives with reports of the detention, interrogation, trial, and execution of a Negro prisoner. The specific act for which the man is condemned is never named. Genet establishes the political nature of the unseen trial and sentence when Newport News tells of its completion: "He has paid. We shall have to get used to the responsibility of executing our own traitors" (111). The prisoner's fate is foretold earlier, when Newport News picks up a revolver and leaves to "question him" under a "Court of Justice." As he departs with the gun, a player named Diouf asks him: "Do you really want to take that object with you? (*pointing to the revolver in Newport News' hand*)." Archibald negates Diouf's hesitancy with muscular resolution: "You're going to urge us to be reasonable, to be conciliatory. But we're bent on being unreasonable, on being hostile" (29) The implication of this bloody subplot is, as Browne summarized: "Essentially, the play is about power and how it corrupts," no matter the racial identity of those who wield that power.[27] Such an ahistorical view of human immorality—which complicates whatever concrete antiracist and anticolonialist meaning one might find within *The Blacks*—elicited objection from some African American commentators. "Buried somewhere in [the play's] obscurities, there seems to be the basic thesis that the white man doesn't exactly have a copyright on the abuse of power and privilege," notes the critic for the *Chi-*

cago Defender. "I don't see how anyone can take it seriously enough either as art or preachment."[28] Or as Baraka put it more bluntly, "The whole theme that Black people are going to replicate white people if they gain equality and self-determination is the master's bullshit. They are always saying stuff like that. . . . That is the master's lie. And maybe some petit bourgeois Negroes."[29]

Here, too, the play's skeptics offers a sound line of critique that cannot be ignored in any analysis of *The Blacks* and its relationship to revolutionary Black culture of the 1960s. Nonetheless, there is a comparison to consider between the subplot of violent retribution against a Black counterrevolutionary figure and the explicit condemnations of "petit bourgeois Negroes" that would emerge a few years later within Black Arts discourse. Baraka's own oeuvre provides several graphic examples—including the beheading of the character Tom at the conclusion of *Slave Ship* (1967), the shootings of Mother and Sister for their devotion to the white Devil Lady in *Madheart* (1967), and the whipping, killing, and dismemberment of Black Cop in *Police* (1968). As Erik Nielson explains, visible throughout the literature and drama of the Black Arts Movement (alongside agitations against white racist oppressors) are evocations of "a kind of metaphorical violence against the 'nigger,' the black man who has allowed himself to become a tool for whites."[30] Such depictions further what Larry Neal defines as the movement's effort to "destroy the double consciousness—the tension that is in the soul of the black folk."[31] Undeniably, a vast distance separates Genet's cynicism from the revolutionary sensibility of the Black Arts Movement. Even so, *The Blacks* provided both cast members and audiences the scenario of a militant Black response to the presence of counterrevolutionary opposition from within Black societies. This strain of the drama was one of several ways that "*The Blacks* was important in opening vistas for the eventual birth of more radical theatre forms" that took shape in its wake.[32]

Given Genet's declaration that *The Blacks* "is intended for a white audience," the off-Broadway production succeeded in finding its envisioned viewers. While detailed demographic data are not available, anecdotal accounts report a largely white audience for the production. In Angelou's estimation, "Each night in the theater whites outnumbered my people four to one, and that fact was befuddling," given what she saw as "the play's obtrusive intent. . . . Why, then, did they crowd into the St. Mark's Playhouse and sit gaping as black actors flung filthy words and even filthier meanings into their faces?" Her account of one backstage interaction with a white theatergoer who had seen the performance five times within the first month provides one possible explanation. This white woman gushed that she and her friends thrilled at the play and wanted to communicate that they "support [the cast]. I mean, we understand what you are saying." But the same woman quickly took umbrage at personal questions from Angelou about her interactions with Black people in her own life: "How many blacks live in your building? . . . How many black friends do you have? I mean, not counting your maid? . . . Would you take me home with you? Would you become my friend?" The woman rushed away from the encounter in annoyance, exclaiming, "You people. You people," leading Angelou to conclude sardonically, "She comes to the theater and allows us to curse and berate her, and that's her contribution to our struggle."[33] This insight aligns with playwright and poet Owen Dodson's 1963 observation that "*The* Blacks . . . is what I call an absolute insult to the white audience. It is a horror, and yet the hordes keep coming on to be insulted."[34] Perhaps the value of the "hate therapy" that Frankel describes was to allow some to unburden themselves of white guilt within the playhouse, so that they could continue to enjoy white privilege without encumbrance everywhere else.

The Blacks did also appeal to some African American spectators. Cheryl Higashida notes that "a range of Black leftists, nationalist, and liberals lauded Genet's play. As cast and audience members, many African Americans appreciated the play's expression of Black anger at a time when formal civil rights could not eradicate white supremacist violence and racial inequities."[35] Arthur French—an accomplished Black actor who was never cast in the production—described the impact that performances of *The Blacks* had on him as a spectator: "After I saw it the first time, I literally saw the play at least four or five times a week, every time it wasn't sold out, because I had never seen anything like it. . . . It hit me in the face and inspired me. It was something different and something that you didn't see" in commercial entertainment.[36] Ossie Davis reported that he "found it a most exciting theatrical production." Despite the excitement, Davis nonetheless took exception to Genet's view that "when the black man gets on top, he will oppress the man on the bottom who happens to be white . . . and we struggle merely to get into position so that we can oppress somebody else." Yet he recognized how "the aims of the author, director and actors were deliberate to be insulting" to whites, and as he saw it, "the insult does have, at its base, a certain amount of validity."[37] In Angelou's remembrance, it was clear that "Blacks understood and enjoyed the play." She notes: "Most blacks in the audience reacted with amusement at our blasphemous disclosures, although there were a few who coughed or grunted disapproval. They were embarrassed at our blatancy, preferring that our people keep our anger behind masks, and as usual under control."[38] Her crediting "our people" as the source of the event's vitriol indicates that the cast's performance praxis functioned as a site of theatrical meaning apart from the white-authored text, and was regularly received in that manner by Black audiences.

The impact of the actors' expressive work was magnified by the social backdrop against which it stood. James Earl Jones notes, "In the early sixties, the play was right for the times. It was one of the most perfectly timed productions I have ever been involved in . . . it provoked a raw, almost religious appeal to conscience,"[39] at a pivotal moment when public discourse on racial injustice was growing markedly more combative. As John Warrick elaborates, the off-Broadway phenomenon of *The Blacks* aligned with the agenda of "certain black radicals [who] began to consider the role of organized violence as a more effective method for attaining full civil rights," and thus became "a vehicle that allowed . . . black performers to express their outrage and anger at white society in the United States" in a novel and liberating manner.[40] That quality was not lost on one prominent champion of Black militancy. As Browne tells it, "When Malcolm saw [*The Blacks*] and he came backstage, he said, 'You need to take this thing all across the country.' Because it was resonant."

GRASPING THE SPEAR OF REVOLUTION IN *LES BLANCS*

That Hansberry's *Les Blancs* is a direct response to Genet's *The Blacks* becomes vivid at one moment of intense debate between the play's protagonist, Tshembe Matose, and his interlocutor, the American journalist Charlie Morris. Though Charlie professes liberalism on race and sympathy toward the colonized subjects of Zatembe (a fictional sub-Saharan nation), his insistent efforts to debate the country's political fortunes with Tshembe betray his ingrained white chauvinism. Tshembe tolerates his American visitor patiently, until hitting a breaking point:

> TSHEMBE: (*Gazing at him with open disgust*) Mr. Morris, have it your way! No matter what delusions of individuality infect *my* mind, to *you* I am not an individual but a tide, a flood, a monolith: "The *Bla-a-acks*!"[41]

Tshembe's "open disgust" with Charlie stands in for Hansberry's open disgust with Genet. *Les Blancs* channels the playwright's antipathy for Genet's racial condescension, his trafficking in colonialist logic, and (as Hansberry puts it) his overarching "distrust of us; his refusal to honor our longings for communion."[42] It is not clear if Tshembe is directly referring to Genet's play in this bit of dialogue. Still, his disdainful, drawn-out delivery points to the depth of Hansberry's revulsion at the work of her French counterpart known as "The *Bla-a-acks.*"

Warrick notes, "The New York production of *The Blacks* made a significant contribution to the development of the African American theatre by inciting controversies of immense aesthetic and political consequence."[43] *Les Blancs* is the most familiar artistic consequence of the backlash against Genet. Hansberry's timely exploration of Black nationalist and anticolonial striving contrasts starkly, by design, with the white chauvinism and philosophical detachment through which Genet approaches race relations in the colonized world. Even so, there is also an axis of alignment that links the efforts of the New York cast of *The Blacks* (as discussed above) and the domestic political implications of *Les Blancs*. Across about four and one-half years of the early 1960s—more or less the same period when Roscoe Lee Browne, James Earl Jones, Maya Angelou, Helen Martin, and their many castmates took the stage with angry fervor at the St. Mark's Playhouse—Hansberry poured her own radical energies into crafting *Les Blancs*. The questions that this African-set drama confronts were of the utmost urgency for the United States during this period of growing unrest within Black political discourse, primarily: "Is violent revolution inevitable in the struggle of oppressed peoples to be free?"[44]

In his published introduction to *Les Blancs*, Nemiroff frames the play within the context of "Lorraine Hansberry's abiding interest in Africa" that originated in her childhood. "Africa had been a conscious part of her almost as far back as consciousness itself."[45] The action of *Les Blancs* connects directly to contemporary anticolonial independence movements unfolding across the continent, particularly in Kenya. The offstage character Amos Kumalo—a moderate diplomatic leader of Zatembe seeking negotiation with the colonial government, only to be imprisoned by that regime—is modeled directly on Kenyan leader Jomo Kenyatta; there are several points of correspondence between *Les Blancs* and Kenyatta's 1938 book about the Kikuyu people, *Facing Mount Kenya*. The play's setting of a hospital run by Western missionaries and the mission's founder, Reverend Torvald Nielsen (another offstage character central to the action), are modeled on the work of Dr. Albert Schweitzer in Gabon. Hansberry also drew inspiration from colonial history and freedom movements in the Congo under Belgian occupation. Through the play's rich allusions to contemporary African political developments and movements, *Les Blancs* becomes in part an exploration of the same "anticolonial, pan-African strands" of geopolitical consciousness that Hansberry had earlier introduced through the character Asagai in *A Raisin in the Sun*.[46]

The resonance of Hansberry's capacious drama extends beyond the African continent. Among the many Hansberry scholars investigating the play, Joy L. Abell is most direct in pursuing a "reading of *Les Blancs* as a political and philosophical commentary on the emerging American Civil Rights movement."[47] Tshembe's return to Zatembe from his life in England for his father's funeral, amid the armed uprising of his countrymen, engulfs him in a conflict that spans the Atlantic Ocean. Through Tshembe's confronting of his own identity, his native country's plight, and his deep knowledge of the ongoing worldwide scourge of white supremacist brutality, Hansberry offers a new vista into the Black freedom struggle in the United States. As Colbert notes, *Les Blancs* is a play that directly "reflects the crossroads Hansberry faced at the end of her life and of the U.S. Civil Rights movement . . . by 1964, the patience of many civil rights activists in the U.S. was wearing thin. Hansberry's play participated in an unresolved conversation among civil rights activists over the merits of nonviolence as *the* protest strategy."[48] The conversation was as active, as urgent, and as unresolved for US citizens of African descent in the early 1960s as it was for revolutionary African political leaders and independence fighters of the era.

The play's central political dynamic arises out of Charlie's arrival at the hospital, when he learns of the region's militant unrest. Alarmed at the gunshots and reports of a local army crackdown, the visiting American asks his hosts, "What about—Kumalo? . . . I mean Amos Kumalo *is* still in Europe? They *are* talking?" Willy DeKoven, a white doctor at the hospital, punctures his naive hopes for diplomatic progress, informing him: "The [white] settlers are outraged because the Foreign Office is talking at all—and the blacks, because talk is no longer enough" (49). The drama hinges upon how Tshembe chooses to act upon the fundamental truth that "talk is no longer enough." Tshembe arrives in the next scene, already skeptical of what Kumalo's diplomacy might accomplish: "Talk, talk, talk. . . . [Kumalo] wanders around in the cold in his thin suits and he *talks*. . . . *That* is what Kumalo has been doing in Europe. *That* is what he will do in Zatembe" (56–57). Even so, though his sympathies are with those resisting the colonizers, Tshembe soon reveals his own wish to detach himself completely from Zatembe's struggles: "It is all over with me and history," he declares (60). Tshembe sidesteps Morris's baiting into political discussion by explaining, "Most of all I [long] to be in a dim little flat off Langley Square, watching the telly with my family" (79).

Yet no matter his affection for his white European wife and his bourgeois family life in England, Tshembe is haunted by a spectral presence:

> She will materialize out of the bush; she will waft up from the savannahs. . . . She will rise up from the smoke outside the huts. I have known her to gaze up at me from the puddles in the streets of London; from vending machines in the New York subways. Everywhere. And whenever I cursed her or sought to throw her off . . . I ended up that same night in her arms! (80)

Hansberry personifies this presence with a silent character, "*A WOMAN, majestic and motionless . . . Black-skinned and imposing, cheeks painted for war*" (41), who surfaces throughout the drama to beckon Tshembe to join the fight for the liberation of Zatembe. Within the otherwise realistic milieu of *Les Blancs,* the Woman is a symbolic presence—an abstract personification of the historical, cultural, and personal imperatives from which Tshembe has tried (unsuccessfully) to separate himself. When she appears at the end of Act 1 to summon him, "*urgently, insistently, unrelenting,*" Tshembe resists her in anguish: "NO! I WILL NOT GO! It is not my affair anymore! . . . I HAVE RENOUNCED ALL SPEARS!" (81).[49] Recognizing the unsustainability of renouncing "all spears" in the face of violent oppression was as urgent a reckoning for activists in the United States as it was for Africans across the globe. As she developed *Les Blancs,* Hansberry pondered just such a reckoning in her letter to a "white farm boy . . . on the Mason-Dixon line" who sought her "views on the 'Negro Question' in the United States . . . and the seemingly diametrically opposite techniques of the various freedom movements." The playwright's answer to this young man speaks to the future ascendency of "a forthcoming generation of Negroes who question even the restraints" shown by Dr. Martin Luther King and his campaign of nonviolent resistance. "The pressure rears up everywhere," she warns her white correspondent; "whether we like it or not, the condition of our people dictates what can only be called revolutionary attitudes."[50]

The force of those same intensifying pressures pushes Tshembe to grasp the spear of righteous revolution. Report comes of the arrest of Amos Kumalo upon his return to Zatembe for talks with the colonial regime. The arrest spurs Tshembe's half brother Eric into action: "They need warriors. . . . I know it is time to drive the invaders into the sea" (107). Soon after, Tshembe's brother Abioseh (educated as a Catholic priest, who stands opposed to the resistance fighters) learns that the local elder Ntali (a servant in the mission, known to the colonizers as "Peter") has been spying for the revolutionary militants. As Abioseh looks to betray Peter's activities to the local army commander Major Rice, Tshembe tries to stop him:

> TSHEMBE: Abioseh, stay out of this. It is not your affair!
> ABIOSEH: (*Taking hold of him*) It is both our affair. Tshembe, come with me!
> TSHEMBE: (*Breaking free*) He is an elder. He helped to raise us. They will kill him, Abioseh . . .
> ABIOSEH: I must go.
> TSHEMBE: No!
>
> (*They grapple and at last* TSHEMBE *flings him to the ground and grabs up the spear to hold him there.*)
>
> ABIOSEH: Then you must *use* the spear! (111)

Tshembe balks at striking his brother at this moment; his hesitancy leads directly to Peter's execution and the further inflaming of local outrage. Tshembe can no longer ignore the call of history. Hansberry's concluding stage direction reinforces his ultimate choice to embrace militancy for the sake of his people's freedom and dignity.

> *TSHEMBE advances. ABIOSEH turns. WARRIORS appear over the rise and at the edges of the stage, rifles in hand. Among them is ERIC—who blocks the way.*
>
> *As ABIOSEH turns back to him, TSHEMBE takes out the pistol he has been concealing . . . then levels it. For a moment the two brothers stand facing each other, aware of all the universal implications of the act; the one pulls the trigger, the other falls.* (128)

Tshembe's fratricide carries more than just familial implications. In an unsuccessful attempt to stop the reporting of Peter's identity to Major Rice, Tshembe lashes out at his brother: "The American blacks have a name for those like you, Abioseh" (110), though he refrains from speaking aloud the epithet "Uncle Tom." Their conflict is fraternal, and also political—with one brother denouncing, and ultimately killing, his kin for betrayal of their country's freedom movement. His completion of the bloody act connects *Les Blancs* not only to the Black Arts plays of Baraka and others (as referenced earlier) by staging the symbolic sacrifice of an "Uncle Tom" figure, but also—in service of a quite different dramatic project—to the offstage events reported by Newport News throughout *The Blacks*.

With this concluding act, Hansberry contemplates the ascent of Black nationalist militancy over the more moderate and collaborative strategies of the "heroic" civil rights period. Abioseh's Christian zeal, and Tshembe's disdain for his brother's professions of religiosity, become particularly resonant within that discussion. Abioseh rationalizes his stance against local militants by proclaiming, "I am committed to God, to civilization—and to Africa! . . . They are murderers, Tshembe. Murderers! . . . Christ leaves me no option" (110–11). Tshembe rejects his brother's religious practice as "another cult—which kept the watchfires of our oppressors for three centuries!" (61–62). As Abell notes, Abioseh's association with Western Christianity, and the untenability of his devotion to nonviolent collaboration with brutal oppressors, "reflect some American activists' growing unhappiness with the presence of religion in the battle for civil rights. . . . Tshembe's attitude toward Christianity, then, aligns Hansberry with those who were uneasy with its often prominent place in the Civil Rights Movement."[51]

Les Blancs concludes with Tshembe joining the uprising for the freedom of Zatembe: a campaign toward which he has reluctantly but inexorably moved throughout the drama. The action concludes with Black revolutionaries overrunning the mission. As flames engulf the hospital, gunfire claims the life of Madame Nielsen—the wife of Reverend Nielsen, and a sympathetic friend to Tshembe. In the wake of the reverend's killing by African fighters, and despite her involvement in the colonialist work of the mission, Madame stands as the play's lone white voice urging Tshembe to take up the spear. "Our country needs *warriors*, Tshembe Matoseh," she tells him. "*Warriors*, Tshembe. Now more than ever" (126). Through this depiction, Hansberry holds open the possibility of white alliance with the cause of revolutionary Black liberation. Madame's killing magnifies the consequences of the agonizing but necessary choice that Tshembe makes as the play concludes: "*TSHEMBE stands alone, MADAME in his arms. As flames envelop the Mission, he sinks to the ground, gently sets her body beside that of his brother, and in his anguish throws back his head and emits an animal-like cry of grief as—in a pool of light facing him—the WOMAN appears*" (128). Those critics who dismissed *Les Blancs* as seeking to incite a race war seem to have missed, or perhaps chose to ignore, the complexities of this final tableau. Hansberry's consideration of Black militancy is nuanced, not propagandist nor bloodthirsty—notwithstanding the howls of certain white reviewers for whom *Les Blancs* "seems to boil down to the fatalistic idea that violence is

Figure 9. L to R: Earle Hyman, James Earl Jones, and Harold Scott in a scene from *Les Blancs* by Lorraine Hansberry at the Longacre Theatrer, New York, NY. Photo: Bill Yoscary.

the black man's only final answer—in short, revolution and the ghetto slogan, '*kill whitey*.'"[52] Hansberry studiously avoids such simple-minded commentary, crafting an honest reckoning with both the urgency and the unavoidable tragic costs of meaningful revolutionary action.

The full implications of Hansberry's vision are most sensitively captured by Clayton Riley, in a *New York Times* essay billed as "A Black Critic on 'Les Blancs.'" Riley's response to the 1970 Broadway debut makes for a needed rejoinder to other (white) critics' overly simplistic readings of this multifaceted drama. Riley celebrates Hansberry's "awareness and exploration of a more contemporaneous reality: ugliness recognized, filth and perversity definitively perceived, in that social order most people will recognize under its formal title—Western Civilization." His analysis continues:

> The play divides people into sectors inhabited on the one hand by those who recognize clearly that a struggle exists in the world today that is about the liberation of oppressed peoples, a struggle to be supported at all costs. In the other camp live those who still accept

> as real the soothing mythology that oppression can be dealt with reasonably—particularly by Black people—if Blacks will just bear in mind the value of polite calm and continuing use of the democratic process.

Hansberry's sympathies for the former group come with a full awareness of "all costs" that the struggle for liberation will incur. Ultimately, the play posits "that there is no compromise with evil, there is only the fight for decency. If even Uncle Sam must die toward that end, 'Les Blancs' implies, then send *him* to the wall."[53]

A POSTSCRIPT: EXCORIATING BOURGEOIS CONFORMISM IN AMIRI BARAKA'S *GREAT GOODNESS OF LIFE*

Riley's metaphor of sending Uncle Sam "to the wall" for the sake of Black liberation foreshadows the central image of a different play that would debut a few years later. Amiri Baraka's 1972 one-act *Columbia, the Gem of the Ocean* (its title taken, sarcastically, from a popular patriotic anthem) dramatizes an "Uncle Sam" character spewing a stream of racist rhetoric and reveling in his power to control and dominate a Black populace—principally by means of a gun. Gradually, a group of Black characters rise up in revolutionary defiance, "*throwing rocks and cans and bottles, & giving them to the audience to throw*" before ending the play in a "*frenzy screaming!!!!* Kill him!"[54] A different short drama by Baraka intervenes even more directly in the theatrical exchange between Genet and Hansberry. As Kimberly Benston notes, before *Les Blancs* was known to the public, "Baraka wrote *Great Goodness of Life* as an explicit answer to Genet's *The Blacks*. . . . The themes, structure, and development of Baraka's play all parallel those of Genet's."[55] *Great Goodness of Life* debuted in November 1967 at the Spirit House in Newark, New Jersey—a theater founded by Baraka expressly as "a Black Nationalist operation" in concert with the "historic work in creating a Black Arts Movement that quickly spread across the country."[56] Though stylistically quite different from *Les Blancs*, Baraka's play shares a project with Hansberry's: to answer Genet's objectionable racial politics with a theatrical consideration of the necessity for Black revolutionary action.

Great Goodness of Life centers on a mysterious trial of a postal worker named Court Royal before an unseen judge—presumably white, present on stage only as a Voice. Accused by the Voice of "shielding a wanted criminal. A murderer,"[57] Court Royal professes himself innocent of all wrongdoing. He defends himself by emphasizing his respectable, middle-class identity: "I'm a good man. I have a car. A home. A club. . . . Please there's some mistake. Isn't there? I've done nothing wrong. I have a family. I work in the Post Office, I'm a supervisor. I've worked for thirty-five years" (56), he protests. The identity of the accused murderer is never specified, though a sequence of projected images links the "wanted criminal" with "*a rapidly shifting series of faces. Malcom. Patrice. Rev. King. Garvey. Dead nigger kids killed by the police. Medgar Evers.*" Court Royal pleads with the Judge, "I never saw that man, it's so many faces, I've never seen those faces . . . never." But the accused soon achieves, under duress, a glimmer of self-awareness about his own bourgeois conformist existence that is removed from most Black people's experiences: "I tried to be a man. I did. I lost my . . . heart . . . please it was so deep, I wanted to do the right thing, just do the right thing" (56–57). The Voice pronounces Court Royal's guilt but offers him a path to freedom; the condemned man can win his release by shooting a hooded prisoner, whom the Voice describes as a "shadow . . . the myth of the murderer . . . the shadow is killed in place of the killer" (61–62). Court Royal accepts the gun and pulls the trigger, proclaiming, "My soul is white as snow. . . . I'm free. My life is a beautiful thing" (63). He resumes his middle-class routine—fully culpable now in a conspiracy to extinguish the transgressive spirit of the subjugated, restless Black masses.

Benston elucidates how *Great Goodness of Life* remixes its source material:

> [Baraka] has taken each of Genet's levels of being and reversed them: what is illusion in *The Blacks* is reality in *Great Goodness of Life* and vice versa. Thus the "court" of masked Negroes comes down form the platform to become the black, middle-class Court Royal, who is put on trial. . . . Whereas the Negroes in *The Blacks* take on roles to divert and deceive their white audience while the Negro rebellion is proceeding outside the theatre, Court Royal's acceptance of the role dictated by the Voice is a concession to white society that allows it to crush the leaders of black revolution. . . . Baraka stages the trial of the black traitor (Court Royal) which is the offstage action of *The Blacks*.

Court Royal's securing of his own personal freedom and his return to material comfort—attained at the price of African American self-determination—renders *Great Goodness of Life* a scathing indictment of the Black middle class's "utter renunciation of black selfhood and complete acceptance of servility."[58] Baraka's theatrical response to *The Blacks*, somewhat like Hansberry's, is ultimately a call to revolutionary action. *Great Goodness of Life* is highly visceral, ironic, and imagistic, in contrast with the mostly realistic, discursive dramaturgy of *Les Blancs*.

Great Goodness of Life stands as one part of what might be understood as an unofficial triptych of theatrical projects that originates with Genet's misguided, self-imposed question, "What is a Black?" The political experience that the off-Broadway cast of *The Blacks* crafted from Genet's text foreshadows Hansberry's uneasy but stirring affirmation of the necessity of Black militancy, which in turn points toward Baraka's harsh excoriation of those African Americans who live their lives in outright denial of that necessity. The trajectory suggested by this trio of theatrical works maps the ascendency of the Black Arts Movement as the defining aesthetic and ideological force in African American theater for the latter phase of the long civil rights movement.

SIX | ". . . But the Show Hasn't Been Written Yet"

"Mississippi Goddam" and Nina Simone's Turn toward Black Nationalism

The five-year span of 1959–1964 saw the debuts of two monumental plays that were profoundly influential within African American theater history. The year 1959 marked the premiere of *A Raisin in the Sun* in Philadelphia, which drama soon became the first from a Black woman playwright to be produced on Broadway. As mentioned previously in this book, critical understanding of the full depth and breadth of Hansberry's dramatic achievement has grown significantly since the play's first appearance. Its transformative impact stemmed in large part from how the playwright delivered her disruptive social critique in a manner that meshed with prevailing "classical" civil rights-era sensibilities. The working-class Younger family's struggles against systemic discrimination, their determination to secure equitable opportunity within the American body politic, and their courage in defying segregationist threats for the sake of family advancement spoke evocatively to mainstream political campaigns for racial justice in the United States. Larry Neal highlights this dimension of *A Raisin in the Sun* in identifying the play as "the embodiment of the liberal integrationism which dominated the black political struggle of the mid-fifties and early sixties . . . in the realist/naturalist tradition."[1] Wilkerson, Colbert, Perry, and other Hansberry scholars expand on *A Raisin in the Sun* as a play predominantly integrationist in its politics and universalizing in its attraction. As Perry notes, "Lorraine mastered the strategic art of the appeal—the use of comfortable conventions for the sake of political argument and subversion. Given that the civil rights movement protest itself was so often a highly aestheticized performance of respectable citizenship, Lorraine's play was consistent with the energy of the struggle in that moment." All the while, beneath its comfortable-seeming surface, *A Raisin in the Sun* gives voice to Hansberry's radical perspectives "as a leftist, a feminist, and a believer in global anticolonial, antiracist politics."[2] Yet it was primarily the play's leveraging of mainstream sensibilities and strategies, rather than its subtle subversions, that brought *A Raisin in the Sun* its initial prominence and wide public celebration.

About five years later, another transformative play appeared as the avatar of a contrasting trajectory. LeRoi Jones / Amiri Baraka's *Dutchman* burst forth in 1964, heralding a new aesthetic and ideological sensibility for the African American stage. Far from a realistic and recognizable fourth-wall portrait of family life, *Dutchman* showcased a heightened, supercharged episode of racial antagonism, "*heaped in modern myth*"[3] and potent with symbolism and visceral power. Its two principal characters—the Black poet Clay and the white temptress Lula—function as archetypes rather than as realistically rendered social portraits. Their encounter turns abruptly from flirtatiousness to hostility, culminating in an outpouring of Black rage from Clay against the insidious, dehumanizing forces of white American hegemony. *Dutchman* gives voice on stage, in a manner not heard previously, to the burgeoning Black nationalist sensibility ascendant in the mid-1960s. In telling contrast to his reading of *A Raisin in the Sun*, Neal argues:

> It was LeRoi Jones' *Dutchman* that radically reordered the internal structure of black theater, first of all by opening up its linguistic range and breaking with the social realism which dominated the forties and fifties, and second . . . through the decidedly utilitarian strategy which informs the play—it is implicitly but very clearly addressed to the radical sector of black socio-political consciousness.

The heightened aesthetics and revolutionary sensibility animating *Dutchman* concretized a new model of Black Arts theater "as a total national institution . . . an instrument for raising the political, ethical, and aesthetic consciousness."[4]

With *Dutchman* too, as with *A Raisin in the Sun*, recent scholarship expands upon a previously incomplete historiography. LaDonna Forsgren warns against a prevailing tendency among Black Arts theater historians to focus exclusively on "Baraka as the 'father' of the movement" and to see *Dutchman* (a hypermasculine cri de coeur whose critique of white supremacy plays out through a misogynistic depiction of sexual devouring) as totemic. Overfixation on Baraka as a playwright, and on *Dutchman* as an originating text, threatens to erase "the contributions of female participants" to the Black Arts Movement, thus flattening "the intricacies of gender and Black Power politics" at work during a dynamic moment of African American cultural production.[5] This context adds nuance to our understanding of *Dutchman*'s position at the leading edge of the Black Arts Movement and allows for wider consideration of the work of Black women artists within the revolutionary movement that erupts in the mid-1960s.

With fuller analyses of these two canonical plays in mind, *A Raisin in the Sun* and *Dutchman* endure as exemplars of the key crosscurrents shaping African American performance culture in this dynamic era. This chapter considers how an interplay between Hansberry's calculated use of familiar aesthetics and Baraka's brash radicalism of expression are contained within the work of one of the era's most influential Black performance artists: Nina Simone. I trace how Simone embodied on the public stage the examples of her contemporary artists Hansberry and Baraka. Within her richly varied and difficult-to-categorize musical repertoire, Simone's signature 1963 song "Mississippi Goddam" becomes a performance text through which the contrasting creative voices associated with *A Raisin in the Sun* and *Dutchman* converge and converse. Perhaps no other cultural product of the era displays such a potent mixture of two disparate ingredients: an incisive social critique strategically crafted within the bounds of mainstream aesthetics on one hand; and a seething, defiant, deliberately impolitic outburst of Black rage on the other.

The biography and musicianship of Nina Simone have been the subject of much scholarship and recent public attention. A comprehensive study of this artist's life, music, and expansive impact is beyond the scope of this chapter. Here my purpose is to highlight one of Nina Simone's most influential songs as emblematic of a key transformation both in its creator's artistic sensibility and in the cultural landscape in which she worked. I use Hansberry's *A Raisin in the Sun* and Baraka's *Dutchman* as orientation points for charting that transformation. My discussion of Simone's musicianship across the 1960s, using key examples of her performance praxis across the decade, positions "Mississippi Goddam" as a nodal point connecting what I see as this musician's largely Hansberry-esque artistry prior to 1963, and the Baraka-like move that she undertakes as a songwriter and performer in the years that follow.

THE ROAD TO "MISSISSIPPI": NINA SIMONE'S EARLY MUSICAL ACTIVITY

Nina Simone and Lorraine Hansberry met in 1960 or 1961 and soon became close friends. They lived near one another in Mount Vernon, New York, and found an affinity as contemporaries and kindred spirits—creative, ambitious, influential Black women artists achieving national prominence at a relatively young age. Hansberry was just twenty-nine when *A Raisin in the Sun* debuted in 1959. Simone, three years her junior, saw her public profile rise quickly at about the same time with the release of her first studio album, *Little Girl Blue,* and thanks to a prestigious solo appearance at New York's Town Hall. Simone would later pay posthumous tribute to her friend with the 1969 anthem "To Be Young, Gifted, and Black"—whose title (taken from a Hansberry speech) also was used for a compendium of unpublished and unfinished writings compiled by Nemiroff (later adapted for the stage). Years before Hansberry coined this phrase and Simone set it to music, these two young, gifted, and Black women artists found themselves drawn together in creative and personal kinship. Simone notes in her memoir how "Lorraine started off my political education"[6] thanks to their close friendship in the early 1960s; her pursuit of an artistry that embraces and trumpets the struggle for Black liberation would intensify in the years following Hansberry's death in 1965.

Nina Simone (born Eunice Waymond) forged a groundbreaking legacy as a singer and songwriter across a broad range of musical styles. Her first artistic aspirations were toward a career as a classical concert pianist. In 1950, after training for several years at the Juilliard School, she auditioned for the prestigious Curtis Institute of Music in Philadelphia, but was denied admission. She notes of this denial, "People who knew—I was told—white people who knew, said the reason I was turned down was because I was black."[7] The setback spurred Simone on a different artistic path. She soon found work playing piano at a bar in Atlantic City, New Jersey. On her first night of improvising her way through piano renditions of familiar songs to entertain patrons, the bar owner approached her. "He was very nice about my playing, said he liked it, but there was just one thing, why hadn't I sung? I looked at him. 'I'm only a pianist,' I said . . . 'Well tomorrow night you're either a singer or you're out of a job.' So the next night I sang as well."[8] This was Simone's first step on a new creative trajectory as a versatile vocalist, whose oeuvre encompassed a wide range of musical styles.

With her ambitions toward advanced classical training limned by racist exclusion, Simone readily found new opportunities as a popular entertainer. She progressed from bars in Atlantic City to upper-crust New York City lounges and supper clubs, and then to larger concert venues. As her profile grew, Simone held on to her original dream. "I still didn't think of my club work as a career at all—it was simply a way to raise money to go back to Juilliard."[9] Biding her time performing in other genres, Simone built through the 1950s and early 1960s a varied repertoire that included popular standards, musical theater, folk songs, spirituals, jazz, blues, and traditional favorites—all infused with a virtuosity and harmonic complexity informed by a grounding in classical music training. Recording contracts with Bethlehem Records and then with Colpix (a studio owned by Columbia Pictures) expanded her audience nationally and internationally. Though not (yet) overtly political in her song selection, Simone's creative output of the 1950s and early 1960s showed some connections to that of Lorraine Hansberry. As an emerging Black woman artist, Simone and her friend both were prominent among New York's interracial avant-garde "who hung out in [Greenwich] Village, the artistic and intellectual crowd" for whom creativity and politics were always "two sides of the same coin."[10]

As her fame grew and her repertory expanded, mainstream tastemakers found it difficult to categorize Simone's work. As she recounted:

> After Town Hall [1959], critics started to talk about what sort of music I was playing and tried to find a neat slot to file it away in. It was difficult for them because I was playing popular songs in a classical style with classical piano technique influenced by cocktail jazz. On top of that I included spirituals and children's songs in my performances, and those sorts of songs were automatically identified with the folk movement. So saying what sort of music I played gave the critics problems because there was something from everything in there, but it also meant I was appreciated across the board.[11]

Mastery of a broad range of musical sensibilities was always central to Simone's creative identity. Even in this early phase, before she addressed racial politics directly in her music, there was an unspoken poetics of defiance and boundary breaking inherent in her public identity as an artist. As Daphne Brooks argues, the "musical heterogeneity that worked to free African Americans from cultural and representational stasis" was for Simone a consistent form of antiracist agitation against the entrenched biases of American popular culture.[12]

Simone's rise to prominence reached a milestone on April 12, 1963, with her first solo engagement at New York's Carnegie Hall. For music critic Alan Light, the concert's eclectic bill of classical, traditional, folk, and popular tunes "reveals the extent to which she was still searching for any material she connected with, regardless of genre."[13] This creative search coincided with a different kind of personal and political exploration for Simone. She reflects on this period of her life: "I was always aware of what the vanguard of black artists and thinkers were concerned with," she writes, "but I wasn't an activist in any sense." That sense of remove from the strug-

Figure 10. Nina Simone, performing at Carnegie Hall, April 12, 1963. Photo: Alfred Wertheimer.

gle for Black liberation began to change in the early 1960s, largely thanks to Hansberry, whom she identifies as "a special kind of friend . . . to pull me into the ideas of the Black Movement and force me to accept that I had to take politics seriously. . . . She understood that I felt separate from what was going on, but told me over and over that like it or not I was involved in the struggle by the fact of being black."[14] This "fact of being black" imprinted itself to varying degrees on Simone's artistic and personal activities between 1959 and 1963. Jazz and blues remained staples within her unique musical repertoire, with some additions of Negro spirituals and African-inspired sounds into her concerts and recordings of this period. In December 1961, she joined Langston Hughes, James Baldwin, and other Black artists and intellectuals on a trip to Lagos, Nigeria, sponsored by the American Society of African Culture. The trip impacted Simone's sense of racial and geopolitical identity: "All around us were black faces, and I felt for the first time the spiritual relaxation any Afro-American feels on reaching Africa. . . . I knew I'd arrived somewhere important and that Africa mattered to me."[15]

Nonetheless, a clear vision of how her artistic and Black sociopolitical identities might inform one another as "two sides of the same coin" had not yet come into sharp focus for Simone. Her Carnegie Hall debut occurred the same day as Martin Luther King's imprisonment in Birmingham, Alabama; King would compose his defiant "Letter from a Birmingham Jail" a few days later. According to biographer Nadine Cohodas, "Lorraine had called Nina right after the Carnegie Hall concert, but it wasn't to congratulate her. She wanted to talk about King's arrest in Birmingham. What was Nina doing for the movement while the reverend and his colleagues were sitting in jail? Nina didn't have a good answer that day."[16] At this moment in history, with no immediate response to her friend's challenge, Simone resembles Hansberry's character Beneatha Younger—idealistic, creative, and curious to "experiment with different forms of expression" and to be "very serious about things,"[17] but still in search of a clear sense of how best to channel her political energies.

Simone found that clarity of vision a few months after the Carnegie Hall concert, after witnessing a horrific three-month period of white supremacist violence in the United States—bookended by the assassination of Medgar Evers in Jackson, Mississippi (on June 12), and the bombing of the Sixteenth Street Baptist Church in Birmingham, killing four young Black girls at Bible study class (on September 15). The musician describes a personal epiphany that grew out of hearing the news of these atrocities:

> It was more than I could take . . . all the truths that I had denied to myself for so long rose up and slapped my face. The bombing of the little girls in Alabama and the murder of Medgar Evers were like the final pieces of a jigsaw that made no sense until you had fitted the whole thing together. I suddenly realized what it was to be black in America . . . it came as a rush of fury, hatred and determination. In church language, the Truth entered me and I "came through."

Simone's immediate impulse was to grab a pistol "to go out and kill someone." With her husband's help, she came to the realization that "I knew nothing about killing and I did know about music." What followed in a generative hour at the piano was a new composition: "Mississippi Goddam." Simone had performed and recorded only a few original compositions prior to writing this song. This musical outpouring of Simone's outrage marked a pivot point for her musicality: "The entire direction of my life shifted."[18] In "Mississippi Goddam," Simone's facility and inventiveness within recognizable musical idioms converges with the overtly radical Black sensibility that would define her artistry across the years that followed. "Mississippi Goddam" now stands as a synecdoche for its entire era: encapsulating the broader transformations of African American performance culture that characterize the long civil rights era.

THE SONG

Several commentators have located the essence of "Mississippi Goddam" within a basic tension between the song's form and its content. To underscore a message of revolutionary defiance (see below for analysis of the lyrics), Simone crafts a musical accompaniment that proceeds in ironic dissonance with the spirit of the words she sings. The song's "euphoria . . . of tempo" and "jaunty ragtime melody" give it an "upbeat vaudevillian quality" that "retains an almost saccharine mirth," in stark contrast with horrifying subject matter.[19] The composition employs the A-A-B-A song structure ubiquitous in American popular music: a melodic and harmonic framework that offers predictability and comfort to the listener. Its central refrain repeats a memorable verse:

> Alabama's got me so upset.
> Tennessee made me lose my rest.
> But everybody knows about Mississippi . . . goddam!

The song delivers smooth and seamless modulations between the keys of C major and A minor—two "relative" keys that utilize the same scale notes. In these ways, Simone anchors her composition in familiar, recognizable musical gestures. During one of the first public performances of the song in the spring of 1964 (in a return solo engagement at Carnegie Hall captured on the album *Nina Simone in Concert*), Simone offered an additional message of reassurance to her audience. In a moment of banter between verses, the singer proclaims to the mostly upper-crust white crowd: "This is a show tune." Here, in an elite venue situated blocks from Broadway, she frames the song as a bit of entertainment offered for mainstream, commercial consumption. Simone then completes the sentence by adding slyly, "But the show hasn't been written for it yet,"[20] eliciting nervous laughter from the crowd. This statement thus becomes an oblique but portentous declaration of the new direction that Simone's musicality, and African American performance culture more broadly, were heading in 1964.

In an incisive and far-reaching analysis of "Mississippi Goddam," Daphne Brooks highlights the rich tensions embedded in the song and captured in several recorded performances from the 1960s. Brooks concludes:

"Brecht is ideologically present in Simone's song of the South."[21] I wish to add Hansberry as another theatrical reference point for conceiving of Simone's musical intervention in the cultural conversation. Using comfortable aesthetics to deliver a Black woman's searing indictment of white racial terror in the United States, "Mississippi Goddam" becomes a potent translation of Hansberry's influence into a new vector of musical activism. Viewed from the opposite perspective, we might reconsider *A Raisin in the Sun* as a theatrical cry of "goddam" with a calculatedly mainstream theatrical profile: "Chicago goddam," "redlining goddam," "American capitalism goddam," and (in light of the foreign student Asagai's impassioned rhetoric about the past and present of his home continent) "colonialism in Africa goddam." Fundamentally, "Mississippi Goddam" was Simone's answer to Hansberry's question of a few months earlier after her performance at Carnegie Hall. *This* is what she would do to advance and energize the movement toward Black liberation. As Tammy Kernodle summarizes, "'Mississippi Goddam' not only marked the awakening of Simone's political beliefs but symbolized the breaking of her musical inhibitions."[22]

This song quickly became a regular part of Simone's concert repertoire, and "remains one of the most powerful pop music protest songs of the Civil Rights era."[23] In performance, Simone kept the lyrics current by adapting them to reflect new episodes of racial violence. In a September 1964 nationwide network TV performance on *The Steve Allen Show*, she changed the second line of the chorus to "St. Augustine made me lose my rest," invoking ongoing protests and racial violence in Florida at the time. (When the program aired, network censors removed the word "goddam" each time it was sung.) Similarly, she sang "Selma made me lose my rest" at a March 1965 concert in Montgomery, Alabama—referencing the widely covered "Bloody Sunday" violence that had erupted just a few days earlier at the Edmund Pettus bridge. Other audiences heard Simone sing that "Watts has made me lose my rest" after riots in Los Angeles, and that "Memphis has made me lose my rest" in 1968, in the wake of Martin Luther King Jr.'s assassination.[24] As Kernodle argues, in contrast to more generic civil rights hymns (such as "We Shall Overcome" or "Go Tell It on the Mountain") and to other topical protest songs "that commented on protest events from a sideline perspective," "Mississippi Goddam" was a potent performance text that functioned as a conduit for immediate, concrete engagement with racial violences as incidents unfolded in real time. As such, the song emerged at the vanguard of a "second generation of freedom songs" that chronicle a rising "black nationalist, black power rhetoric" during the mid-1960s.[25]

Simone delivers the shock of that rhetoric before the song even begins, with a deliberately profane title—a provocation that (no matter the melodic and rhythmic lightness of the music) captures both the visceral urgency of the life-and-death struggle Simone has joined, and a rejection of the "classical" civil rights movements' reliance on well-mannered persuasion and respectability politics. That an African American woman artist would dare—whether on a commercially released single, on national network television, or in an elite concert venue—to blaspheme so publicly and unapologetically was unheard of. As Simone started the song's bouncy introduction from the Carnegie Hall stage, she announced to her audience, "The name of this song is 'Mississippi Goddam,'" eliciting nervous giggles. She then added, to a smaller swell of laughter, "And I mean every word of it."[26] Perhaps the word most sincerely meant was the one already causing unease and smashing bourgeois social norms: the word that summons divine damnation upon a state infamous for its racial terrors. From its title forward, "Mississippi Goddam" aligns itself with a Black Arts mission for performances that capture "the mad cries of the poor," "stagger through our universe correcting, insulting, preaching, spitting craziness," and do not hesitate to "Accuse and Attack anything that can be accused and attacked."[27]

The lyrics of "Mississippi Goddam" amplify the radical implications of its titular expletive. Stark imagery evokes the violent tumult created and enforced by white supremacy in the United States:

> Hound dogs on my trail
> School children sitting in jail
> Black cat cross my path
> I think every day's gonna be my last.
> Lord have mercy on this land of mine.
> We all gonna get it in due time.

The song projects the unsustainability of a gruesome status quo and the looming inevitability of a massive disruption:

> Can't you see it?
> Can't you feel it?
> It's all in the air.
> I can't stand the pressure much longer. . . .
> Don't tell me, I tell you
> Me and my people just about due.

Simone's lyrics lay bare the rank hypocrisy at the heart of national life, and foresee a grotesque resolution soon to arrive:

> Picket lines, and schoolboy cops.
> They try to say it was a Communist plot.
> All I want is equality
> For my sister, my brother, my people, and me.
> Yes, you lied to me all these years. . . .
> Oh but this whole country is full of lies.
> You're all gonna die and die like flies.

From beginning to end, the language of "Mississippi Goddam" offers no relief from provocation, no promise of hope or transcendence, no vision of reform or progress toward justice.

As "Mississippi Goddam" builds toward a conclusion, its narrator renounces integrationist ideology, rejecting the very model of pluralistic progress pursued by Hansberry's Younger family: "You don't have to live next to me. / Just give me my equality." This thought launches the song into its finale, in which Simone repeats a reminder three times (with variation) of what "everybody knows," then ends by sustaining the final epithet for several beats. In concert, Simone habitually punctuated the song's ending with a two-word declaration that follows the band's final chord:

> Everybody knows about Mississippi
> Everybody knows about Alabama
> Everybody knows about Mississippi, goooood daaaaam!
> *[Spoken] That's it!*[28]

With its violent imagery, deep cynicism about the promises of integrationist politics, and an unshakable sense of future violence, "Mississippi Goddam" aligns more closely with Baraka's fatalistic voice in *Dutchman* than with the more hopeful strategy Hansberry employs in *A Raisin in the Sun*. Danielle C. Heard argues that the song vividly "anticipates the project of black arts articulated by Amiri Baraka and others . . . whereby the urge for physical violence as a revolutionary tactic was transferred into cultural productions determined by an aesthetic of violence."[29]

A bridge section found twice within "Mississippi Goddam" presents a revealing variation on Simone's musical strategy. Simone sings:

Don't tell me, I tell you
Me and my people just about due
I've been there so I know
They keep on saying, "Go slow!"

With a contrast established between justice denied and overdue to "my people," and a nation obstructing progress with the demand to "Go slow," a rapid back-and-forth exchange between Simone and her band members follows. This section employs a call-and-response pattern (essential in African diasporic and African American music) to situate the song's commentary within a wider social context. At the same time, this dialogic section makes good on Simone's promise that "Mississippi Goddam" is fundamentally a theatrical experience, or as she put it, a "show tune." Kernodle transcribes the dialogue of this section in the following manner (with the band's answers in parentheses):

But that's just trouble (go slow). Washing the windows (go slow)
Picking the cotton (go slow). You're just plain rotten (go slow)
You're too damn lazy (go slow). Thinking crazy (go slow)
Where am I going? What am I doing? I don't know, I don't know.[30]

In this interpretation, the band members repeat the phrase "Go slow" intoned earlier in the song—as an incessant reminder of the obstructionist slogan that "they keep on saying" in response to demands for justice. The band's spoken calls echo and amplify the boiling frustration and cynicism that propel the song as a whole.

Extant concert recordings of "Mississippi Goddam" are not entirely clear, however, on exactly how the band members answer Simone in this bridge section. Without a separate microphone to capture the musicians' speech, their voices sound faint and muddy in each live capturing I found. As a result, scholars have interpreted their calls within the song differently. For example, Brooks records the band's interjections as "Do it slow!"—an imperative construction that suggests the band members are taking on the voices of the white American power structure as the song plays. This reading puts the band in active conflict with Simone's narrator (rather than positioning them as a validating echo of a line she has previously sung). Several others, such as La Marr Jurelle Bruce, transcribe the band's response as "*Too slow!*": an intriguing possibility that imbues this voice with some dramatic agency. This alternate interpretation transforms the line into a defiant "fight chant to drown out hegemonic calls for patience or a rally cry to jump-start liberation."[31] Such a reading brings the song's revolutionary potentialities more forcefully to the surface, allowing listeners to bear witness to how cries of "goddam" can spark radical defiance among Black communities. The same call-and-response technique returns later in the song with another bridge section. Following Bruce's rendering:

> But that's just the trouble (*Too slow!*). Desegregation (*Too slow!*).
> Mass participation (*Too slow!*). Reunification (*Too slow!*).
> Do things gradually (*Too slow!*). But bring more tragedy (*Too slow!*).
> Why don't you see it? Why don't you feel it?
> I don't know. I don't know.[32]

Here the song speaks not only to persistent white intransigence toward social reform, but also on the inadequacy of prevailing "classical" civil rights strategies. The band's words reinforce a view that these particular tactics fail to meet the urgency of the moment, and become a repeated call for more rapid and forceful liberatory action.

The immediacy and potency of this protest anthem, and the continuing evolution of Simone's musical politics, are captured in another concert recording from a few years later. On April 7, 1968, Simone performed at the Westbury Music Fair in Westbury, New York. The concert occurred just three days following the assassination of Martin Luther King Jr. in Memphis, Tennessee. Simone memorialized the slain leader by performing a three-song cycle that came to be known as the "Dr. Martin Luther King Jr. Suite"—which was captured and distributed on the 1968 RCA/Victor album *'Nuff Said*. First in the trio of songs was "Sunday in Savannah," a song written by Hugh Mackay in 1959 depicting a quotidian church day in King's home state of Georgia. Simone's band followed this with a brand-new composition entitled "Why? (The King of Love Is Dead)"—a mournful twelve-minute-long elegy composed by bassist Gene Taylor only the previous day in remembrance of the slain leader. "Mississippi Goddam," now a staple of Simone's repertoire, came third in the song suite and took on a striking new urgency in light of recent traumatic events.

For this performance, Simone inserted a pointed change to the lyrics during her second delivery of the chorus: "Memphis has made me lose my rest." A few moments after singing this verse, as the band vamped, Simone engaged audiences with banter of a very different nature than what had been recorded in Carnegie Hall four years earlier. "If you have been moved at all, and you know my songs at all," she urged, "for God's sake, join me. Don't sit back there. The time is too late now. Good God. You know?" The plea to "join me" is vaguely worded, but its implication to listeners is clear: abandon passivity, and, as Simone has exemplified through "my songs" (particularly the one currently being performed), be active in expressing outrage. Simone continued: "The King is dead. The King of love is dead. *I ain't 'bout to be nonviolent, honey. . . .* Oh no," she declared, to some delighted applause.[33] Here Simone shared publicly a moment from a private exchange she had with King himself when they had met backstage in Montgomery a few days after the "Bloody Sunday" massacre in Selma. Simone was about to headline a benefit performance to raise money for a protest march that King was soon to lead. As retold by Simone's longtime guitarist Al Schackman:

> We were at a fundraiser and we approached Martin and he put his hand out. And before anything else could happen, [Simone] just in a very strong voice looked at him and said, "I'm not nonviolent!" And he said, "Oh, that's OK, sister. You don't have to be."[34]

Inserting a variation on this statement into her rendition of "Mississippi Goddam" offered in the wake of King's murder, Simone reaffirmed her rejection of the tactics of nonviolent disobedience that were identified with the slain leader. Thus a moment of mourning and an expression of love for King became the singer's platform for embracing and advocating for a platform of Black militancy.

NINA SIMONE AND BLACK MILITANCY IN PERFORMANCE

Simone's evolving militant sensibility could also be seen elsewhere in her performance at the Westbury Music Fair, particularly in her rendition of another original composition, "Backlash Blues." Like "Mississippi Goddam," this song had become one of Simone's more familiar political anthems. The song sets to music the following poem written by the singer's close friend, Langston Hughes:

> Mister Backlash, Mister Backlash,
> Just who do you think I am?
> You raise my taxes, freeze my wages,
> Send my son to Vietnam.
> You give me second-class houses,
> Second-class schools.

Do you think that colored folks
Are just second-class fools?
When I try to find a job
To earn a little cash,
All you got to offer
Is a white backlash.
But the world is big,
Big and bright and round—
And it's full of folks like me who are
Black, Yellow, Beige, and Brown.
Mister Backlash, Mister Backlash,
What do you think I got to lose?
I'm gonna leave you, Mister Backlash,
Singing your mean old backlash blues.
    You're the one
    Will have the blues.
    Not me—
    Wait and see![35]

In an earlier July 1967 performance of "Backlash Blues" at the Newport Jazz Festival, less than two months after the poet's death, Simone described the poem as Hughes's "final slap in the face of the white backlash of this country." At Westbury, "Backlash Blues" (though not part of the trio of songs specifically dedicated to Dr. King) reflected potently on King's legacy and memory. Simone's voice crackles with anger and passion in a brand-new verse for the song not heard on the earlier recordings: one that draws pointedly upon the urgency of the moment:

When Langston Hughes died, he told me many months before,
He said, "Nina, keep on workin' 'till they open up the door."
One of these days when you made it, the doors will open wide
Make sure you tell 'em exactly where it's at,
so they will have no place to hide.[36]

This live variation on existing song lyrics—a creative gesture that Simone increasingly used in performance as her music grew more political in orientation—reflects the intensifying militancy of Simone's outlook and of the entire era of Black performance culture.

About a year later, in April 1968, Simone unveiled her song "To Be Young, Gifted, and Black" at a jazz festival at Morgan State College in

Baltimore—while the play of the same name (adapted from Hansberry's writings) was also running in New York. Simone composed the song with her music director Weldon Irvine Jr. It is a gesture of loving tribute to Hansberry's memory, with a resonance that extends well beyond their relationship. Within Simone's oeuvre of political songs, "To Be Young, Gifted, and Black" was distinctive as an unadulterated expression "of inspiration and uplift rather than fury."[37] Its lyrics begin:

> Young, gifted and black
> Oh what a lovely precious dream
> To be young, gifted and black
> Open your heart to what I mean
> In the whole world you know
> There's a million boys and girls
> Who are young, gifted and black
> And that's a fact.

The lyrics takes one brief detour into pessimism, when Simone sings, "There are times when I look back / And I am haunted by my youth." But this change of tone soon gives way to the anthem's hopeful conclusion:

> Oh but my joy of today
> Is that we can all be proud to say
> To be young, gifted and black
> is where it's at!

"To Be Young, Gifted and Black" was a direct musical affirmation of the era's "Black is Beautiful" sociocultural ethos. By emphasizing the potential of African American youth and envisioning a bright future led by a rising generation ("There's a world waiting for you / Yours is the quest that's just begun"),[38] Simone provides a forward-looking rejoinder to the sense of outrage and cynicism expressed in "Mississippi Goddam" and "Backlash Blues." As Shana L. Redmond argues in a comprehensive analysis of the song and its impact, "Simone's 'To Be Young, Gifted and Black' is a continuation of Hansberry's project of identification and critique" of racial injustice in the United States; in alignment *A Raisin in the Sun* as well as Hansberry's other writings, the song functions as "an organizing text that acknowledged despair but led the listener toward its alternative."[39]

Simone's triumphant embrace of Black strength, beauty, and achievement resonated within the radicalized political discourse of its moment.

Two years after the song's release, the Congress on Racial Equality (CORE) officially recognized "To Be Young, Gifted and Black" as the "Black National Anthem." This designation came following CORE's distinct turn away from a strategy of nonviolence in 1966—when Floyd McKissick replaced James Farmer as the organization's national director and steered the group in a distinctly more militant direction. Such recognition for Simone's song reinforced the musician's deepening connections to radical Black politics. Redmond historicizes "To Be Young, Gifted and Black" as a work that "articulates the transition from the civil rights activity of the 1950s and early 1960s to the Black Power methodologies of the middle to late 1960s and early 1970s. . . . 'To Be Young, Gifted and Black' did more than inspire; its heightened function as an anthem highlighted its didactic function within the Black nation [and] signaled a new phase of Black liberation struggles" unfolding in the long civil rights era.[40]

The growing prominence of Nina Simone's music within Black nationalist culture points to the vital and frequently overlooked contributions made by women artists to the Black Arts Movement. Within her repertoire, "the dynamic relationship between the black liberation and feminist movements" and the complex "intricacies of gender and racial inequality"[41] become most palpable in the 1966 ballad "Four Women." This song is essentially theatrical. A quartet of first-person soliloquies dramatizes the distinctive experiences of four archetypal female characters: the "black" matriarch Aunt Sarah, the "yellow" mixed-race Saffronia, the "tan" escort Sweet Thing, and the "brown" street tough Peaches. Simone's lyrics speak of suppressed anger, sexual violence, and desperation—but also strength and resilience, reinforced by an abrupt and triumphant resolution in its final line that modulates to an uplifting major key. Due to its frank and explicit content, "Four Women" elicited significant controversy. Several Black newspapers denounced the song, and some Black radio stations refused to play it, subscribing to a misguided interpretation of the lyrics as insulting to Black women. In truth, as "the first song to insert gender into the context of the Black Arts Movement," "Four Women" was a daring intervention into 1960s Black cultural discourse that delivered "one of the strongest pronouncements of black women's experiences in America."[42] As Simone herself reflected, "The song told a truth that many people in the USA—especially black men—simply weren't ready to acknowledge at the time."[43] As she contributed to the cultural politics of the Black Arts Movement, Simone used her platform to advocate for African American women within that cultural field.

Simone's prominence within Black nationalist culture reached a notable high point on August 17, 1969, with her performance at the Harlem Cultural Festival. Archival video of this performance (not widely seen for decades) is now available and richly contextualized within Ahmir "Questlove" Thompson's 2021 documentary film *Summer of Soul*. The film tells the story of a multiday celebration that drew more than three hundred thousand people to Harlem's Mount Morris Park for a gathering of African American musical performers that came to be known as the "Black Woodstock." Simone appeared at the festival wearing an African print dress and an intricately braided hairstyle, backed by an all-Black band clad in matching dashikis. The venue for the Harlem Cultural Festival was situated just a few miles uptown from Juilliard, Carnegie Hall, and the other midtown venues that had fostered this musician's emergence as a popular performer earlier in the decade. But since those younger days, Simone had traveled a vast distance—culturally, politically, spiritually—with her artistry. As she took the stage in Mount Morris Park, the festival announcer introduced her as "a young lady who tells a story about the troubles and tribulations of the ghetto, the new Black struggle, the first lady of soul: Nina Simone!"[44]

To live up to this introduction, Simone performed several of her most potent political songs; she also continued with her performance praxis of riffing on her own material to add texture and power to her messages. Her Harlem festival rendition of "Backlash Blues" set aside the traditional swing blues feel heard on other recordings for a more contemporary, driving, funk-inspired pulse. Relaying the wisdom of Langston Hughes (in the verse cited earlier in this chapter), Simone varied her own lyrics to amp up the urgency. "Make sure you *sock it to 'em where they live*, so they'll have no place to hide," she sang, improvising freely on the melody and rhythm of the passage. Despite the controversy that "Four Women" had engendered, Simone boldly delivered that anthem of Black womanhood to the masses gathered in Harlem. At the same concert, her rendition of "To Be Young, Gifted and Black" was noticeably more driving, insistent, and urgent in tone. Midway through the song, overtaken with passion, she lifted her hands from the piano to give four forceful claps and a direct scream to the audience. "Do you hear what I say!? Do you hear what I say!?" she asks the crowd—a group overflowing with members from the ascendant African American generation to whom the song is dedicated and addressed. As the music swelled toward its conclusion, Simone encouraged her band onward. "Hit it! Hit it! Hit it! Hit it!"[45] she called to them, urging a crescendo of intensity to punctuate her musical affirmation of Black youth ascendancy.

The Harlem festival set also included another selection that was both an original song of Simone's and, simultaneously, a provocative revision of

Figure 11. Nina Simone, performing at the Harlem Cultural Festival, August 17, 1969. From the film *Summer of Soul* (dir. Ahmir "Questlove" Thompson), 2021.

familiar material. Her remixed version of the 1968 Beatles hit "Revolution" built on the harmonic structure of John Lennon and Paul McCartney's traditional rock-and-roll composition, transforming it into a rhythm-and-blues manifesto for Black liberation. The Beatles' original song, a meditation on the worldwide political upheaval of 1968, gives voice to a philosophical and detached sensibility. "You say you'll change the constitution / Well, you know, we'd all love to change your head," sings Lennon. Simone's variation converts this passage into a call to social rather than internal change: "We're in the middle of a revolution, cause I see the face of things to come / Oh, your Constitution, well, my friend, its gonna have to bend." Rather than asking (as the Beatles do) "When you talk about destruction / Don't you know that you can count me out?" Simone proclaims: "I'm here to tell you about destruction. / All the evil that will have to end." Both versions of "Revolution" offer a repeated and reassuring refrain: "It's gonna be all right. / Everything's gonna be all right." But in lieu of Lennon and McCartney's suggestion of a transformation of consciousness ("You tell me it's the institution, / Well, you know, you better free your mind instead"), Simone demands radical upheaval of existing power structures as crucial to making everything "all right": "The only way that we can stand, in fact / Is when they get their foot off our back." Much more than simply a cover of a popular tune, this new "Revolution" was a radical intervention into and transformation of white popular music that Simone delivered to the Harlem masses assembled at the "Black Woodstock."[46]

To conclude her set at the Harlem Cultural Festival, this classically trained musician offered a drastic departure from her familiar repertoire. Rising from the piano, she finished her set with an impassioned recitation of a poem, "Are You Ready, Black People?" by Dahveed Nelson (a member of the Harlem-based Black Arts collective The Last Poets). Addressing the crowd directly from the lip of the stage, she told the audience, "This is for you," before confessing, "I didn't memorize it enough, so I have to read it." With text in hand, backed only by drums and repeated unison chants from her band, Simone delivered a spoken-word performance of Nelson's poem, which consists of a series of portentous, open-ended questions:

> Are you ready, Black people? Are you really ready?
> Ready to do what is necessary? To do what is necessary to do?
> Are you ready to kill if necessary? . . .
> Are you ready to smash white things? To burn buildings? Are you ready?
> Are you ready to build Black things?
> Are you ready to give yourself, your love, your soul, your heart, to create life? Are you ready to create out of nothing?
> Black man, Black woman, Black youth, Black everybody:
> Are you really, really, really, ready? . . .
> Are you ready to call the wrath of Black gods, Black magic, to do your bidding?
> Are you ready to use whatever is necessary?

As Simone passionately intoned these queries, the crowd answered back their collective affirmation, fueling Simone with additional performative energy in each cycle of call-and-response. Swaying to the drummer's rhythm, her voice swelling in volume and intensity, Simone builds toward a raucous final communion with her audience: "Are you ready to change yourself, turn yourself, inside out, through and through, and make yourself a through and through and through and through and through and through and through real Black person? *I say: are you ready!?*"[47] The crowd roared its agreement, bringing the entire performance to a raucous, communal endorsement of revolutionary action.

In its medium, its aesthetics, its performative dynamic, and its social outlook, "Are You Ready, Black People?" is as drastic a departure as one can imagine from Simone's youthful plan to make her name as a virtuoso of classical music. The performance brings full circle a reflection from a 1989 interview that Simone offered about the artistic aspirations that launched her musical journey: "I wanted to be a classical pianist because there was no black classical pianist, but I wasn't focused on 'black,' if you understand the difference."[48] Nowhere was this musician's understanding of that difference more evident in her performance work or more legible to an audience than on the Harlem Cultural Festival stage in August 1969, where her embrace of militant Black nationalist creative expression comes into its clearest focus.

Nina Simone's work as an inventive, boundary-crossing artist would continue for several more decades, outlasting the Black Arts Movement and stretching toward the end of the twentieth century. (She released her final album, *A Single Woman*, in 1993; her final concert performance took place in April 2002, as part of a benefit at Carnegie Hall.) This latter phase of her career unfolded under the shadow of many cascading personal challenges: marital and familial strife, legal entanglements, mental health struggles, alcohol abuse, and ultimately, a diagnosis of breast cancer that claimed her life about a year later. Another headwind facing Simone was political: the aftermath of her turn toward radical, militant ideals that started in 1963. For a March 1986 *Jet* magazine profile, Simone spoke of having been "so torn by her emotions in the freedom struggle that she sent herself into self-imposed exile in Europe and Africa in 1974." From that point forward, this transformational American artist—embraced by audiences from Carnegie Hall to Harlem—lived an itinerant life abroad, with brief residences in Barbados, Liberia, Switzerland, England, the Netherlands, and France (interrupted by a few brief returns to the United States). In Simone's telling to *Jet*, the root cause of her disaffection with her home country, and the prime factor in her decision to emigrate, was the hostility elicited by one particular song:

> "I wouldn't change being a part of the civil rights movement. I wouldn't change that, but some of the songs that I sang, I would have changed because they hurt my career." Asked which song did the most damage to her career, she unhesitatingly responded: "*Mississippi Goddam!*"[49]

That this artist's most galvanizing song of protest stood for her in retrospect as a site of professional "damage" is a curious assessment. Such an interpretation perhaps speaks more to the consumerist cultural climate of the 1980s (when it was offered) than it does to any questions of creative, cultural, or social impact. The reflection also shines a light on the role that gatekeepers—invariably white men in positions of power and outsized influence—exerted on Simone and continue to exert on Black creators, in validating and circulating their creative efforts. Though the pronouncement is valid with respect to mainstream commercial considerations, Amiri Baraka or Lorraine Hansberry would never have concurred. Whatever impact "Mississippi Goddam" might have had on the career of its creator, the song marks Simone's revolutionary transformation—in alignment with its moment in Black cultural history—from a versatile, popular, and largely apolitical crooner into one of the era's boldest and most radical muses of Black pride and liberation.

Conclusion

The evening of June 16, 1966, in the rural town of Greenwood, Mississippi, is a time and place that historians cite as transformational for the Black freedom struggle in the United States. Mark Whitaker identifies this as "the moment that would change [the] movement forever." The occasion was the Meredith March Against Fear: a protest march across the state, inspired by voting rights activist James Meredith, to promote Black ballot access and decry violent voter suppression in Mississippi and throughout the Jim Crow South. On this occasion, upon a "makeshift stage" consisting of "a flatbed truck [surrounded] with generator-powered floodlights," a performer entered "as though he had stepped into the lights of Broadway." Stokely Carmichael, newly appointed chair of SNCC, had come to address this audience directly from prison, following his unjust detention by local police for most of that day. Whitaker describes the scene:

> Gazing down at hundreds of moonlit faces looking up at him, [Carmichael] raised his right arm and clenched his hand into a fist. Then he clutched a small silver microphone and spoke in a voice filled with anger not only at the infuriating events of the day but at all the indignities he had suffered and witnessed in five years of working in the South.
>
> "This is the twenty-seventh time that I have been arrested, and I ain't going to jail no more! I ain't going to jail no more!"
>
> The crowd cheered and clapped, and Carmichael repeated the line with even more urgency. "I *ain't going* to jail no more!" he cried . . .
>
> "We've been saying 'Freedom Now' for six years and we ain't got nothing. What we're gonna start saying now is: 'Black Power'!"
>
> "*Black Power!*" the crowd roared back. . . .
>
> "We want Black Power!" Carmichael shouted.
>
> "*Black Power!*" the crowd cried.
>
> "We want Black Power!"

"Black Power!" . . .

Then Carmichael rephrased the refrain as a question, and the answer came back even louder.

"What do you want?" Carmichael asked.

"Black Power!" the crowd screamed.

"What do you want?"

"Black Power!"

"That's right," Carmichael shouted. "That's what we want, Black Power! We don't have to be ashamed of it. . . . From now on, when they ask you what you want, you know what you tell them? What do we want?"

"Black Power!" the crowd roared again.[1]

The nationwide reverberations that flowed from this staged moment demonstrate the explosive power of live performance to impact the national zeitgeist. Carmichael presented no new policy position for SNCC, nor proposed any particular strategy for political action in this address. The phrase "Black Power" had already appeared from time to time within African American political discourse, but to this point had gained little traction among the public. Enacting a calculated script at an explosive moment before a combustible group of spectators, Carmichael used the alchemy of performance—that spontaneous fusion of live presence, forceful language, physicality, and visceral aurality—to supercharge the slogan "Black Power" and catalyze Black nationalist politics. Peniel Joseph's account of the rally reads: "As the crowd chanted 'Black Power' in unison, the rhythmic call and response between speaker and audience electrified some, frightened others, and marked a turning point for the African American freedom movement."[2] Within days, the cry "Black Power" overtook the nation's conversations on racial justice: emboldening activists toward greater militancy and provoking concern among those of a more measured temperament (both within and outside of Black political communities).

It is hard to imagine any written treatise, radio broadcast, or even a televised address having an equivalent impact. Theatricality was the power source that charged the phrase "Black Power" with its distinctive urgency and efficacy. Carmichael's performance achieved the essence of what Amiri Baraka had envisioned for a new "Revolutionary Theatre": namely, a public and participatory airing of "the mad cries of the poor" that could effectively "moves victims to look at the strength in their minds and their bodies."[3] Without the use of dramatic narrative, or scenery, or rehearsal, or much else in the way of conventional aesthetics or mechanics of the theater, Carmichael's corporeal presence—the physicalized anger and determina-

Figure 12. Stokely Carmichael, delivering his famous "Black Power" speech in Greenwood, MS, June 16, 1966. Photo: Bob Fitch. Bob Fitch Photography Archive, Department of Special Collections, Stanford University Library.

tion he personified for his community, in defiance of the white supremacist order that had targeted and detained him that day—helped fortify bonds of African American solidarity. Or, as Baraka forecast it: "Our theatre will show victims so that their brothers in the audience will be better able to understand that they are the brothers of victims, and that they themselves are victims, if they are blood brothers. And what we show must cause the blood to rush. . . . And it will cause their deepest souls to move, and they find themselves tensed and clenched, even ready to die, at what the soul has been taught."[4] This performance by Stokely Carmichael is a vivid example of the linkage between Black political and theatrical cultures of the era. As Mike Sell argues, "The peculiar ontologies and epistemologies of performance are foundational dynamics of both the Black Power and Black Arts Movements."[5]

The synergies between the politics of Black nationalism and the aesthetics of Black Arts theater have been widely studied and justifiably celebrated as a disruptive and transformative development within African American theatrical history. How the artists of an earlier so-called classical civil rights period helped move Black theater and performance culture toward that point of disruption and transformation is a less familiar story—one that this study seeks to illuminate. In doing so, I do not intended to suggest that the artists discussed in the chapters of this book were always in close political alignment with Carmichael and other Black militant activists. As strident Black nationalist voices gained influence within midcentury racial politics, prominent cultural figures like Jackie Robinson, Alice Childress, Beulah Richardson, Ossie Davis, and others sometimes sought to distance themselves from the rhetoric and the politics of "Black Power." Indeed, among the subjects discussed in this this book, Nina Simone stands as a clear counterexample who proves the rule.

In July 1966, just a few weeks after the Mississippi speech that solidified Carmichael's status as the "'father' of the 'Black Power' theory," Simone joined the SNCC leader onstage at a rally in Philadelphia. Carmichael used the event to advocate for "dynamite, if necessary, to rid this country of discrimination," to decry white liberal meddling in Black communities, and to denounce the racial inequities of the US military involvement in Vietnam. Hearing his arguments, the musician's eyes welled with tears. "Miss Simone was so moved before the overflow crowd . . . that she was lost for words but finally said, 'I have been thinking of some of these things I have heard tonight since I was three years old.'"[6] This event occurred approximately three years following the release of "Mississippi Goddam," after the transformation of her artistry and public identity discussed in Chapter 6 had taken root. But for many of her contemporaries who had also launched their creative lives in the postwar period, their negotiations of the tensions between integrationist and nationalist politics proved more uneasy.

No matter where these public figures positioned themselves within the freedom struggle, their work in the realms of theater and performance merits reconsideration for how it prefigured and facilitated the emergence of a Black Arts revolution. Performing militant defiance of white supremacy amid a storm of forbidding societal headwinds—including American geopolitical triumphalism, the influence of integrationist politics, the prominence of white liberals, and mounting Cold War paranoia—was a fraught enterprise for artists of the postwar years. Whether through a lens of late-1960s and 1970s Black nationalism, or from a contemporary vantage point, it can be tempting to allow what might seem like compromises made and punches pulled by African American artists of the period to dominate our view. If unabashed alignment with totalizing revolution is how we measure Black radicalism, many of the efforts of Black artists presented during the late 1940s to early 1960s will inevitably seem inadequate.

Nonetheless, just as "the 'origins' of Black Power rhetoric, ideology, and militancy are to be found by taking a fresh look at . . . the *heroic period* of the civil rights era,"[7] so too are the roots of Black Arts performance praxis to be found in the years that preceded the mid-1960s. The rhetoric produced by Black Arts theorists offers a different interpretation of the past. Baraka begins his manifesto by declaring, "The Revolutionary Theatre should force change, it should be change." Larry Neal (quoting "Brother Knight") offers this analysis: "The Black artist must create new forms and new values, sing new songs (or purify old ones); and along with other Black authorities, he must create a new history, new symbols, myths and legends (and purify old ones by fire)." Or as Ron Karenga puts it, "All art that does not discuss or contribute to revolutionary change is invalid. . . . We have come to change reality."[8] Demands for *change*, venerations of things *new*, and calls for the obliteration of all that is *old* pervade Black Arts theory, wrapping the movement within a cloak of complete historical disjuncture and total reinvention. Such a narrative served the movement's larger objectives, and accounts for its abundant bravura. But to romanticize Black Arts theater as completely and irrevocably severed from its immediate past can obscure how African American artists working between the late 1940s and the early 1960s made strategic, courageous, influential advances into the cultural territory upon which the new wave of late-1960s revolutionaries then boldly planted their flag.

As I write these words in 2023, by many accounts, a new transformative Black cultural revolution is underway. A nationwide movement to combat white supremacy and protest racism and anti-Black violence has coalesced under the banner of Black Lives Matter (BLM). The rallying cry "Black Lives Matter"—first circulated in 2012, following the acquittal of Florida vigilante George Zimmerman for the shooting of Trayvon Martin (an unarmed African American teenager)—continues to acquire new currency in US political discourse. The slogan returns to the forefront of the national discourse with each prominent instance of racial violence, particularly in response to the killings of unarmed Black Americans by police that are a frighteningly regular occurrence within the national news. Like its predecessor "Black Power," the phrase "Black Lives Matter" speaks more to a broad social ethos than to any specific policy platform, strategy, or organized political party. It articulates a fierce determination that racial justice in the United States can only be meaningfully pursued through a radical disruption and reordering of social values. And like their predecessors of the Black Power movement, BLM activists and organizers harness the power of theatricality to advance their aims. As Jeffrey C. Alexander notes:

> In the years since 2012, . . . a performatively powerful black civil rights movement has begun to take shape. . . . As they unfolded on television and computer screens, the unprecedented wave of demonstrations against police brutality looked spontaneous, as if they were grassroots, springing up from the underclass victims themselves. Yet, this was not the case. Certainly, the demonstrations were heartfelt. Their authenticity, however, was choreographed, their verisimilitude the result of a singular fusion between actors and audiences enhanced by performative effect.[9]

As the performative politics of BLM (and the predictable right-wing backlash that such activities tend to elicit) continue to impact the nation's public life, it is fitting that theater artists have stood at the forefront of a cultural reckoning with the movement and its implications. Khalid Y. Long notes, "Similar to the impact made by artists during the Black Arts Movement of the 1960s and '70s . . . we are witnessing a commitment to radical art" among a new vanguard of African American theater artists of the new century. "The burgeoning wave of creative works by artist-activists such as Reginald Edmund, Simeilia Hodge-Dallaway, James Ijames, Dominique Morriseau, and Idris Goodwin, among others, is a cultural revolution that most certainly falls under the rubric: theatre of the Black Lives Matter movement." Also included under this rubric are various activist campaigns directed against theatrical institutions and leaders, spurred by a vocal coalition of Black, Indigenous, and People of Color artist-activists named We See You White American Theatre, to address a culture of white supremacy throughout the theater industry and to promote a new ethics of equity and care for the professional stage.[10]

Much remains to be experienced, and written, to assess the significance of BLM as a political and cultural inflection point for the United States. Such an assessment (beyond the purpose of this study) has been a focus for contemporary journalists, cultural critics, and sociologists since the movement's inception in the early 2010s. That analysis will inevitably be taken up by future cultural, social, and political historians reflecting on US society of the early twenty-first century. With the perspective of time, a fuller analysis of the transformational impact of the theater of BLM will surely emerge. As with the genealogy of mid-twentieth-century Black theater, our historical understanding should also credit the innovations and advances of a preceding group of writers and performers, whose work actively helped the nation get ready for the revolution to come.

Notes

INTRODUCTION

1. Imani Perry, *Looking for Lorraine: The Radiant and Radical Life of Lorraine Hansberry* (Boston: Beacon Press, 2018), 2.

2. Perry, *Looking for Lorraine*, 100.

3. For biographies of Hansberry, see also Soyica Diggs Colbert, *Radical Vision: A Biography of Lorraine Hansberry* (New Haven: Yale University Press, 2021), and Charles J. Shields, *Lorraine Hansberry: The Life behind A Raisin in the Sun* (New York: Henry Holt, 2022). For studies of *A Raisin in the Sun* and Hansberry's other dramatic writing, see, for example, Stephen R. Carter, *Hansberry's Drama: Commitment amid Complexity* (New York: Penguin, 1991); Anne Cheney, *Lorraine Hansberry* (Boston: Twayne, 1994).

4. James Baldwin, "Sweet Lorraine," in *To Be Young, Gifted, and Black: Lorraine Hansberry in Her Own Words*, ed. Robert Nemiroff (New York: Vintage Books, 1995), xvii.

5. Colbert, *Radical Vision*, 69–70.

6. Ben Keppel, *The Work of Democracy: Ralphe Bunche, Kenneth B. Clark, Lorraine Hansberry, and the Cultural Politics of Race* (Cambridge, MA: Harvard University Press, 1995), 22.

7. Harold Cruse, *The Crisis of the Negro Intellectual* (New York: William Morrow, 1967), 278, 280.

8. Lloyd W. Brown, "Lorraine Hansberry as Ironist: A Reappraisal of *A Raisin in the Sun*," *Journal of Black Studies* 4, no. 3 (March 1974): 237.

9. Amiri Baraka, "A Critical Reevaluation: *A Raisin in the Sun*'s Enduring Passion," in Lorraine Hansberry, *A Raisin in the Sun and The Sign in Sidney Brustein's Window* (New York: Vintage, 1995), 19.

10. Amiri Baraka, "The Black Arts Movement," in *SOS—Calling All Black People: A Black Arts Movement Reader*, ed. John H. Bracey et al. (Amherst: University of Massachusetts Press, 2014), 11.

11. Baraka, "The Black Arts Movement," 16–18.

12. James Smethurst, *The Black Arts Movement: Literary Nationalism in the 1960s and 1970s* (Chapel Hill: University of North Carolina Press, 2005), 56.

13. Peniel E. Joseph, "The Black Power Movement: A State of the Field," *Journal of American History* 96, no. 3 (December 2009): 759–60, 775.

14. Jacquelyn Dowd Hall, "The Long Civil Rights Movement and the Political Uses of the Past," *Journal of American History* 91, no. 4 (March 2005): 1234–35.

15. Margo Natalie Crawford, *Black Post-Blackness: The Black Arts Movement and Twenty-First Century Aesthetics* (Urbana: University of Illinois Press, 2017), 39. Chapter 1 of Crawford's study focuses on several texts from the Harlem Renaissance of the 1920s and how they anticipate the Black Arts Movement's promotion of a Black aesthetic, as a prelude to its analysis of the Black Arts Movement's anticipation of contemporary "post-Black" literature. The book skips over the period under consideration here.

16. Manning Marable, *Race, Reform, and Rebellion: The Second Reconstruction in Black America, 1945–1990* (Jackson: University of Mississippi Press, 1991), 15, 17.

17. Julius B. Fleming Jr., *Black Patience: Performance, Civil Rights, and the Unfinished Project of Emancipation* (New York: NYU Press, 2022), 40.

18. Mary Helen Washington, *The Other Blacklist: The African American Literary and Cultural Left of the 1950s* (New York: Columbia University Press, 2014), 4.

19. Martha Biondi, *To Stand and Fight: The Struggle for Civil Rights in Postwar New York City* (Cambridge, MA: Harvard University Press, 2009), 4–5.

20. Washington, *The Other Blacklist*, 22–23.

21. Marable, *Race, Reform, and Rebellion*, 20.

22. Larry Neal, "The Black Arts Movement," *TDR: The Drama Review* 12, no. 4 (Summer 1968): 28–39.

23. Nikhil Pal Singh, *Black Is a Country: Race and the Unfinished Struggle for Democracy* (Cambridge, MA: Harvard University Press, 2004), 6.

CHAPTER 1

1. Arthur Daley, "At the Baseball Writers Show," *New York Times*, February 4, 1946, https://www.nytimes.com/1946/02/04/archives/sports-of-the-times-at-the-baseball-writers-show.html

2. Wendell Smith, "The Sports Beat," *Pittsburgh Courier*, February 23, 1946, ProQuest Historical Newspapers.

3. Jackie Robinson, quoted in Jules Tygiel, *Baseball's Great Experiment: Jackie Robinson and His Legacy* (New York: Oxford University Press, 1997), 71.

4. "Rickey Claims That 15 Clubs Voted to Bar Negroes from the Majors," *New York Times*, February 18, 1948, https://www.nytimes.com/1948/02/18/archives/rickey-claims-that-15-clubs-voted-to-bar-negroes-from-the-majors.html

5. Carl Rowan with Jackie Robinson, *Wait Till Next Year: The Story of Jackie Robinson* (New York: Random House, 1960), 139.

6. Rowan with Robinson, *Wait Till Next Year*, 117.

7. David Naze, *Reclaiming 42: Public Memory and the Reframing of Jackie Robinson's Radical Legacy* (Lincoln: University of Nebraska Press, 2019), 16.

8. Naze, *Reclaiming 42*, 3.

9. Rowan with Robinson, *Wait Till Next Year*, 117.

10. Rowan with Robinson, *Wait Till Next Year*, 117–18.

11. Douglas A. Jones Jr., "Slavery, Performance, and the Design of African American Theatre," in *The Cambridge Companion to African American Theatre*, ed. Harvey A. Young (Cambridge: Cambridge University Press, 2012), 16.

12. Harvey Young, *Embodying Black Experience: Stillness, Critical Memory, and the Black Body* (Ann Arbor: University of Michigan Press, 2010), 6.

13. Augusto Boal, *Theatre of the Oppressed*, trans. Charles A. McBride and Maria-Odilia Leal McBride (New York: Theatre Communications Group, 1993), 141.

14. Jackie Robinson, *I Never Had It Made* (New York: HarperCollins, 1995), 58–59.

15. Koritha Mitchell, "Identifying White Mediocrity and Know-Your-Place Aggression: A Form of Self-Care," *African American Review* 51, no. 4 (Winter 2018): 253.

16. Jules Tygiel, "Jackie Robinson: 'A Lone Negro' in Major League Baseball," in *Sport and the Color Line: Black Athletes and Race Relations in Twentieth-Century America*, ed. Patrick B. Miller and David Kenneth Wiggins (New York: Routledge, 2004), 204.

17. Jackie Robinson, "Jackie Robinson Says," *Pittsburgh Courier*, May 3, 1947, 15, ProQuest Historical Newspapers.

18. Jackie Robinson, "Jackie Robinson Says," *Pittsburgh Courier*, May 17, 1947, 14, ProQuest Historical Newspapers.

19. Jackie Robinson, quoted in Harvey Frommer, *Jackie Robinson* (New York: Franklin Watts, 1984), 51.

20. Bill Nunn Jr., "Robinson Ejected from His First Major League Game," *Pittsburgh Courier*, September 4, 1948, 12, ProQuest Historical Newspapers.

21. Robinson, *I Never Had It Made*, 75.

22. Leo Durocher and Ed Linn, *Nice Guys Finish Last* (Chicago: University of Chicago Press, 2009), 207, 208.

23. Neil Lanctot, *Campy: The Two Lives of Roy Campanella* (New York: Simon & Schuster, 2011), 172.

24. William C. Kashatus, *Jackie & Campy: The Untold Story of Their Rocky Relationship and the Breaking of Baseball's Color Line* (Lincoln: University of Nebraska Press, 2014), 4, 142.

25. Robinson, *I Never Had It Made*, 77.

26. Robinson, *I Never Had It Made*, 79.

27. "Jackie Returns to American Party," *Sporting News*, June 13, 1951, 12.

28. Rowan with Robinson, *Wait Till Next Year*, 183.

29. Robinson, *I Never Had It Made*, 81.

30. "Bums Set to Protest Slurs against Robinson, Black," *Pittsburgh Courier*, June 21, 1952, 25, ProQuest Historical Newspapers. It is not clear if O'Malley followed through and formally lodged a complaint with the National League, or if Giles took any action.

31. Wendell Smith, "Robinson Almost Found a Target," *Pittsburgh Courier*, September 8, 1956, 22, ProQuest Historical Newspapers.

32. Arnold Rampersad, *Jackie Robinson: A Biography* (New York: Ballantine Books, 1997), 258.

33. US Congress, Committee on Un-American Activities, *Hearings Regarding Communist Infiltration of Minority Groups—Part 1* (July 13, 14, and 18, 1949) (Washington, DC: US Government Printing Office, 1949), Google Books, https://www.google.com/books/edition/Hearings_Regarding_Communist_Infiltratio/UsJGAQAAMAAJ

34. US Congress, *Hearings Regarding Communist Infiltration*, 482.

35. Robinson, *I Never Had It Made*, 83.

36. "Big League Moguls Get Plea for Negro Players," *Chicago Defender*, December 11, 1943, 1, ProQuest Historical Newspapers.

37. US Congress, *Hearings Regarding Communist Infiltration*, 481–82.

38. US Congress, *Hearings Regarding Communist Infiltration*, 481.

39. Naze, *Reclaiming* 42, 93.

40. "Robinson Charges Yankee Race Bias," *New York Times*, December 1, 1952, 31, https://www.nytimes.com/1952/12/01/archives/robinson-charges-yankee-race-bias-dodger-negro-second-baseman-cites.html

41. "Robinson Says Frick Didn't Silence Him," *Pittsburgh Courier*, December 27, 1952, 20, ProQuest Historical Newspapers.

42. "Robinson Should Be Player—Not Crusader," *Sporting News*, December 10, 1952, 12.

43. Wendell Smith, "The Yankees May, or May Not, Be Guilty . . . ," *Pittsburgh Courier*, December 13, 1952, 17, ProQuest Historical Newspapers.

44. Jackie Robinson, "Our Policy," *Our Sports* 1, no. 1 (May 1953): 3.

45. Jimmy Cannon, *New York Post*, May 10, 1947, quoted in Tygiel, *Baseball's Great Experiment*, 188.

46. Letter to Jackie Robinson, July 18, 1962, Jackie Robinson Papers, National Baseball Hall of Fame Museum and Archive, Series III, box 2, folder 7.

47. Walter F. Scott Jr., Letter to the Editor, *New York Amsterdam News*, December 7, 1963, 12, ProQuest Historical Newspapers.

48. Ron Briley, "A Cold War State of Mind: Jackie Robinson and the Anticommunist Crusade," *Black Ball* 8 (2015): 6, 17.

49. Jackie Robinson, interview by Theodore Granik, "Youth Wants to Know," April 1967, Jackie Robinson Papers, Series VI, box 1, folder 10.

50. Rampersad, *Jackie Robinson*, 303–4.

51. Rampersad, *Jackie Robinson*, 321–23.

52. Rampersad, *Jackie Robinson*, 378.

53. Rampersad, *Jackie Robinson*, 392.

54. Jackie Robinson, quoted in Louis Lautier, "Jackie Speaks His Mind: Says NAACP Leaders Overlook 'Little Man,'" *Cleveland Call and Post*, July 19, 1958, 3, ProQuest Historical Newspapers.

55. Jackie Robinson, quoted in James Booker, "Demand 'Integration Now': Jackie, Judge Delany Blast Roy Wilkins," *New York Amsterdam News*, August 9, 1958, 9, ProQuest Historical Newspapers.

56. Jackie Robinson, "A Negro First," *New York Amsterdam News*, July 4, 1964, 19, ProQuest Historical Newspapers.

57. Gertrude Wilson, "Jackie Robinson Battles Goldwater," *New York Amsterdam News*, July 18, 1964, 19, ProQuest Historical Newspapers.

58. Jackie Robinson, letter to Nelson Rockefeller, October 7, 1964, Jackie Robinson Papers, Series III, Box 1, folder 13.

59. Jackie Robinson, "Mixed Emotions over Boycott of Olympics," *New York Amsterdam News*, December 16, 1967, 17, ProQuest Historical Newspapers.

CHAPTER 2

1. Amiri Baraka, "The Revolutionary Theatre," *Liberator*, July 1965, 4.

2. Aimee Zygmonski, "Amiri Baraka and the Black Arts Movement," in *Cambridge Companion to African American Theatre*, ed. Young, 148.

3. LaDonna Forsgren, *In Search of Our Warrior Mothers: Women Dramatists of the Black Arts Movement* (Evanston, IL: Northwestern University Press, 2018), x.

4. Baraka, "The Revolutionary Theatre," 5.

5. Barbara Ann Teer, "We Can Be What We Were Born to Be," *New York Times*, July 7, 1968.

6. Neal, "The Black Arts Movement," 29, 30.

7. Brian Dolinar, *The Black Cultural Front: Black Writers and Artists of the Depression Generation* (Jackson: University of Mississippi Press, 2012), 8.

8. For more on the Black Cultural Front, see, for example, Marc Naison, *Communists in Harlem during the Depression* (Urbana: University of Illinois Press, 2014); James Edward Smethurst, *The New Red Negro: The Literary Left and African American Poetry, 1930–1946* (New York: Oxford University Press, 1996); Washington, *The Other Blacklist*; James Ziegler, *Red Scare Racism and Cold War Black Radicalism* (Jackson MS: University of Mississippi Press, 2015).

9. Theodore Ward, quoted in D. Gobbins, "Story of Theodore Ward, Leading Negro Playwright," *Daily Worker*, March 9, 1947, 10.

10. Theodore Ward, quoted in James Hatch, "Theodore Ward, Black American Playwright," Theodore Ward Collection, 1902–1983, Stuart A. Rose Manuscript, Archives, and Rare Book Library, Emory University, box 1, folder 18.

11. Julie Burrell, "Reinventing Reconstruction and Scripting Civil Rights in Theodore Ward's *Our Lan'*," *Theatre History Studies* 39 (2020): 216.

12. Owen E. Brady, "Theodore Ward's *Our Lan'*: From the Slavery of Melodrama to the Freedom of Tragedy," *Callaloo* 21 (Spring–Summer 1984), 42.

13. Brady, "Theodore Ward's *Our Lan'*," 42.

14. Theodore Ward, *Our Lan'*, in *Black Drama in America: An Anthology*, ed. Darwin T. Turner (New York: Faucett Publishers, 1971), 92–93. Parenthetical citations that follow refer to this edition of the play.

15. The inevitability of the African American farmers' defeat is reinforced with a final sound effect: "*Just as the curtain closes completely, there is the sound of a cannon being fired*" (145). As Darwin T. Turner explains in his introduction to the play in the anthology *Black Drama in America*, "According to the author, when the play was taken to Broadway a decision was made to eliminate the sound of the cannon at the end of the play. It was feared that that final shock might produce panic in an audience already strained to an almost unbearable tension" (73). The stage direction indicating the cannon sound was restored for publication at Ward's request.

16. Paul Robeson, "Plain Talk: From South Africa to B'way," *People's Voice*, October 18, 1947, Theodore Ward Collection, box 1, folder 32.

17. Alan M. Wald, "Theodore Ward," in *Writers of the Black Chicago Renaissance*, ed. Stephen C. Tracy (Urbana: University of Illinois Press, 2011), 334, Project Muse, http:// muse.jhu.edu/book/18395

18. Michelle Y. Gordon, "Theodore Ward and the Black Arts Movement," Race and Difference Colloquium Series, Emory University, Atlanta, GA, filmed April 14, 2016, video recording, https://youtu.be/GtnzN1sZD5Q

19. Theodore Ward, interviewed by Mike Cook, *Afrika Must Unite: An International Journal of Current Afrikan Affairs*, undated clipping, 10, Theodore Ward Collection, box 1, folder 32. *Afrika Must Unite* was a small journal dedicated to the politics and culture of the African diaspora, published by Chicago's Arusha-Konakri Institute from 1972 to 1973.

20. Lorraine Hansberry, "CNA Presents Exciting New Dramatic Revue," *Freedom* 2 (May 1952): 7.

21. "C.N.A." promotional flier, Schomburg Clipping File—"Committee for the Negro in the Arts" folder, Schomburg Center for Research in Black Culture, New York Public Library, New York.

22. Ed Strickland, Letter from Committee for the Negro in the Arts to W. E. B. Du Bois, June 7, 1951, W. E. B. Du Bois Papers (MS 312), Special Collections and University Archives, University of Massachusetts, Amherst Libraries.

23. Cruse, *Crisis of the Negro Intellectual*, 208, 211.

24. Washington, *The Other Blacklist*, 129.

25. Alice Childress, "For a Strong Negro People's Theatre," *Daily Worker*, February 16, 1951, 11, ProQuest Historical Newspapers.

26. W. E. B. Du Bois, "Krigwa Players Little Negro Theatre," *Crisis* 32 (July 1926): 134.

27. Childress, "Strong Negro People's Theatre," 11.

28. Alice Childress, *Gold Through the Trees*, in *Selected Plays*, ed. Kathy A. Perkins (Evanston, IL: Northwestern University Press, 2011), 25. Parenthetical citations that follow in this section refer to this edition of the play.

29. Elizabeth Smith, "Against the Grain: Alice Childress and the Black Arts Movement," in *With Fists Raised: Radical Art, Contemporary Activism, and the Iconoclasm of the Black Arts Movement*, ed. Tru Leverette (Liverpool: Liverpool University Press, 2021), 85, JSTOR, https://www.jstor.org/stable/j.ctv1prsrhz

30. Alice Childress, *Gold Through the Trees*, in Alice Childress Papers, Schomburg Center for Research in Black Culture, box 20, folder 6. The scenes entitled "The Haitian Vendor" and "In the West Indes" are not included in the version of *Gold Through the Trees* published in *Selected Plays*. Manuscript copies of these scenes survive in the Alice Childress Papers archive. Published reviews of Club Baron's 1951 production confirm that these scenes were included in the play's debut production.

31. John Hudson Jones, "'*Gold Through Trees*' Has Beauty and Power," review of *Gold Through the Trees* by Alice Childress at Club Baron, *Daily Worker*, April 10, 1952.

32. Alvin "Chick" Webb, "*In Splendid Error* is Splendid Drama," review of *In Splendid Error* by William Branch at the Greenwich Mews Theatre, *New York Amsterdam News*, December 4, 1954, 29, ProQuest Historical Newspapers.

33. William Branch, interviewed by N. Graham Nesmith, "William Branch: (A Conversation) Reminiscence," *African American Review* 38, no. 3 (Autumn 2004): 484.

34. William Branch, *In Splendid Error*, in *Black Theater: A 20th Century Collection of the Work of Its Best Playwrights*, ed. Lindsay Patterson (New York: Dodd Mead, 1971), 97. Parenthetical citations that follow in this section refer to this edition of the play.

35. The character Shields Green, like John Brown and Frederick Douglass, is based in history and arises out of Branch's research. As depicted in the play, Green was rescued by and lived with Douglass until he met John Brown and joined the raid on Harper's Ferry. Accounts of Green are recorded in several of Douglass's speeches and writings. For more information, see Louis DeCaro Jr., *The Untold Story of Shields Green: The Death of a Harpers Ferry Raider* (New York: NYU Press, 2020).

36. Miles Jefferson, "The Negro on Broadway, 1954–55: More Spice Than Substance," *Phylon* 16, no. 3 (1955): 309.

37. Webb, "Splendid Drama," 29.

38. L. F., "'In Splendid Error' Opens at Greenwich Mews," review of *In Splendid Error* by William Branch at the Greenwich Mews Theatre, *New York Times*, October 27, 1954, https://www.nytimes.com/1954/10/27/archives/in-splendid-error-opens-at-greenwich-mews.html

39. William Branch, quoted in Doris E. Abramson, *Negro Playwrights in the American Theatre, 1925–1959* (New York: Columbia University Press, 1969), 187–88.

CHAPTER 3

1. James Baldwin, "Sidney Poitier," *Look*, July 22, 1968, 57.

2. Maxine Hall Elliston, "Two Sidney Poitier Films," *Film Comment* 5, no. 4 (Winter 1969): 28.

3. Ossie Davis, in Lisa Gay Hamilton, dir., *Beah: A Black Woman Speaks*, 2003, Home Box Office, HBOMax. Transcribed by author.

4. Baldwin, "Sidney Poitier," 54, 55.

5. Dayo F. Gore, "*A Black Woman Speaks:* Beah Richards's Life of Protest and Poetry," in *Lineages of the Literary Left: Essays in Honor of Alan M. Wald*, ed. Howard Brick et al. (Ann Arbor: Maize Books / Michigan Publishing Services, 2015), http://dx.doi.org/10.3998/maize.13545968.0001.001

6. Washington, *The Other Blacklist*, 12.

7. "Negro Woman Poet to Appear at Wm. Patterson Birthday Rally," *Daily Worker*, August 17, 1951, 2, Chronicling America: Historic American Newspapers.

8. Margaret Wilkerson, introduction to *A Black Woman Speaks*, in *Nine Plays by Black Women*, ed. Margaret Wilkerson (New York: New American Library, 1986), 27.

9. Sue-Ellen Case, *Feminism and Theatre* (New York: Methuen, 1988), 56.

10. Kate Dossett, *Radical Black Theatre in the New Deal Era* (Chapel Hill: University of North Carolina Press, 2020), 11.

11. Erik S. McDuffie, *Sojourning for Freedom: Black Women, American Communism, and the Making of Black Left Feminism* (Durham, NC: Duke University Press, 2011), 3. McDuffie credits the phrase "black left feminism" to literary historian Mary Helen Washington, and defines the movement as "a path-breaking brand of feminist politics that centers working-class women by combining black nationalist and American Communist Party (CPUSA) positions on race, gender, and class with black women radicals' own lived experiences" (3).

12. "Foreword," in Beulah Richardson, *A Black Woman Speaks . . . of White Womanhood, of White Supremacy, of Peace* (New York: American Women for Peace, 1951).

13. Gore, "*A Black Woman Speaks*."

14. Yvonne Gregory, "Beulah Richardson: Poet Demands Equality for Negro Womanhood," *Freedom* 1, no. 8 (September 1951): 7, Tamiment Library, New York University, http://dlib.nyu.edu/freedom/books/tamwag_fdm000009/#1

15. Wilkerson, "Introduction" to *A Black Woman Speaks*, 27–28.

16. Annette Wannamaker, "Present(ing) Historical Memory: Beah Richards' 'A Black Woman Speaks,' Performance, and a Pedagogy of Whiteness," *Theatre Topics* 14, no. 1 (March 2004): 340.

17. Richardson, *A Black Woman Speaks*. All quotations from *A Black Woman Speaks* in this chapter are taken from the original published edition, which was

published without page numbers. I have indicated line breaks as they appear in this edition.

18. For more information about Rosa Ingram, see the section below on Richardson's play *The Revolt of Rosa Ingram*. Rosalee McGee was the wife of Willie McGee, an African American man from Mississippi wrongfully sentenced to death in 1945 for the rape of a white woman. Years later, Richardson reminisced that *A Black Woman Speaks* "came right out of that meeting with Rosalee McGee" (Hamilton, *Beah: A Black Woman Speaks*) and the inspiration that the young writer felt from McGee's public campaign on her husband's behalf. Despite Rosalee McGee's years-long efforts and a legal and political campaign waged by leftist activists, the state of Mississippi executed Willie by electrocution on May 8, 1951, just a few months before the first performance of *A Black Woman Speaks*.

19. Gregory, "Beulah Richardson," 7.

20. Joanna Schneider Zangrando and Robert L. Zangrando, "Black Protest: A Rejection of the American Dream," *Journal of Black Studies* 1, no. 2 (December 1970): 142.

21. Neal, "The Black Arts Movement," 30.

22. Boal, *Theatre of the Oppressed*, 122.

23. Wannamaker, "Present(ing) Historical Memory," 348.

24. John Hudson Jones, "New Negro People's Poet Talks of Art and Liberation," *Daily Worker*, October 14, 1951, 7, Chronicling America: Historic American Newspapers.

25. Beulah Richardson, *Genocide*, Civil Rights Congress records, 1946–1955, Schomburg Center for Research in Black Culture, Part 2, folder M114. 11. Citations that follow in this section refer to this manuscript.

26. Gore, "*A Black Woman Speaks.*"

27. Charles H. Martin, "Internationalizing 'The American Dilemma': The Civil Rights Congress and the 1951 Genocide Petition to the United Nations," *Journal of American Ethnic History* 16, no. 4 (Summer 1997): 56.

28. "Miss Richardson Interviewed," *Daily Worker*, November 9, 1951, 7, Chronicling America: Historic American Newspapers.

29. John Hudson Jones, "Denounce Florida Judge's Whitewash of Murderer," *Daily Worker*, November 14, 1951, 6, Chronicling America: Historic American Newspapers. Hilda Haynes was an actress who had previously been active with the American Negro Theatre in Harlem in the 1940s. She enjoyed a prominent decades-long career in theater, television, and film until the early 1980s, including work with the Negro Actors' Guild and the Negro Ensemble Company. I could find no additional information about Elyce Weir.

30. Gore, "*A Black Woman Speaks.*"

31. Martin, "Internationalizing 'The American Dilemma,'" 52.

32. Richardson, *A Black Woman Speaks*.

33. Dayo F. Gore, *Radicalism at the Crossroads: African American Women Activists in the Cold War* (New York: NYU Press, 2011), 74, 76.

34. Charles H. Martin, "Race, Gender, and Southern Justice: The Rosa Lee Ingram Case," *American Journal of Legal History* 29, no. 3 (July 1985): 252.

35. Gore, *Radicalism at the Crossroads*, 76.

36. Gore, "*A Black Woman Speaks*."

37. Belle Sundeen, "I Saw the Face of a New Georgia," *Daily Worker*, December 27, 1953, 13, Chronicling America: Historic American Newspapers.

38. Beulah Richardson, *The Revolt of Rosa Ingram*, in Civil Rights Congress records 1946–1955, Schomburg Center for Research in Black Culture, Part 2, folder N218. 1. Citations in this section refer to this edition of the play.

39. Byline for Beulah Richardson, "Paul Robeson," *Freedom* 1, no. 6 (June 1951): 7, Tamiment Library, New York University, New York, http://dlib.nyu.edu/freedom/books/tamwag_fdm000007/#1

40. Rev. George Robert Garner III, "Negro Art Theatre Triumphs," *Los Angeles Sentinel*, June 21, 1951, B3, ProQuest Historical Newspapers.

41. "Negro Art Group Honors Actress," *Los Angeles Daily News*, June 12, 1951, 19, ProQuest Historical Newspapers.

42. Beah Richards, *One Is a Crowd*, unpublished manuscript, Abbey Lincoln Collection, 1949–2008, Institute of Jazz Studies, Rutgers University Libraries, box 15, folder 7. Citations in this section refer to this edition of the play. Because the manuscript shows the author's name as "Beah Richards," it likely originates with the 1971 production rather than from the play's original composition of 1950 (before Richardson started using her adopted stage name).

43. Dan Knapp, "Beah Richards Tells What Her Play Is All About," *Los Angeles Times*, May 23, 1971, Q32, ProQuest Historical Newspapers.

44. Dan Sullivan, "Beah Richards in 'Crowd,'" review of *One Is a Crowd* at Inner City Repertory, *Los Angeles Times*, May 31, 1971, F11, ProQuest Historical Newspapers.

45. Beah Richards, in Hamilton, *Beah*.

46. Sullivan, "Beah Richards in 'Crowd,'" F11.

CHAPTER 4

1. Ossie Davis, interviewed by Julieanna L. Richardson, March 9, 2001, *The HistoryMakers Digital Archive*, Session 1, tape 1, story 7. Ossie Davis recalls a racist incident from his childhood.

2. Ossie Davis, interviewed by Julieanna L. Richardson, tape 3, story 2. Ossie Davis talks about the early years of his marriage and surviving McCarthyism.

3. Ossie Davis, quoted in Joseph Wershba, "A Negro Playwright Tries to Kill Segregation with Laughter," *New York Post*, October 11, 1961, 52.

4. Mel Watkins, *On the Real Side: Laughing, Lying and Signifying; the Underground Tradition of African-American Humor That Transformed American Culture, from Slavery to Richard Pryor* (New York: Touchstone, 1994), 27–28.

5. Ossie Davis, quoted in Thomas Lask, "Farce—Not Force," *New York Times*, September 24, 1961, X1, https://timesmachine.nytimes.com/timesmachine/1961/09/24/97247637.html

6. Ossie Davis, *Purlie Victorious: A Commemorative* (New Rochelle, NY: Emmalyn Enterprises, 1993), 1.

7. Ossie Davis, in Ossie Davis and Ruby Dee, *With Ossie and Ruby: In This Life Together* (New York: William Morrow, 1998), 291–92.

8. Baraka, "The Revolutionary Theatre," 4.

9. Ossie Davis, *Purlie Victorious*, in *Black Theater: A 20th Century Collection of the Work of Its Best Playwrights*, ed. Lindsay Patterson (New York: Dodd Mead, 1971), 318. Parenthetical citations that follow in this chapter refer to this edition of the play.

10. Henry D. Miller, *Theorizing Black Theatre: Art versus Protest in Critical Writings, 1898–1965* (Jefferson, NC: McFarland, 2011), 189.

11. See, for example, Bambi Haggins, *Laughing Mad: The Black Comic Persona in Post-soul America* (New Brunswick, NJ: Rutgers University Press, 2007); Lawrence W. Levine, *Black Culture and Black Consciousness: Afro-American Folk Thought from Slavery to Freedom* (New York: Oxford University Press, 1978); William Schechter, *The History of Negro Humor in America* (New York: Fleet, 1970); Terrence T. Tucker, *Furiously Funny: Comic Rage from Ralph Ellison to Chris Rock* (Gainesville: University Press of Florida, 2017); Watkins, *On the Real Side.*

12. Tucker, *Furiously Funny*, 2–3.

13. Daryl C. Dance, "Contemporary Militant Black Humor," *Negro American Literature Forum* 8, no. 2 (Summer 1974): 217.

14. Ossie Davis, quoted in Den Ross, "The Slapstick Side of Segregation," *New York Herald Tribune*, September 24, 1961.

15. Ossie Davis, quoted in Thomas Lask, "Farce—Not Force," *New York Times*, September 24, 1961.

16. "Broadway Yells 'No, No' as Ossie Davis Play Opens," *Chicago Defender*, October 2, 1961.

17. Davis, *Purlie Victorious* (1971), 1.

18. David Gillota, "Black Nerds: New Directions in African American Humor," *Studies in American Humor* 3, no. 28 (2013): 20.

19. Simon Weaver, "The 'Other' Laughs Back: Humor and Resistance in Anti-racist Comedy," *Sociology* 44, no. 1 (2010): 33.

20. Ossie Davis, quoted in William Glover, "Angry Young Author Satirizes Segregation," unidentified clipping, Ossie Davis and Ruby Dee Papers, Schomburg Center for Research in Black Culture.

21. "'Purlie Victorious' Mocks White Negro Stereotypes," *The Delphian*, January 11, 1962, Ossie Davis and Ruby Dee Papers. My emphasis.

22. Sylvester Leaks, "Theater: Purlie Emerges Victorious," *Freedomways* 1, no. 3 (Fall 1961): 347.

23. Watkins, *On the Real Side*, 27.

24. W. E. B. Du Bois, *The Souls of Black Folk* (Chicago: A.C. McClurg, 1904), 3.

25. Watkins, *On the Real Side*, 27.

26. Henry Louis Gates Jr., *The Signifying Monkey: A Theory of African-American Literary Criticism* (Oxford: Oxford University Press, 1989), 19, 100.

27. Carol Bunch Davis, "'Be Loyal to Yourselves': Jim Crow Segregation, Black Cultural Nationalism, and US Cultural Memory in Ossie Davis' *Purlie Victorious*," in *Critical Insights: Civil Rights Literature, Past and Present*, ed. Christopher A. Varlack (Hackensack, NJ: Salem Press, 2011), 38.

28. Davis, "Be Loyal to Yourselves," 40.

29. Gates, *The Signifying Monkey*, 45.

30. Ossie Davis, "Purlie Told Me!," *Freedomways* 2, no. 2 (January 1962): 157–58.

31. Dave Hepburn, "The Go, Go Kids of Broadway," *Amsterdam News*, March 31, 1962, A15, ProQuest Historical Newspapers.

32. "Their Theatre Parties a Boon to Purlie," *New York Amsterdam News*, November 18, 1961, 31, ProQuest Historical Newspapers.

33. Davis, "Purlie Told Me!," 158.

34. Davis, *Purlie Victorious* (1971), 1.

35. Davis, *With Ossie and Ruby*, 294.

CHAPTER 5

1. Jean Genet, *The Blacks: A Clown Show*, trans. Bernard Frechtman (New York: Grove Press, 1960), 3–4.

2. John McClain, "A Vigorous, Fascinating Play," review of *The Blacks* by Jean Genet at St. Marks Playhouse, New York, *New York Journal American*, May 5, 1961, 23.

3. Robert Brustein, "Genet's Call to the Colors: *The Blacks* by Jean Genet," review of *The Blacks* by Jean Genet at St. Marks Playhouse, *New Republic*, May 29, 1961, 21.

4. John McClain, "Joke's on Us!," *New York Journal-American*, May 13, 1961; John Gassner, "Broadway in Review," *Educational Theatre Journal* 13, no. 3 (October 1961): 217; Richard Cooke, "Sardonic Circus," review of *The Blacks* by Jean Genet at St. Marks Playhouse, *Wall Street Journal*, June 9, 1961, 6.

5. Lorraine Hansberry, "Genet, Mailer, and the New Paternalism," *Village Voice*, June 1, 1961, https://www.villagevoice.com/2020/06/30/genet-mailer-the-new-paternalism/

6. Robert Nemiroff, "A Critical Background," in Lorraine Hansberry, *Les Blancs: The Collected Last Plays of Lorraine Hansberry*, ed. Nemiroff (New York: Vintage Books, 1972), 32.

7. Richard Watts, "Grim Fruits of Colonialism," review of *Les Blancs* by Lorraine Hansberry at the Longacre Theatre, New York, November 16, 1970, in *New York Theatre Critics Reviews, 1970–71* (New York: Theatre Critics Reviews, 1971), 154; John Simon, "Shaffer's Shafts and Storey Theater," *New York*, November 30, 1970, 56; *Playboy*, quoted in Robert Nemiroff, "Postscript," in Hansberry, *Les Blancs*, 133.

8. David Saltz, "What Theatrical Performance Is (Not): The Interpretation Fallacy," *Journal of Aesthetics and Art Criticism* 59, no. 3 (Summer 2001): 302.

9. Genet, *The Blacks*, 3. Parenthetical citations in this section refer to this edition of the play.

10. Una Chaudhuri, "The Politics of Theater: Play, Deceit, and Threat in Genet's *The Blacks*," *Modern Drama* 28, no. 3 (Fall 1985): 364, 366.

11. Chaudhuri, "The Politics of Theater," 366.

12. James Earl Jones and Penelope Niven, *Voices and Silences* (New York: Limelight Press, 2002), 120.

13. Maya Angelou, *Heart of a Woman* (New York: Random House, 1981), 173, 178.

14. Gene Frankel, interviewed by Studs Terkel, July 15, 1963, Studs Terkel Radio Archive, https://studsterkel.wfmt.com/programs/interviewing-gene-frankel-director-blacks-jean-genet. Transcribed by author.

15. Stuart W. Little, *Off-Broadway: The Prophetic Theater* (New York: Coward, McCann & Geoghegan, 1972), 125–26.

16. Roscoe Lee Browne, HistoryMakers Digital Archive, clip A2005.234, interviewed by Paul Brock, March 30, 2006.

17. Angelou, *Heart of a Woman*, 178.

18. Jones and Niven, *Voices and Silences*, 120.

19. Hansberry, "Genet, Mailer."

20. Amiri Baraka, in "Jean Genet's *The Blacks*: A Panel Discussion," February 3, 2003, video recording, Theatre on Film and Tape, New York Public Library for the Performing Arts, New York. Transcribed by author. The panel discussion, held in conjunction with the Classical Theatre of Harlem's revival of *The Blacks*, was moderated by Michael Dinwiddie. Other panelists (some quoted below) included Roscoe Lee Browne, Ed Bullins, Vinie Burrows, Gene Frankel, Arthur French, Judith Malina, and Ty Jones.

21. Genet, *The Blacks*, 33, 39. Parenthetical citations that follow in this section of the chapter refer to this edition.

22. James Earl Jones, HistoryMakers Digital Archive, clip A2016.007, interviewed by Julieanna L. Richardson, August 10, 2016.

23. Vinie Burrows, in "Jean Genet's *The Blacks*."

24. Angelou, *Heart of a Woman*, 179, 183.

25. Frantz Fanon, *Black Skin, White Masks*, trans. Richard Philcox (New York: Grove Press, 2008), 90.

26. Angelou, *Heart of a Woman*, 179.

27. Roscoe Lee Browne, in "Jean Genet's *The Blacks*." Browne went on to

explain, "As soon as we actors discovered not to mistake the metaphor for the theme, we played it well." I read that statement to mean that Browne and his fellow actors came to view the social relations revealed in the play as a *metaphor* that points to a more general thesis about the corrupting tendencies of political power, not a direct *message* that endorses racist thinking or colonialist exercises of power.

28. "'The Blacks,' New Bias Hit on Broadway," review of *The Blacks* by Jean Genet at St. Marks Playhouse, New York, *Chicago Defender*, May 13, 1961, 10, ProQuest Historical Newspapers.

29. Amiri Baraka, in "Jean Genet's *The Blacks*."

30. Erik Nielson, "White Surveillance of the Black Arts," *African American Review* 47, no. 1 (Spring 2014): 166.

31. Larry Neal, "And Shine Swam On," quoted in Nielson, "White Surveillance," 161.

32. Mance Williams, *Black Theatre in the 1960s and 1970s: An Historical-Critical Analysis of the Movement* (Westport, CT: Greenwood Press, 1985), 13.

33. Angelou, *Heart of a Woman*, 183, 184–85.

34. Owen Dodson, quoted in "A Symposium: The Negro Writer in America," *Negro Digest* 12, no. 8 (June 1963): 63.

35. Cheryl Higashida, *Black Internationalist Feminism: Women Writers on the Black Left, 1945–1995* (Urbana: University of Illinois Press, 2011), 62.

36. Arthur French, in "Jean Genet's *The Blacks*."

37. Ossie Davis, quoted in "A Symposium: The Negro Writer in America," 63.

38. Angelou, *Heart of a Woman*, 183.

39. Jones and Niven, *Voices and Silences*, 118.

40. John Warrick, "*The Blacks* and Its Impact on African American Theatre in the United States," in *Jean Genet: Performance and Politics*, ed. C. Finburgh et al. (London: Palgrave Macmillan UK, 2006), 131.

41. Hansberry, *Les Blancs*, 91.

42. Hansberry, "Genet, Mailer."

43. Warrick, "*The Blacks* and Its Impact," 132.

44. Margaret B. Wilkerson, "The Dark Vision of Lorraine Hansberry: Excerpts from a Literary Biography," *Massachusetts Review* 28, no. 4 (Winter 1987): 647.

45. Nemiroff, "A Critical Background," 27.

46. Higashida, *Black Internationalist Feminism*, 63.

47. Joy L. Abell, "African/American: Lorraine Hansberry's *Les Blancs* and the African Civil Rights Movement," *African American Review* 35, no. 3 (Fall 2001): 461, 462.

48. Colbert, *Radical Vision*, 203.

49. A 2020 revival of *Les Blancs* at London's National Theatre moved this scene to later in the play, at the end of the scene corresponding to Act 2, Scene

3 in the published script—using this as a moment of pronounced internal conflict leading into the production's intermission. The National Theatre worked with the Lorraine Hansberry Literary Trust to assemble a new version of *Les Blancs* based more faithfully than the published version on Hansberry's notebooks and surviving drafts. Another notable departure from the published script in the National Theatre's production is that, in this newly revised version, Amos Kumalo is executed by the colonialist authorities (not simply imprisoned).

50. Lorraine Hansberry, in *To Be Young, Gifted, and Black: An Informal Autobiography of Lorraine Hansberry*, adapted by Robert Nemiroff (New York: Signet, 1970), 221–22.

51. Abell, "African/American," 463.

52. Hobe, review of *Les Blancs* by Lorraine Hansberry at the Longacre Theatre, New York, *Variety*, November 18, 1970, 82.

53. Clayton Riley, "A Black Critic on 'Les Blancs': An Incredibly Moving Experience," *New York Times*, November 29, 1970, 3, 20, https://timesmachine.nytimes.com/timesmachine/1970/11/29/82166271

54. Amiri Baraka, *Columbia, the Gem of the Ocean*, in *Black Drama: African, African American and Diaspora, 1850 to Present*, Alexander Street Press, https://search.alexanderstreet.com/view/work/bibliographic_entity%7Cbibliographic_details%7C3607010, n.p. August Wilson used the same song title for his 2003 drama *Gem of the Ocean* (set in Pittsburgh in 1904).

55. Kimberly W. Benston, *Baraka: The Renegade and the Mask* (New Haven, CT: Yale University Press, 1978), 215–16. See 212–17 for Benston's full analysis of *Great Goodness of Life*.

56. Amiri Baraka, "Spirit House, the New Fortress," October 14, 2013, *Rise Up Newark*, 2, https://riseupnewark.com/wp-content/uploads/2016/09/Spirit-House-The-New-Fortress-by-Amiri-Baraka-ilovepdf-compressed.pdf

57. Amiri Baraka (LeRoi Jones), *Great Goodness of Life: A Coon Show*, in *Four Revolutionary Plays* (New York: Bobbs Merrill, 1969), 46. Parenthetical citations in this section refer to this edition of the play.

58. Benston, *Baraka*, 215–16.

CHAPTER 6

1. Larry Neal, "Into Nationalism, Out of Parochialism," in *The Theatre of Black Americans: A Collection of Critical Essays*, ed. Errol Hill (New York: Applause Books, 1987), 295.

2. Perry, *Looking for Lorraine*, 102.

3. LeRoi Jones, *Dutchman*, in *"Dutchman" and "The Slave": Two Plays* (New York: William Morrow, 1964), 3.

4. Neal, "Into Nationalism," 296.

5. Forsgren, *In Search*, 6.

6. Nina Simone with Stephen Cleary, *I Put a Spell on You: The Autobiography of Nina Simone* (New York: Da Capo, 1993), 86–87.

7. Simone with Cleary, *I Put a Spell on You*, 42.

8. Simone with Cleary, *I Put a Spell on You*, 51.

9. Simone with Cleary, *I Put a Spell on You*, 56.

10. Simone with Cleary, *I Put a Spell on You*, 67.

11. Simone with Cleary, *I Put a Spell on You*, 68.

12. Daphne Brooks, "Nina Simone's Triple-Play," *Callaloo* 34, no. 1 (Winter 2011): 178.

13. Alan Light, *What Happened, Miss Simone? A Biography* (New York: Crown Archetype, 2016), 94.

14. Simone with Cleary, *I Put a Spell on You*, 86.

15. Simone with Cleary, *I Put a Spell on You*, 80.

16. Nadine Cohodas, *Princess Noire: The Tumultuous Reign of Nina Simone* (New York: Pantheon Books, 2010), 138.

17. Lorraine Hansberry, *A Raisin in the Sun* (New York: Vintage Books, 1994), 48, 63.

18. Simone with Cleary, *I Put a Spell on You*, 89–91.

19. See Brooks, "Nina Simone's Triple-Play," 183; Bridget R. Cooks and Graham Eng-Wilmot, "Sound of the Break: Jazz and the Failures of Emancipation," *American Quarterly* 68, no. 2 (June 2016): 330; Malik Gaines, *Black Performance on the Outskirts of the Left: A History of the Impossible* (New York: NYU Press, 2017), 30; Danielle C. Heard, "'Don't Let Me Be Misunderstood': Nina Simone's Theater of Invisibility," *Callaloo* 35, no. 4 (Fall 2012): 1066. See also Tammy L. Kernodle, "'I Wish I Knew How It Would Feel to Be Free': Nina Simone and the Redefining of the Freedom Song of the 1960s," *Journal of the Society of American Music* 2, no. 3 (2008): 295–317.

20. Nina Simone, "Mississippi Goddam," track 7 on *Nina Simone in Concert*, Philips, 1964.

21. Brooks, "Nina Simone's Triple-Play," 184.

22. Kernodle, "I Wish I Knew," 305.

23. Brooks, "Nina Simone's Triple-Play," 182.

24. Nadine Cohodas, "'Mississippi Goddam'—Nina Simone (1964)," National Recording Preservation Board, Library of Congress, 2018, https://www.loc.gov/static/programs/national-recording-preservation-board/documents/MississippiGoddam.pdf

25. Kernodle, "I Wish I Knew," 295–96.

26. Simone, "Mississippi Goddam."

27. Baraka, "The Revolutionary Theatre," 4.

28. Simone, "Mississippi Goddam."

29. Heard, "Don't Let Me Be Misunderstood," 1068.

30. Simone, "Mississippi Goddam."

31. La Marr Jurelle Bruce, "Interludes in Madtime: Black Music, Madness and Metaphysical Syncopation," *Social Text* 35, no. 4 (December 2017): 2.

32. Simone, "Mississippi Goddam."

33. Nina Simone, "Mississippi Goddam," track 12 on *'Nuff Said*, RCA, 1968.

34. Al Schackman, interview by Joe Hagan, "'I Am Not Nonviolent': New Nina Simone Film Captures Singer and Activist's Uncompromising Voice," *Democracy Now!*, June 24, 2015, https://www.democracynow.org/2015/6/24/new_nina_simone_documentary_what_happened

35. Langston Hughes, "The Backlash Blues," in *The Collected Poems of Langston Hughes*, ed. Arnold Rampersad (New York: Random House, 1995), 552.

36. Nina Simone, "The Backlash Blues," track 3 on *'Nuff Said*, RCA, 1968.

37. Light, *What Happened, Miss Simone?*, 167.

38. Nina Simone, "To Be Young, Gifted, and Black," track 7 on *Black Gold*, RCA, 1970.

39. Shana L. Redmond, *Anthem: Social Movements and the Sound of Solidarity in the African Diaspora* (New York: NYU Press, 2013), 199.

40. Redmond, *Anthem*, 181, 192.

41. Forsgren, *In Search*, 4–5.

42. Kernodle, "I Wish I Knew," 310.

43. Simone with Cleary, *I Put a Spell on You*, 117.

44. Questlove (Ahmir Thompson), *Summer of Soul (. . . or, When the Revolution Could Not Be Televised)*, Onyx Collective / Searchlight Pictures, 2021, Hulu. Transcribed by author.

45. Nina Simone, in Questlove, *Summer of Soul*. Transcribed by author.

46. The Beatles, "Revolution 1," track B of single "Hey Jude"/"Revolution," EMI, 1968; Nina Simone, "Revolution," as performed at Harlem Cultural Festival, August 17, 1969, video recording, https://www.dailymotion.com/video/x1tffkh. Simone's performance of "Revolution" at the festival does not appear in *Summer of Soul*.

47. Davheed Nelson, "Are You Ready, Black People?," as performed by Nina Simone, in Questlove, *Summer of Soul*. Transcribed by author.

48. Nina Simone, quoted in Light, *What Happened, Miss Simone?*, 96.

49. "Nina Simone Reveals: 'Mississippi Goddam' Song 'Hurt My Career,'" *Jet*, March 24, 1996, 54–55.

CONCLUSION

1. Mark Whitaker, *Saying It Loud: 1966—the Year Black Power Challenged the Civil Rights Movement* (New York: Simon & Schuster, 2022), 164–65.

2. Peniel Joseph, "Introduction: Toward a Historiography of the Black Power Movement," in *The Black Power Movement: Rethinking the Civil Rights–Black Power Era*, ed. Joseph (New York: Routledge, 2006), 2.

3. Baraka, "The Revolutionary Theatre," 5.

4. Baraka, "The Revolutionary Theatre," 5.

5. Mike Sell, "The Black Arts Movement: Performance, Neo-orality, and the Destruction of the 'White Thing,'" in *African American Performance and Theater History: A Critical Reader*, ed. Harry J. Elam Jr. and David Krasner (New York: Oxford University Press, 2001), 56, 57.

6. Chet Coleman, "'Black Power,' Beauty, Unity Rally Themes: Blast War in Vietnam, Phony Civil Righters," *Philadelphia Tribune*, July 19, 1966, 1, ProQuest Historical Newspapers.

7. Joseph, "Introduction," 8.

8. Baraka, "The Revolutionary Theatre," 5; Neal, "The Black Arts Movement," 30; Ron Karenga, "On Black Art," *Black Theatre* 3 (1968): 9–10.

9. Jeffrey C. Alexander, "Seizing the Stage: Social Performances from Mao Zedong to Martin Luther King Jr., and Black Lives Matter Today," *TDR: The Drama Review* 61, no. 1 (Spring 2017): 29, 30.

10. Khalid Y. Long, "Staging Black Lives Matter," in *The Cambridge Companion to African American Theatre*, 2nd ed., ed. Harvey Young (New York: Cambridge University Press, 2023), 284–85.

Bibliography

ARCHIVAL COLLECTIONS

Abbey Lincoln Collection, 1949–2008. Institute of Jazz Studies. Rutgers University Libraries. Newark, NJ.

Alice Childress Papers. Schomburg Center for Research in Black Culture. New York Public Library. New York.

Civil Rights Congress records, 1946–1955. Schomburg Center for Research in Black Culture. New York Public Library, New York.

Gene Frankel Papers. Billy Rose Theatre Collection. New York Public Library for the Performing Arts, New York.

Jackie Robinson Papers. National Baseball Hall of Fame Museum and Archive. Cooperstown, NY.

Lorraine Hansberry Papers. Schomburg Center for Research in Black Culture. New York Public Library, New York.

Ossie Davis and Ruby Dee Papers. Schomburg Center for Research in Black Culture. New York Public Library, New York.

Schomburg Clipping File. Schomburg Center for Research in Black Culture. New York Public Library. New York.

Theater Stills Collection. Photographs and Prints Division. Schomburg Center for Research in Black Culture. New York Public Library, New York.

Theodore Ward Collection, 1902–1983, Stuart A. Rose Manuscript, Archives, and Rare Book Library. Emory University. Atlanta, GA.

W. E. B. Du Bois Papers. Special Collections and University Archives, University of Massachusetts Amherst Libraries. Amherst, MA.

PLAY SCRIPTS

Baraka, Amiri. *Columbia, the Gem of the Ocean*. In *Black Drama: African, African American and Diaspora, 1850 to Present*. Alexander Street Press, https://search.alexanderstreet.com/view/work/bibliographic_entity%7Cbibliographic_details%7C3607010

Baraka, Amiri. *Dutchman*. In *Dutchman and The Slave: Two Plays*. New York: William Morrow, 1964. 3–38.

Baraka, Amiri. *Great Goodness of Life: A Coon Show*. In *Four Revolutionary Plays*. New York: Bobbs Merrill, 1969. 41–64.

Branch, William. *In Splendid Error*. In *Black Theater: A 20th Century Collection of the Work of Its Best Playwrights*. Ed. Lindsay Patterson. New York: Dodd Mead, 1971. 95–133.

Childress, Alice. *Gold Through the Trees*. In *Selected Plays*. Ed. Kathy A. Perkins. Evanston, IL: Northwestern University Press, 2011. 23–46.

Davis, Ossie. *Purlie Victorious*. In *Black Theater: A 20th Century Collection of the Work of Its Best Playwrights*. Ed. Lindsay Patterson. New York: Dodd Mead, 1971. 279–318.

Genet, Jean. *The Blacks: A Clown Show*. Trans. Bernard Frechtman. New York: Grove Press, 1960.

Hansberry, Lorraine. *Les Blancs*. In *Les Blancs: The Collected Last Plays of Lorraine Hansberry*. Ed. Robert Nemiroff. New York: Vintage Books, 1994. 37–139.

Hansberry, Lorraine. *A Raisin in the Sun*. New York: Vintage Books, 1994.

Richardson, Beulah. *A Black Woman Speaks . . . of White Womanhood, of White Supremacy, of Peace*. New York: American Women for Peace, 1951.

Richardson, Beulah. *Genocide*. Civil Rights Congress records, 1946–1955. Schomburg Center for Research in Black Culture. New York Public Library, New York. Part 2, folder M114.

Richardson, Beulah. *One Is a Crowd*. Abbey Lincoln Collection, 1949–2008. Institute of Jazz Studies. Rutgers University Libraries. Newark, NJ. Box 15, folder 7.

Richardson, Beulah. *The Revolt of Rosa Ingram*. In Civil Rights Congress records 1946–1955. Schomburg Center for Research in Black Culture. New York Public Library, New York. Part 2, folder N218.

Ward, Theodore. *Our Lan'*, In *Black Drama in America: An Anthology*. Ed. Darwin T. Turner. New York: Faucett Publishers, 1971. 73–145.

AUDIOVISUAL MATERIALS

The Beatles. "Revolution 1." Track B of "Hey Jude"/"Revolution." EMI, 1968.

Hamilton, Lisa Gay, director. *Beah: A Black Woman Speaks*. 2003: Home Box Office. 1 hr. 30 min. HBOMax.

Questlove (Ahmir Thompson). *Summer of Soul (. . . or, When the Revolution Could Not Be Televised)*. Onyx Collective / Searchlight Pictures, 2021. 1 hr., 58 min. Hulu.

Simone, Nina, "Backlash Blues." Track 3 on *'Nuff Said*. RCA, 1968.

Simone, Nina. "Mississippi Goddam." Track 7 on *Nina Simone in Concert*. Philips, 1964.

Simone, Nina. "Mississippi Goddam." Track 12 on *'Nuff Said*. RCA, 1968.

Simone, Nina. "To Be Young, Gifted, and Black." Track 7 on *Black Gold*. RCA, 1970.

ARTICLES, BOOKS, AND INTERVIEWS

Abell, Joy L. "African/American: Lorraine Hansberry's *Les Blancs* and the American Civil Rights Movement." *African American Review* 35, no. 3 (Fall 2001): 459–70.

Abramson, Doris E. *Negro Playwrights in the American Theatre, 1925–1959*. New York: Columbia University Press, 1969.

Alexander, Jeffrey C. "Seizing the Stage: Social Performances from Mao Zedong to Martin Luther King Jr., and Black Lives Matter Today." *TDR: The Drama Review* 61, no. 1 (Spring 2017): 14–42.

Angelou, Maya. *Heart of a Woman*. New York: Random House, 1981.

Baldwin, James. "Sidney Poitier." *Look*, July 22, 1968. 50–57.

Baldwin, James. "Sweet Lorraine." In *To Be Young, Gifted, and Black: Lorraine Hansberry in Her Own Words*. Ed. Robert Nemiroff. New York: Vintage Books, 1995. xi–xv.

Baraka, Amiri. "The Black Arts Movement." In *SOS—Calling All Black People: A Black Arts Movement Reader*. Ed. John H. Bracey et al. Amherst: University of Massachusetts Press, 2014. 11–19.

Baraka, Amiri. "A Critical Reevaluation: *A Raisin in the Sun*'s Enduring Passion." In Lorraine Hansberry, *A Raisin in the Sun and The Sign in Sidney Brustein's Window*. New York: Vintage, 1995. 9–20.

Baraka, Amiri. "The Revolutionary Theatre." *Liberator*, July 1965. 4–6.

Baraka, Amiri. "Spirit House, the New Fortress." October 14, 2013, *Rise Up Newark*. 2. https://riseupnewark.com/wp-content/uploads/2016/09/Spirit-House-The-New-Fortress-by-Amiri-Baraka-ilovepdf-compressed.pdf

Benston, Kimberly W. *Baraka: The Renegade and the Mask*. New Haven, CT: Yale University Press, 1978.

"Big League Moguls Get Plea for Negro Players." *Chicago Defender*, December 11, 1943. 1. ProQuest Historical Newspapers.

Biondi, Martha. *To Stand and Fight: The Struggle for Civil Rights in Postwar New York City*. Cambridge, MA: Harvard University Press, 2009.

"'The Blacks,' New Bias Hit on Broadway." Review of *The Blacks* by Jean Genet at St. Marks Playhouse, New York. *Chicago Defender*, May 13, 1961. 10. ProQuest Historical Newspapers.

Boal, Augusto. *Theatre of the Oppressed*. Trans. Charles A. McBride and Maria-Odilia Leal McBride. New York: Theatre Communications Group, 1993.

Booker, James. "Demand 'Integration Now': Jackie, Judge Delany Blast Roy Wilkins." *New York Amsterdam News*, August 9, 1958. 1, 9. ProQuest Historical Newspapers.

Brady, Owen E. "Theodore Ward's *Our Lan'*: From the Slavery of Melodrama to the Freedom of Tragedy." *Callaloo* 21 (Spring–Summer 1984): 40–56.

Briley, Ron. "A Cold War State of Mind: Jackie Robinson and the Anticommunist Crusade." *Black Ball* 8 (2015): 5–24.

Brooks, Daphne. "Nina Simone's Triple-Play." *Callaloo* 34, no. 1 (Winter 2011): 176–97.

Brown, Lloyd W. "Lorraine Hansberry as Ironist: A Reappraisal of *A Raisin in the Sun*." *Journal of Black Studies* 4, no. 3 (March 1974): 237–47.

Browne, Roscoe Lee. Interview by Paul Brock. March 30, 2006. HistoryMakers Digital Archive.

Bruce, La Marr Jurelle. "Interludes in Madtime: Black Music, Madness and Metaphysical Syncopation." *Social Text* 35, no. 4 (December 2017): 1–31.

"Bums Set to Protest Slurs against Robinson, Black." *Pittsburgh Courier*, June 21, 1952. 25. ProQuest Historical Newspapers.

Burrell, Julie. "Reinventing Reconstruction and Scripting Civil Rights in Theodore Ward's *Our Lan'*." *Theatre History Studies* 39 (2020): 215–24.

Case, Sue Ellen. *Feminism and Theatre*. New York: Methuen, 1988.

Chaudhuri, Una. "The Politics of Theater: Play, Deceit, and Threat in Genet's *The Blacks*." *Modern Drama* 28, no. 3 (Fall 1985): 362–76.

Childress, Alice. "For a Strong Negro People's Theatre." *Daily Worker*, February 16, 1951. 11. Chronicling America: Historical American Newspapers.

Cohodas, Nadine. "'Mississippi Goddam'—Nina Simone (1964)." National Recording Preservation Board. Library of Congress. 2018. https://www.loc.gov/static/programs/national-recording-preservation-board/documents/MississippiGoddam.pdf

Cohodas, Nadine. *Princess Noire: The Tumultuous Reign of Nina Simone*. New York: Pantheon Books, 2010.

Colbert, Soyica Diggs. *Radical Vision: A Biography of Lorraine Hansberry*. New Haven: Yale University Press, 2021.

Coleman, Chet. "'Black Power,' Beauty, Unity Rally Themes: Blast War in Vietnam, Phony Civil Righters." *Philadelphia Tribune*, July 19, 1966. 1. ProQuest Historical Newspapers.

Cooks, Bridget R. and Graham Eng-Wilmot. "Sound of the Break: Jazz and the Failures of Emancipation." *American Quarterly* 68, no. 2 (June 2016): 315–38.

Crawford, Margo Natalie. *Black Post-Blackness: The Black Arts Movement and Twenty-First Century Aesthetics*. Urbana: University of Illinois Press, 2017.

Cruse, Harold. *The Crisis of the Negro Intellectual*. New York: William Morrow, 1967.

Daley, Arthur. "At the Baseball Writers Show." *New York Times*, February 4, 1946. https://www.nytimes.com/1946/02/04/archives/sports-of-the-times-at-the-baseball-writers-show.html

Davis, Carol Bunch. "'Be Loyal to Yourselves': Jim Crow Segregation, Black Cultural Nationalism, and US Cultural Memory in Ossie Davis' *Purlie Victorious*." In *Critical Insights: Civil Rights Literature, Past and Present*. Ed. Christopher A. Varlack. Hackensack, NJ: Salem Press, 2011. 36–52.

Davis, Ossie. Interview by Julieanna L. Richardson. March 9, 2001. HistoryMakers Digital Archive.

Davis, Ossie. "Purlie Told Me!" *Freedomways* 2, no. 2 (January 1962): 155–59.

Davis, Ossie. *Purlie Victorious: A Commemorative*. New Rochelle, NY: Emmalyn Enterprises, 1993.

Davis, Ossie and Ruby Dee. *With Ossie and Ruby: In This Life Together*. New York: William Morrow, 1998.

DeCaro, Louis, Jr. *The Untold Story of Shields Green: The Death of a Harpers Ferry Raider*. New York: NYU Press, 2020.

Dolinar, Brian. *The Black Cultural Front: Black Writers and Artists of the Depression Generation*. Jackson: University of Mississippi Press, 2012.

Dossett, Kate. *Radical Black Theatre in the New Deal Era*. Chapel Hill: University of North Carolina Press, 2020.

Du Bois, W. E. B. "Krigwa Players Little Negro Theatre." *Crisis* 32 (July 1926): 134–36.

Du Bois, W. E. B. *The Souls of Black Folk*. Chicago: A.C. McClurg, 1904.

Durocher, Leo and Ed Linn. *Nice Guys Finish Last*. Chicago: University of Chicago Press, 2009.

Elliston, Maxine Hall. "Two Sidney Poitier Films." *Film Comment* 5, no. 4 (Winter 1969): 26–33.

Fanon, Frantz. *Black Skin, White Masks*. Trans. Richard Philcox. New York: Grove Press, 2008.

Fleming, Julius B., Jr., *Black Patience: Performance, Civil Rights, and the Unfinished Project of Emancipation*. New York: NYU Press, 2022.

Forsgren, LaDonna. *In Search of Our Warrior Mothers: Women Dramatists of the Black Arts Movement*. Evanston, IL: Northwestern University Press, 2018.

Frankel, Gene. Interview by Studs Terkel. July 15, 1963. Studs Terkel Radio Archive. https://studsterkel.wfmt.com/programs/interviewing-gene-frankel-director-blacks-jean-genet

Frommer, Harvey. *Jackie Robinson*. New York: Franklin Watts, 1984.

Gaines, Malik. *Black Performance on the Outskirts of the Left: A History of the Impossible*. New York: NYU Press, 2017.

Garner, Rev. George Robert, III. "Negro Art Theatre Triumphs." *Los Angeles Sentinel*, June 21, 1951. B3. ProQuest Historical Newspapers.

Gates, Henry Louis, Jr. *The Signifying Monkey: A Theory of African-American Literary Criticism*. Oxford: Oxford University Press, 1989.

Gillota, David. "Black Nerds: New Directions in African American Humor." *Studies in American Humor* 3, no. 28 (2013): 17–30.

Gobbins, D. "Story of Theodore Ward, Leading Negro Playwright." *Daily Worker*, March 9, 1947. 10. Chronicling America: Historic American Newspapers.

Gordon, Michelle Y. "Theodore Ward and the Black Arts Movement." Race and Difference Colloquium Series. Emory University, Atlanta, GA. Filmed April 14, 2016. Video recording. https://youtu.be/GtnzN1sZD5Q

Gore, Dayo F. "*A Black Woman Speaks:* Beah Richards's Life of Protest and

Poetry." In *Lineages of the Literary Left: Essays in Honor of Alan M. Wald*. Ed. Howard Brick et al. Ann Arbor: Maize Books / Michigan Publishing Services, 2015. http://dx.doi.org/10.3998/maize.13545968.0001.001

Gore, Dayo F. *Radicalism at the Crossroads: African American Women Activists in the Cold War*. New York: NYU Press, 2011.

Gregory, Yvonne. "Beulah Richardson: Poet Demands Equality for Negro Womanhood." *Freedom* 1, no. 8 (September 1951): 7. Tamiment Library, New York University. http://dlib.nyu.edu/freedom/books/tamwag_fdm000009/#1

Hall, Jacquelyn Dowd. "The Long Civil Rights Movement and the Political Uses of the Past." *Journal of American History* 91, no. 4 (March 2005): 1233–63.

Hansberry, Lorraine. "I Presents Exciting New Dramatic Revue." *Freedom* 2 (May 1952): 7. Tamiment Library. New York University. http://dlib.nyu.edu/freedom/books/tamwag_fdm000017/#1

Hansberry, Lorraine. "Genet, Mailer, and the New Paternalism." *Village Voice*, June 1, 1961. https://www.villagevoice.com/2020/06/30/genet-mailer-the-new-paternalism/

Hansberry, Lorraine. *Les Blancs: The Collected Last Plays*. Ed. Robert Nemiroff. New York: Vintage Books, 1972.

Hansberry, Lorraine. *To Be Young, Gifted, and Black: An Informal Autobiography of Lorraine Hansberry*. Adapted by Robert Nemiroff. New York: Signet, 1970.

Heard, Danielle C. "'Don't Let Me Be Misunderstood': Nina Simone's Theater of Invisibility." *Callaloo* 35, no. 4 (Fall 2012): 1056–84.

Hepburn, Dave. "The Go, Go Kids of Broadway." *Amsterdam News*, March 31, 1962. A15. ProQuest Historical Newspapers.

Higashida, Cheryl. *Black Internationalist Feminism: Women Writers on the Black Left, 1945–1995*. Urbana: University of Illinois Press, 2011.

Hobe. Review of *Les Blancs* by Lorraine Hansberry at the Longacre Theatre, New York. *Variety*, November 18, 1970. 78, 82.

Hughes, Langston. "The Backlash Blues." In *The Collected Poems of Langston Hughes*. Ed. Arnold Rampersad. New York: Random House, 1995. 552.

"Jackie Returns to American Party." *Sporting News*, June 13, 1951. 12.

"Jean Genet's *The Blacks*: A Panel Discussion." February 3, 2003. Video recording. Theatre on Film and Tape, New York Public Library for the Performing Arts, New York.

Jefferson, Miles. "The Negro on Broadway, 1954–55: More Spice Than Substance." *Phylon* 16, no. 3 (Third Quarter 1955): 303–12.

Jones, Douglas A., Jr., "Slavery, Performance, and the Design of African American Theatre." In *The Cambridge Companion to African American Theatre*. Ed. Harvey A. Young. Cambridge: Cambridge University Press, 2012. 15–33.

Jones, James Earl. Interview by Julieanna L. Richardson. August 10, 2016. HistoryMakers Digital Archive.

Jones, James Earl and Penelope Niven. *Voices and Silences*. New York: Limelight Press, 2002.

Jones, John Hudson. "Denounce Florida Judge's Whitewash of Murderer." *Daily Worker*, November 14, 1951. 6. Chronicling America: Historic American Newspapers.

Jones, John Hudson. "*Gold Through Trees* Has Beauty and Power." Review of *Gold Through the Trees* by Alice Childress at Club Baron, *Daily Worker*, April 10, 1952. Chronicling America: Historic American Newspapers.

Jones, John Hudson. "New Negro People's Poet Talks of Art and Liberation." *Daily Worker*, October 14, 1951. 7. Chronicling America: Historic American Newspapers.

Joseph, Peniel E. "The Black Power Movement: A State of the Field." *Journal of American History* 96, no. 3 (December 2009): 751–76.

Joseph, Peniel E. "Introduction: Toward a Historiography of the Black Power Movement." In *The Black Power Movement: Rethinking the Civil Rights–Black Power Era*. Ed. Joseph. New York: Routledge, 2006. 1–25.

Karenga, Ron. "On Black Art." *Black Theatre* 3 (1968): 9–10.

Kashatus, William C. *Jackie & Campy: The Untold Story of Their Rocky Relationship and the Breaking of Baseball's Color Line*. Lincoln: University of Nebraska Press, 2014.

Keppel, Ben. *The Work of Democracy: Ralphe Bunche, Kenneth B. Clark, Lorraine Hansberry, and the Cultural Politics of Race*. Cambridge, MA: Harvard University Press, 1995.

Kernodle, Tammy L. "'I Wish I Knew How It Would Feel to Be Free': Nina Simone and the Redefining of the Freedom Song of the 1960s." *Journal of the Society of American Music* 2, no. 3 (2008): 295–317.

Knapp, Dan. "Beah Richards Tells What Her Play Is All About." *Los Angeles Times*, May 23, 1971. Q32. ProQuest Historical Newspapers.

Lanctot, Neil. *Campy: The Two Lives of Roy Campanella*. New York: Simon & Schuster, 2011.

Lask, Thomas. "Farce—Not Force: Ossie Davis Contends Humor Is a Weapon." *New York Times*, September 24, 1961. X1, X3. https://timesmachine.nytimes.com/timesmachine/1961/09/24/97247637.html

Lautier, Louis. "Jackie Speaks His Mind: Says NAACP Leaders Overlook 'Little Man." *Cleveland Call and Post*, July 19, 1958. 1A, 3. ProQuest Historical Newspapers.

Leaks, Sylvester. "Theater: Purlie Emerges Victorious." *Freedomways* 1, no. 3 (Fall 1961): 347.

L. F. "'In Splendid Error' Opens at Greenwich Mews." Review of *In Splendid Error* by William Branch at the Greenwich Mews Theatre. *New York Times*, October 27, 1954. https://www.nytimes.com/1954/10/27/archives/in-splendid-error-opens-at-greenwich-mews.html

Light, Alan. *What Happened, Miss Simone? A Biography*. New York: Crown Archetype, 2016.

Little, Stuart W. *Off-Broadway: The Prophetic Theater*. New York: Coward, McCann & Geoghegan, 1972.

Long, Khalid Y. "Staging Black Lives Matter." In *The Cambridge Companion to African American Theatre*, 2nd ed. Ed. Harvey Young. New York: Cambridge University Press, 2023. 283–99.

Marable, Manning. *Race, Reform, and Rebellion: The Second Reconstruction in Black America, 1945–1990*. Jackson: University of Mississippi Press, 1991.

Martin, Charles H. "Internationalizing 'The American Dilemma': The Civil Rights Congress and the 1951 Genocide Petition to the United Nations." *Journal of American Ethnic History* 16, no. 4 (Summer 1997): 35–61.

Martin, Charles H. "Race, Gender, and Southern Justice: The Rosa Lee Ingram Case." *American Journal of Legal History* 29, no. 3 (July 1985): 251–68.

McClain, John. "A Vigorous, Fascinating Play." Review of *The Blacks* by Jean Genet at St. Marks Playhouse, New York. *New York Journal American*, May 5, 1961. 23.

McDuffie, Erik S. *Sojourning for Freedom: Black Women, American Communism, and the Making of Black Left Feminism*. Durham, NC: Duke University Press, 2011.

Miller, Henry D. *Theorizing Black Theatre: Art versus Protest in Critical Writings, 1898–1965*. Jefferson, NC: McFarland, 2011.

"Miss Richardson Interviewed." *Daily Worker*, November 9, 1951. 7. Chronicling America: Historic American Newspapers.

Mitchell, Koritha. "Identifying White Mediocrity and Know-Your-Place Aggression: A Form of Self-Care." *African American Review* 51, no. 4 (Winter 2018): 253–62.

Naison, Mark. *Communists in Harlem during the Depression*. Urbana: University of Illinois Press, 2014.

Naze, David. *Reclaiming 42: Public Memory and the Reframing of Jackie Robinson's Radical Legacy*. Lincoln: University of Nebraska Press, 2019.

Neal, Larry. "The Black Arts Movement." *TDR: The Drama Review* 12, no. 4 (Summer 1968): 28–39.

Neal, Larry. "Into Nationalism, out of Parochialism." In *The Theatre of Black Americans: A Collection of Critical Essays*. Ed. Errol Hill. New York: Applause Books, 1987. 293–300.

"Negro Art Group Honors Actress." *Los Angeles Daily News*, June 12, 1951. 19. ProQuest Historical Newspapers.

"Negro Woman Poet to Appear at Wm. Patterson Birthday Rally." *Daily Worker*, August 17, 1951. 2. Chronicling America: Historic American Newspapers.

Nesmith, N. Graham and William Branch. "William Branch: (A Conversation) Reminiscence." *African American Review* 38, no. 3 (Autumn 2004): 477–88.

Nielson, Erik. "White Surveillance of the Black Arts." *African American Review* 47, no. 1 (Spring 2014): 161–77.

"Nina Simone Reveals: 'Mississippi Goddam' Song 'Hurt My Career." *Jet*, March 24, 1996. 54–55.

Nunn, Bill, Jr. "Robinson Ejected from His First Major League Game." *Pittsburgh Courier*, September 4, 1948, 12. ProQuest Historical Newspapers.

Perry, Imani. *Looking for Lorraine: The Radiant and Radical Life of Lorraine Hansberry*. Boston: Beacon Press, 2018.

Rampersad, Arnold. *Jackie Robinson: A Biography*. New York: Ballantine Books, 1997.

Redmond, Shana L. *Anthem: Social Movements and the Sound of Solidarity in the African Diaspora*. New York: NYU Press, 2013.

Richardson, Beulah. "Paul Robeson." *Freedom* 1, no. 6 (June 1951): 7. Tamiment Library, New York University, New York. http://dlib.nyu.edu/freedom/books/tamwag_fdm000007/#1

"Rickey Claims That 15 Clubs Voted to Bar Negroes from the Majors." *New York Times*, February 18, 1948. https://www.nytimes.com/1948/02/18/archives/rickey-claims-that-15-clubs-voted-to-bar-negroes-from-the-majors.html

Riley, Clayton. "A Black Critic on 'Les Blancs': An Incredibly Moving Experience." *New York Times*, November 29, 1970, 3, 20. https://timesmachine.nytimes.com/timesmachine/1970/11/29/82166271

Robinson, Jackie. *I Never Had It Made*. New York: HarperCollins, 1995.

Robinson, Jackie. "Jackie Robinson Says." *Pittsburgh Courier*, May 3, 1947. 15. ProQuest Historical Newspapers.

Robinson, Jackie. "Jackie Robinson Says." *Pittsburgh Courier*, May 17, 1947. 14. ProQuest Historical Newspapers.

Robinson, Jackie. "Mixed Emotions over Boycott of Olympics." *New York Amsterdam News*, December 16, 1967. 17. ProQuest Historical Newspapers.

Robinson, Jackie. "A Negro First." *New York Amsterdam News*, July 4, 1964. 19. ProQuest Historical Newspapers.

Robinson, Jackie. "Our Policy." *Our Sports* 1, no. 1 (May 1953): 3.

"Robinson Charges Yankee Race Bias." *New York Times*, December 1, 1952. 31. https://www.nytimes.com/1952/12/01/archives/robinson-charges-yankee-race-bias-dodger-negro-second-baseman-cites.html

"Robinson Says Frick Didn't Silence Him." *Pittsburgh Courier*, December 27, 1952, 20. ProQuest Historical Newspapers.

"Robinson Should Be Player—Not Crusader." *Sporting News*, December 10, 1952. 12.

Rowan, Carl with Jackie Robinson. *Wait Till Next Year: The Story of Jackie Robinson*. New York: Random House, 1960.

Saltz, David. "What Theatrical Performance Is (Not): The Interpretation Fallacy." *Journal of Aesthetics and Art Criticism* 59, no. 3 (Summer 2001): 299–306.

Schackman, Al. Interview by Joe Hagan. "'I Am Not Nonviolent': New Nina Simone Film Captures Singer and Activist's Uncompromising Voice." *Democracy Now!*, June 24, 2015. https://www.democracynow.org/2015/6/24/new_nina_simone_documentary_what_happened

Scott, Walter F., Jr. Letter to the Editor. *New York Amsterdam News*, December 7, 1963. 12. ProQuest Historical Newspapers.

Sell, Mike. "The Black Arts Movement: Performance, Neo-orality, and the Destruction of the 'White Thing.'" In *African American Performance and Theater History: A Critical Reader*. Ed. Harry J. Elam Jr. and David Krasner. New York: Oxford University Press, 2001. 56–80.

Shields, Charles J. *Lorraine Hansberry: The Life behind "A Raisin in the Sun"*. New York: Henry Holt, 2022.

Simon, John. "Shaffer's Shafts and Storey Theater." *New York*, November 30, 1970. 56.

Simone, Nina with Stephen Cleary. *I Put a Spell on You: The Autobiography of Nina Simone*. New York: Da Capo, 1993.

Singh, Nikhil Pal. *Black Is a Country: Race and the Unfinished Struggle for Democracy*. Cambridge, MA: Harvard University Press, 2004.

Smethurst, James. *The Black Arts Movement: Literary Nationalism in the 1960s and 1970s*. Chapel Hill: University of North Carolina Press, 2005.

Smethurst, James. *The New Red Negro: The Literary Left and African American Poetry, 1930–1946*. New York: Oxford University Press, 1996.

Smith, Elizabeth. "Against the Grain: Alice Childress and the Black Arts Movement." In *With Fists Raised: Radical Art, Contemporary Activism, and the Iconoclasm of the Black Arts Movement*. Ed. Tru Leverette. Liverpool: Liverpool University Press, 2021. 85–106.

Smith, Wendell. "Robinson Almost Found a Target." *Pittsburgh Courier*, September 8, 1956. 22. ProQuest Historical Newspapers.

Smith, Wendell. "The Sports Beat." *Pittsburgh Courier*, February 23, 1946. ProQuest Historical Newspapers.

Smith, Wendell. "The Yankees May, or May Not, Be Guilty . . ." *Pittsburgh Courier*, December 13, 1952. 17. ProQuest Historical Newspapers.

Sullivan, Dan. "Beah Richards in 'Crowd.'" Review of *One Is a Crowd* at Inner City Repertory. *Los Angeles Times*, May 31, 1971. F11. ProQuest Historical Newspapers.

Sundeen, Belle. "I Saw the Face of a New Georgia." *Daily Worker*, December 27, 1953. 13. Chronicling America: Historic American Newspapers.

"A Symposium: The Negro Writer in America." *Negro Digest* 12, no. 8 (June 1963): 54–65.

Teer, Barbara Ann. "We Can Be What We Were Born to Be." *New York Times*, July 7, 1968. D1. https://www.nytimes.com/1968/07/07/archives/-we-can-be-what-we-were-born-to-be-we-can-be-what-we-were-born-to.html

"Their Theatre Parties a Boon to Purlie." *New York Amsterdam News*, November 18, 1961. 31. ProQuest Historical Newspapers.

Tygiel, Jules. *Baseball's Great Experiment: Jackie Robinson and His Legacy*. New York: Oxford University Press, 1997.

Tygiel, Jules. "Jackie Robinson: 'A Lone Negro' in Major League Baseball." In *Sport and the Color Line; Black Athletes and Race Relations in Twentieth-Century America*. Ed. Patrick B. Miller and David Kenneth Wiggins. New York: Routledge, 2004. 167–90.

US Congress, Committee on Un-American Activities. *Hearings Regarding Communist Infiltration of Minority Groups—Part 1*. July 13, 14, and 18, 1949. Washington, DC: US Government Printing Office, 1949. Google Books. https://www.google.com/books/edition/Hearings_Regarding_Communist_Infiltratio/UsJGAQAAMAAJ

Wald, Alan M. "Theodore Ward." In *Writers of the Black Chicago Renaissance*. Ed. Stephen C. Tracy. Urbana: University of Illinois Press, 2011. 320–40.

Wannamaker, Annette. "Present(ing) Historical Memory: Beah Richards' 'A Black Woman Speaks,' Performance, and a Pedagogy of Whiteness." *Theatre Topics* 14, no. 1 (March 2004): 339–51.

Warrick, John. "*The Blacks* and its Impact on African American Theatre in the United States." In *Jean Genet: Performance and Politics*. Ed. C. Finburgh et al. London: Palgrave Macmillan UK, 2006. 131–42.

Washington, Mary Helen. *The Other Blacklist: The African American Literary and Cultural Left of the 1950s*. New York: Columbia University Press, 2014.

Watkins, Mel. *On the Real Side: Laughing, Lying and Signifying; the Underground Tradition of African-American Humor That Transformed American Culture, from Slavery to Richard Pryor*. New York: Touchstone, 1994.

Watts, Richard. "Grim Fruits of Colonialism." Review of *Les Blancs* by Lorraine Hansberry at the Longacre Theatre, New York. *New York Post*, November 16, 1970. In *New York Theatre Critics Reviews, 1970–71*. New York: Theatre Critics Reviews, 1971. 154.

Weaver, Simon. "The 'Other' Laughs Back: Humor and Resistance in Anti-racist Comedy." *Sociology* 44, no. 1 (2010): 31–48.

Webb, Alvin. "*In Splendid Error* is Splendid Drama." Review of *In Splendid Error* by William Branch at the Greenwich Mews Theatre. *New York Amsterdam News*, December 4, 1954. 29. ProQuest Historical Newspapers.

Wershba, Joseph. "A Negro Playwright Tries to Kill Segregation with Laughter." *New York Post*, October 11, 1961. 52.

Whitaker, Mark. *Saying It Loud: 1966—the Year Black Power Challenged the Civil Rights Movement*. New York: Simon & Schuster, 2022.

Wilkerson, Margaret B. "The Dark Vision of Lorraine Hansberry: Excerpts from a Literary Biography." *Massachusetts Review* 28, no. 4 (Winter 1987): 642–50.

Wilkerson, Margaret B., ed. *Nine Plays by Black Women*. New York: New American Library, 1986.

Williams, Mance. *Black Theatre in the 1960s and 1970s: An Historical-Critical Analysis of the Movement*. Westport, CT: Greenwood Press, 1985.

Wilson, Gertrude. "Jackie Robinson Battles Goldwater." *New York Amsterdam News*, July 18, 1964. 19. ProQuest Historical Newspapers.

Young, Harvey. *Embodying Black Experience: Stillness, Critical Memory, and the Black Body*. Ann Arbor: University of Michigan Press, 2010.

Zangrando, Joanna Schneider and Robert L. Zangrando. "Black Protest: A Rejection of the American Dream." *Journal of Black Studies* 1, no. 2 (December 1970): 141–59.

Ziegler, James. *Red Scare Racism and Cold War Black Radicalism*. Jackson: University of Mississippi Press, 2015.

Zygmonski, Aimee. "Amiri Baraka and the Black Arts Movement." In *Cambridge Companion to African American Theatre*. Ed. Harvey Young. Cambridge: Cambridge University Press, 2012. 137–54.

Index